Sociology

William Sims Bainbridge

Director of Sociology
National Science Foundation*

* The views expressed in this book do not necessarily represent the
views of the National Science Foundation or the United States.

BARRON'S

All inquiries should be addressed to:
Barron's Educational Series, Inc.
250 Wireless Boulevard
Hauppauge, New York 11788

Library of Congress Catalog Card No. 97-6360

International Standard Book No. 0-8120-9920-6

Library of Congress Cataloging-in-Publication Data

Bainbridge, William Sims.
  Sociology / William Sims Bainbridge.
    p.   cm. — *(College review series)*
  Includes index.
  ISBN 0-8120-9920-6
  1. Sociology.   I. Title.   II. Series.
HM51.B175   1997
301—dc21   97-6360
                                                      CIP

PRINTED IN THE UNITED STATES OF AMERICA

9 8 7 6 5 4 3 2 1

CONTENTS

PREFACE

Sociology is the scientific study of social interaction and of the structures and institutions that arise from it. This guide summarizes many of the greatest works of sociology, both old and very new, to help students understand the full breadth of the field and to guide instructors in preparing their own classroom surveys. It is designed to be the ideal intellectual companion for students of introductory sociology and undergraduate sociology majors.

To select the best and most representative works for this guide, I scrutinized the bibliographies of eight of the most widely used introductory texts, examined the books that have received awards from the American Sociological Association, and reflected upon my own experience as a sociology professor and as the director of the chief federal program that supports sociological research.

In writing this review, I have tried to communicate the major ideas and findings of each sociological work clearly and faithfully, with a minimum of my own analysis. The arrangement of the chapters and the brief connecting passages set out the intellectual structure of sociology.

The first chapter examines a single classic, Emile Durkheim's *Suicide*, to see how a great work of sociology builds on what went before, how it contributes fresh insights and research methods, and how it is reconsidered and its findings modified in the light of subsequent research.

The remaining chapters cover the topics most often raised by introductory textbooks, and they integrate many of the subdisciplines of sociology that are the focus of upper-division undergraduate college courses. These fifteen chapters are arranged in three sections. The first ("Individual in Society") begins with the fundamental principles of social interaction that place the individual in groups, networks, and the moral order sustained by intimate social relationships. The second ("Large-Scale Social Structures") considers phenomena and institutions beyond the individual: the community, occupations, organizations, stratification, and ethnic relations. The third ("Societal Transformation") is devoted to the massive processes that sustain or transform society over long periods of time: religion, social movements, politics, social change, and population.

I dedicate this guide to the five thousand students from whom I had the privilege of learning, and to the one thousand reviewers who now evaluate research proposals for me. I am deeply in their intellectual debt.

INTRODUCTION

1
THE SCOPE OF SOCIOLOGY

WORKS AT A GLANCE

A Classic

Suicide by Emile Durkheim (1897)

Earlier Works

"Statistics of Insanity in the United States" by Edward Jarvis (1842)
The Regularity of Apparently Voluntary Human Behavior
by Adolf Heinrich Gotthilf Wagner (1864)
Suicide by Henry Morselli (1879)
History of American Socialisms by John Humphrey Noyes (1870)

Later Publications on Religion
and Suicide

Suicide and Homicide by Andrew F. Henry and James F. Short, Jr. (1954)
"Sociology's 'One Law'" by Whitney Pope and Nick Danigelis (1981)
"Durkheim, Suicide, and Religion: Toward a Network Theory of Suicide"
by Bernice A. Pescosolido and Sharon Georgianna (1989)

The Proper Scope of Sociology

"Evolutionary Universals in Society" by Talcott Parsons (1964)
"Bringing Men Back In" by George C. Homans (1964)

We begin with an extremely influential, century-old book that continues to stimulate students and guide researchers today: *Suicide,* by the great French sociologist Emile Durkheim. By focusing for this first chapter on a single work and the context around it, we show how sociological studies connect to each other, and how great questions call forth the efforts of many social scientists. We see that a study can be extremely valuable even if the specific results are not always scientifically valid, and that ideas are at least as valuable as facts are for sociology.

Durkheim relied heavily upon earlier social scientists, even as he tried to develop the new discipline of sociology. In *Suicide,* he considered some of the central human questions, such as the relationship between the individual and the society, and the value of life in a world where values themselves are precarious. These were also the themes of pioneering works by the early American sociologists Edward Jarvis and John Humphrey Noyes. Scientific studies of suicide by the German Adolf Wagner and the Italian Henry Morselli were superior to Durkheim's work in their wealth of data, perhaps in their variety of hypotheses, and certainly in their caution in accepting general theories about society on the basis of relatively limited suicide statistics. Durkheim's work is superior chiefly in the way it attempted to claim distinctive intellectual territory for sociology and in the inspiration it provided for the subsequent century of sociology.

Since Durkheim wrote, research has tended to contradict his theories as well as sometimes to support them, as we see in the studies by Henry and Short, Pope and Danigelis, and Pescosolido and Georgianna. Durkheim argued that sociology should concern itself with the social facts of society as a whole, and many later sociologists, such as Talcott Parsons, agreed. Others, like George Homans, have argued instead that sociology should focus on the small groups and individual human beings that create society. By focusing on such an individual act as suicide, and showing that it was influenced by the condition of society as a whole, Durkheim demonstrated the importance of a science of society.

A Classic

Durkheim, Emile
   1897 *Suicide*. New York: Free Press [1951].

Emile Durkheim's aim in this classic sociological study of suicide was not merely to understand why people take their own lives, but to use this question to convince his reader that sociology was a science of great power and scope. He begins by noting that the word *sociology* had become widely familiar only around 1890, and grave doubts persisted whether it was capable of becoming a valuable science. Suicide seems to be the most solitary of human acts, so if Durkheim can show that it can be understood only by analysis of society, then sociology has great scope and even is superior to psychology.

Durkheim asserts that *social facts* must be studied as phenomena that exist above and beyond the individual. He goes so far as to claim that sociology cannot exist unless societies themselves exist in a very real sense, and that societies cannot be reduced to the desires and actions of individuals. Durkheim has no fear about the future of sociology, however, because he is convinced that each individual is dominated by the collective, moral reality that exists around him or her. Each nation or ethnic group has a characteristic rate of suicide—a relatively constant number of self-murders per 100,000 population every year—which could not be possible if suicide were strictly an individual act. Every regularity in suicide statistics is a social fact that reveals the crucial importance of sociology.

Rather than offer a sociological theory and then test it with suicide data, Durkheim takes the opposite approach. He tantalizes the reader with perplexing facts, considers non-sociological theories that do not seem to explain these facts, and only then offers a sociological explanation, like the climax of a mystery story. Is suicide the result of insanity? Durkheim argues that diagnosis of insanity is very difficult, but clearly many suicides are committed by people who had not previously been diagnosed as suffering from mental illness. He offers statistics indicating that insanity is slightly more common among women than among men, but men are far more likely to kill themselves. If suicide were hereditary, one would think that it would afflict young people, but in fact suicide is more common among the elderly. Suicide is more common in the cold nations of Europe, but in warm months of the year, so climate is not a clear cause. After discussing all these matters, Durkheim arrives at the social explanations fully a third of the way into his book. He suggests there are really four kinds of suicide, which he calls egoistic, altruistic, anomic, and fatalistic.

Durkheim's presentation of egoistic suicide begins with a bewildering array of facts. Protestant nations of Europe seem to have much higher suicide rates than do Catholic countries. Durkheim says this is true because the Protestant faith encourages "free inquiry" by the individual into religious matters, and this causes fragmentation of the church into many competing sects and denominations. Similarly, education creates intellectual independence, and more highly educated people are more apt to kill themselves. Single people are more likely to kill themselves than are married people, and any factor that strengthens the family reduces suicide. Nations undergoing political crisis or war have low rates of suicide. After spending two chapters discussing all these statistical findings, Durkheim finally explains that each of these factors concerns the degree of social solidarity surrounding the individual. For example, Catholic societies are more strongly integrated than are Protestant societies, and nations at war temporarily achieve high solidarity. *Egoism* (note, this word is different from "egotism") is excessive individualism in which a person lacks the moral support of society, and much self-murder is *egoistic suicide*.

If excessive individualism causes suicide, so does the opposite, insufficient individuation. In *altruistic suicide*, people sacrifice themselves out of duty to the society. One example is religious martyrdom; another is the high suicide rate among military personnel, quite apart from the risks they take in war. In societies that are very high in social solidarity, the suicide rate will be low, because egoistic suicide is absent, but the rate will not be zero because altruistic suicide remains. In addition, Durkheim argues, homicide rates are high in such societies.

Economic crisis increases the suicide rate, but so does exceptional economic prosperity. Suicide rates tend to be low in poor societies, so poverty itself cannot be the factor increasing suicide during economic depressions. Thus, the principle at work must be that sudden change and uncertainty aggravate suicide. Here, Durkheim introduces his most influential concept, *anomie* (occasionally spelled "anomy"). Human beings need a sense of stable goals within definite limits, and disruption in the norms and values that guide an individual's life is harmful anomie that may cause *anomic suicide*. Anomie is primarily a quality of society, not of the individual, and is exemplified by the loss or breakdown of traditional standards for behavior.

Durkheim mentions *fatalistic suicide*, his fourth kind of self-murder, only in a footnote, because it tells us little about society. Slaves may kill themselves in order to escape oppression, and an inability to do anything about their fates may bring people to kill themselves.

Few of the students who read Durkheim's classic today have any idea of the extensive research by others that preceded him throughout the entire nineteenth century, and few examine closely the many more recent works that have addressed the issues in *Suicide* with modern methods and theories. The remainder of this chapter considers the place of Durkheim's classic in that wider context.

Earlier Works

Jarvis, Edward
   1842 "Statistics of Insanity in the United States," *Boston Medical and Surgical Journal* 27:116–121, 281–282.

Contemporary American sociology traces its origins from French and German social thought of a century ago, and it ignores the splendid work done by several American researchers as early as the 1830s that laid the basis for modern theory-driven, quantitative sociology. Edward Jarvis lived from 1803 to 1884 and was gone from the scene a decade before the first sociology courses were taught in American universities and two decades before the founding of the American Sociological Association. But he was president of the American Statistical Association for thirty years, and in 1865 he was instrumental in the creation of the American Social Science Association. He never called himself a "sociologist," and the word did not become fashionable in America until after his death, but he published in several fields that today are included within sociology, and one of his articles on immigration is considered here in Chapter 16.

The 1840 census of the United States tried to count all the insane residents in each part of the country so that communities could decide whether they needed to build mental hospitals, but the data were soon put to other uses, both political and scientific. As soon as the census reports were published in 1842, attention focused on the insanity statistics for African Americans. *The Southern Literary Messenger*, an intellectual leader for the forces that later created the Confederacy, pointed out that rates of insanity were much higher among free blacks than among slaves, and Southern political leaders as influential as John C. Calhoun used this research in their defense of slavery. According to Calhoun, African Americans were not capable of handling freedom, and their high rate of insanity in the Northern states was supposedly proof of this.

When Jarvis saw the census data, probably in June 1842, he immediately calculated insanity rates and discovered the same thing that the Southern proslavery intellectuals had found, but he gave the finding a very different meaning. Jarvis was a vocal foe of slavery, and he did not think that blacks and whites differed in the factors that harmed or protected their sanity. Indeed, he believed that social research on African Americans could reveal principles that were true of all human beings. He calculated that the insanity rate for African Americans in free Northern states was 616 per 100,000, compared with only 64 per 100,000 in the slave states of the South. He knew there were errors in these data, but at first he thought they might be small enough that the general result was reliable. Jarvis quickly wrote up a journal article reporting his discovery and offering a theoretical explanation very much like Durkheim's concept of anomie half a century later.

Jarvis suggested that slavery limits psychological and intellectual development. "By refusing man many of the hopes and responsibilities which the free, self-thinking and self-acting enjoy and sustain, of course it saves him from some of the liabilities and dangers of active self-direction. If the mental powers and the propensities are kept comparatively dormant, certainly they must suffer much less from misdirection or over-action. So far as this goes, it proves the common notion, that in the highest state of civilization and mental activity there is the greatest danger of mental derangement; for here, where there is the greatest mental torpor, we find the least insanity.... It is a common and a probable theory, that the development of insanity has kept pace with the progress of civilization; and that the great disproportion between the number of lunatics among the free whites and the slave blacks in the United States, surely tends to corroborate this doctrine."

Like Durkheim, Jarvis was passionately attached to his own theories. Thus it was a remarkable turnabout in November 1842 when Jarvis repudiated his own analysis. Delving deeper into the data, he had discovered profound flaws. For example, he discovered that the census reports claimed that Worcester, Massachusetts, had 133 insane blacks, when these were actually the white residents of the Worcester insane asylum. Seven towns in Maine with no black residents were credited with 26 insane or "idiotic" blacks. Jarvis concluded that the private companies that tabulated and published the census volumes, and that had been involved in scandalous cost overruns, had simply done an incompetent job. Often they, or the census-takers themselves, had written numbers in the wrong columns on their forms, and the effect was greatly inflating the apparent insanity rates among free blacks. This is an early example of how social science can become involved in politics, because advocates of slavery rampaged across the pages of the nation's magazines and newspapers, claiming the census proved that slavery was good. Jarvis soon was leading a national crusade to refute these lies and to improve the quality of census data, in which he was joined by Northern free black organizations.

Jarvis's work on the 1840 census is today seen as a milestone in the development of rigorous social science. He was a consultant for the census of 1850, wrote the mortality volume of the 1860 census, and was a consultant again for the 1870 census. In 1855 he published a book based on a major survey of all the insane persons of Massachusetts, finding a close connection between poverty and insanity, a fact that sociologists of the twentieth century had to rediscover for themselves, because by the 1930s, Jarvis had been completely forgotten.

Wagner, Adolf Heinrich Gotthilf
  1864 *The Regularity of Apparently Voluntary Human Behavior from the Standpoint of Statistics* [*Die Gesetzmässigkeit in den Scheinbar Willkürlichen Menschlichen Handlungen vom Standpunkte der Statistik*]. Hamburg: Boyes und Geisler.

Durkheim took most of his data on suicide from earlier works. The study by Adolf Wagner is a remarkably painstaking analysis of European social statistics showing that human behavior follows regular laws, and offering judicious observations about the meaning of the findings. Wagner reports that earlier writers had suspected Protestants were more liable to commit suicide than Catholics, and he marshals a tremendous amount of data about Germany to demonstrate that this is so. He also shows that suicide is associated with higher levels of education, as Jarvis would have suspected. Unfortunately, Wagner's fine book was never translated into either French or English, and academic sociology took no notice of it until 130 years after it was published.

Morselli, Henry
  1879 *Suicide: An Essay on Comparative Moral Statistics*. New York:
    Appleton (1882).

Originally published in Italian, Morselli's book was quickly translated into English, and it became the standard social-scientific text on the topic of suicide until Durkheim's book superceded it. Morselli employed a tremendously wide range of statistics beyond suicide rates to explore every conceivable factor that might affect self-murder, from the climates of different countries to apparent psychological motives. His central theme is sociological, however: suicide is steadily increasing because civilization itself promotes it. Suicide is greater among better educated populations, in cities, and where high development of the railroads and of magazine publishing indicates commerce and communication. He hints that suicide may be increased by a weakening of traditional religious faith, but he explains the higher rate for Protestants as the result of their distinctive religious psychology: "Protestantism, denying all materialism in external worship and encouraging free enquiry into dogmas and creeds, is an eminently mystic religion, tending to develop the reflective powers of the mind and to exaggerate the inward struggles of the conscience" (p. 125).

Noyes, John Humphrey
  1870 *History of American Socialisms*. Philadelphia: Lippincott.

Throughout the nineteenth century, European and American intellectuals were simultaneously imagining new forms of society and thinking up theories about the communities in which they lived. Among the most remarkable of these social theorists was John Humphrey Noyes, who created a religious movement with branches at Oneida, New York, and Wallingford, Connecticut. At Oneida all shared the wealth and an experimental system of free love replaced the conventional family. All across America, other groups were experimenting with voluntary communism, some of them religious, and others based on non-religious socialist ideas. Hoping to determine the factors that led to success or failure for these utopian experiments, Noyes undertook a great study of their histories. Part of his research required tracking down a lost trunk containing data about these communes, including questionnaires members had filled out and eyewitness observations of their lifestyles, that had been collected by A. J. MacDonald, who died fifteen years earlier.

Noyes found that all of the non-religious socialist communes in nineteenth-century America failed, most of them very quickly. Some of the religious communes lasted for decades, Oneida among them. The quickest and often most disastrous failures were socialist experiments that brought together a group of strangers who had never learned to trust each other and who had no commitment to each other. Noyes described his findings in a way that presaged Durkheim's distinction between anomie and egoism: "Judging from all our experience and observation, we should say that the two most essential requisites for the formation of successful Communities, are *religious principle* and *previous acquaintance* of the members" (p. 57). If the members of a community share a coherent set of religious beliefs and practices, they will be protected from anomie. And if they have developed strong social relationships over a period of years, they are protected from egoism. Thus, their community will have a strong moral and social basis.

Later Publications on Religion and Suicide

Henry, Andrew F., and James F. Short, Jr.
  1954 *Suicide and Homicide.* Glencoe, Illinois: Free Press.

Calling Durkheim's work "the most important theoretical contribution to the understanding of suicide," Henry and Short focused on the correlation between suicide rates and changing economic conditions, using data on the United States in 1929–1949. Like Durkheim, they believed homicide was in some sense the opposite of suicide, so something about suicide could be learned by examining homicide as well. Henry and Short argued that both kinds of killing were caused by frustration, and social scientists had long argued that frustration often led to aggression. In suicide, the aggression was directed inward toward the person feeling it, whereas in homicide the aggression was directed outward toward other people. Like Durkheim, they found that suicide rates increased during times of economic depression, but their results refuted Durkheim's claim that suicide rates also increased during exceptionally good economic times.

This discovery was like a dagger plunged into the heart of Durkheim's theory of anomie. He had said that suicide rates were relatively low during times of economic stability, and they were high whenever economic conditions were either very bad or very good. If suicides increased only when the economy became unusually bad, then we could conclude that economic depression causes psychological depression, leaving little room for a sociological explanation. But if suicides also increase during exceptionally good economic times, then we could conclude that anything disrupting stable social life could aggravate suicide. By the mid-1950s, however, sociologists had found so many applications for the concept of anomie that they were not about to abandon it (see for example Merton's article in Chapter 5). The precise meaning of "anomie" has been hotly disputed, and many sociologists have expanded the definition to include egoism and other forms of social disorganization.

Pope, Whitney, and Nick Danigelis
   1981 "Sociology's 'One Law,'" *Social Forces* 60:496–514.

Pope and Danigelis test Durkheim's claim that Protestants have higher suicide rates than Catholics, using data covering 1919 to 1972 on twelve European nations. Seven of the nations were predominantly Catholic (Austria, Belgium, Ireland, Italy, Luxembourg, Portugal, Spain), and five were predominantly Protestant (Denmark, Finland, Iceland, Norway, Sweden). On average, the Protestant countries had a suicide rate of 14.3 per 100,000 population, compared with 11.4 per 100,000 in the Catholic countries. So at first it appears that Durkheim was right. However, modern statistical methods allowed Pope and Danigelis to test Morselli's theory that a nation's level of cultural development determines its suicide rate. In general, the five Protestant nations had achieved a higher level of development, as measured by such things as the proportion of households who had telephones. Using statistical methods to control for level of development, Pope and Danigelis found that the Protestant-Catholic suicide differences vanished. Statistical controls allow us to see how the nations would differ in suicide if they did not differ in technology and economics. If all twelve nations were at the same level of development, there would be no suicide difference between the Protestant or Catholic ones. Although such statistical methods seldom give a conclusive answer, they help us understand which of several social factors are really at work in a complex situation. Here, they raise serious questions about Durkheim's analysis and suggest that Morselli's might be closer to the truth.

Pescosolido, Bernice A., and Sharon Georgianna
   1989 "Durkheim, Suicide, and Religion: Toward a Network Theory of
   Suicide," *American Sociological Review* 54:33–48.

This study uses data on suicides, religion, and many other variables for 404 groups of American counties in 1970. Pescosolido and Georgianna analyze the relationships between the strengths of different denominations and the suicide rates, controlling statistically for other social factors. Rather than comparing Protestants with Catholics, they examine different Protestant denominations separately. The data show that the suicide rate tends to be low where the Catholic church is strong, but it is low also where *evangelical* Protestant denominations are strong, such as Nazarenes, Evangelical Baptists, Seventh-day Adventists, and the Church of God. In contrast, the suicide rate tends to be high where religion is dominated by *mainstream* Protestant churches such as the Episcopalians, institutional Presbyterians and Methodists, or the United Church of Christ. Pescosolido and Georgianna note there are many possible explanations for their findings, but they are especially interested in Durkheim's suggestion that stable social relationships deter suicide. Members of suicide-preventing denominations attend church more often than other people do, and they have a greater tendency to marry members of their own denomination, so the power of these denominations to deter suicide may result from their stronger social bonds.

The Proper Scope of Sociology

Parsons, Talcott
  1964 "Evolutionary Universals in Society," *American Sociological Review*
  29:339–357.

Talcott Parsons was among the greatest defenders of Durkheim's view that sociology should concern large-scale social phenomena such as society itself, and should not analyze everything in terms of the behavior of individuals. In this article, Parson's topic is nothing less than the evolution of human society over thousands of years, and the emergence of large-scale societal institutions that are so important that they are required for further progress. All societies possess four features of supreme importance: religion, communication with language, social organization through kinship, and technology. Thus, Parsons deduces, each of these four is essential to humanity. Six other major features are lacking in the most simple societies but emerge over the course of history and are found in all advanced nations: social stratification, cultural legitimation, bureaucratic organization, money and markets, generalized universalistic norms, and the democratic association. He focuses on these six as prerequisites for the development of modern society.

Social stratification is the development of different classes or gradations in wealth and influence that give some people more power than others. Parsons does not say that stratification is unjust; rather he argues that effective leadership and the development of modern conceptions of justice are based on the emergence of social inequality. *Cultural legitimation* is the development of ideological belief systems that support the society's institutions, including a sense of citizenship in the society and loyalty to the governing powers. *Bureaucratic organization* is an institutionalized hierarchy of authority that emerges first in government and then becomes characteristic of all large social organizations because it is so effective. Efficient *markets* based on *money* are a system of distributing wealth that competes with means for sharing wealth based on political, ethnic, or religious membership. *Universalistic norms* are standards for behavior that make no special distinctions based on the family, race, or group to which people belong, treating everyone in some sense equally. A *democratic association* is a political system of an organization or nation in which leaders are elected through voting by all members of the group, who are either citizens or voluntary participants. These features of society fit together into a mutually-reinforcing structure. For example, without cultural legitimation money would be worthless, and bureaucratic organization makes no sense without stratification. Without universalistic norms, democracy is impossible.

Parson's analysis is a kind often called *functionalist*. He analyzes each institution or feature of society in terms of what it accomplishes for the society as a whole. That is, he seeks the natural function of each societal feature, and he is not concerned about how the actions and interactions of individuals might create or sustain that feature. This approach is also called *structuralist* or *structural-functionalist*, because it assumes that the institutions of society fit together into a logical structure in which each institution supports the others. Although Parsons goes far beyond Durkheim, many writers have found the roots of structural-functionalism in Durkheim's work.

Homans, George C.
1964 "Bringing Men Back In," *American Sociological Review* 29:809–818.

In his presidential address to the American Sociological Association, George Homans criticized structural-functionalists for having taken Durkheim's approach to its illogical extreme. In particular, he condemned Durkheim's idea that social facts could not be derived from the actions of individuals, and thus that sociology could not be reduced to psychology. For Homans this was as ridiculous as saying that biologists did not need to worry about chemicals, because chemicals were the province of chemists, and chemists did not need to worry about atoms, because atoms were the province of physicists. For Homans, sociologists needed to find explanations for all social phenomena, and this would often mean analyzing how they arose in the interactions among individuals, with full attention to individual psychology.

A key problem with functionalism, Homans argued, was that it did not understand the nature of theory. Functionalists might assert that a particular societal institution served a particular function for the society, but they would not explain the precise mechanism by which it accomplishes this nor the exact series of steps by which it came into existence to serve the given function. A scientific theory, for Homans, consists of a set of formal statements, which he calls *propositions* of the theory. Each one states the relationship between properties of nature, which are well-defined phenomena that can be observed and measured, at least in principle. These propositions are arranged in a deductive system. At the top are general statements that may relate to a range of phenomena, and at the bottom are specific propositions that need to be explained. The system is like Greek geometry. The general propositions are the axioms of the system, and the lesser propositions are theorems that must be deduced from the axioms. (More detailed examination of how Homans thought this could be done is in Chapter 2.)

Homans said that Durkheim was a great sociologist, and that he often went beyond the limitations of structural-functionalism. But it was a mistake, according to Homans, to focus early in the history of sociology on large-scale structures and systems of institutions. Far better would be to understand relatively small and simple social structures through analysis of how individual human actions created them. And it was a mistake to build an intellectual wall between sociology and psychology, because often the best explanation of a social institution would be a deductive analysis of how it arose in the needs and actions of individuals. For Homans, defending the independence and supremacy of sociology was far less important than discovering the truth about human society, wherever that truth could be found. By "men" in the title of his influential paper, Homans meant "individual human beings." And sociology, he thought, needed to be reminded that the basis of all social life was the individual person.

INDIVIDUAL IN SOCIETY

2
SYMBOLIC INTERACTION AND EXCHANGE

WORKS AT A GLANCE

Symbolic Interactionism

Human Nature and the Social Order by Charles Horton Cooley
(1902, 1922)
Symbolic Interactionism: Perspective and Method
by Herbert Blumer (1969)
The Presentation of Self in Everyday Life by Erving Goffman (1959)

Exchange Theory

Social Behavior: Its Elementary Forms by George Caspar Homans
(1961, 1974)
Exchange and Power in Social Life by Peter Blau (1964)

We begin our survey of sociology with the individual human being and the relations with other individuals that link him or her to the immediate group and to the larger society. This is the domain of sociological social psychology, although many psychologists also claim this territory. Within sociology the dominant approach to social psychology is *symbolic interactionism*, which emphasizes the communications that provide the individual with a personal identity and with socially-scripted roles to play. *Exchange theory* is another important perspective that argues that humans develop relationships because of the rewards they can provide each other. Both symbolic interactionism and exchange theory examine the give-and-take between individuals, but the first believes that symbols have great power of their own, whereas the second asserts that symbols have power only to the extent that they guide the person in achieving rewarding goals.

In 1937 Herbert Blumer coined the term *symbolic interactionism,* but this perspective was created at the very beginning of the century, chiefly by American writers such as Charles Horton Cooley. To symbolic interactionists, a person's self-image is very important, and people labor to create a good impression in the minds of others. Cooley believed that humans have an innate need to feel that life is meaningful and that they themselves behave properly. Blumer stresses the fact that human beings are constantly redefining situations and actions, creating fresh meanings through social interaction. Erving Goffman agreed with Blumer that individuals are active creators of the world of meanings they inhabit, and he emphasized more than any other major theorist the ways that people may consciously scheme to make a good impression and manipulate other people's images of them. Modern symbolic interactionists use a wide variety of research methods, but much of the work is similar to humanistic literature, in which a perceptive writer observes the world and responds with fresh insights and critical arguments.

Sociological exchange theory draws heavily upon economics and upon behaviorist psychology. Although many sociologists have always been influenced by these other sciences, exchange theory in sociology did not really consolidate until the work of George Homans in the 1950s and the later efforts of Peter Blau and James Coleman (see Coleman in Chapter 10 and Chapter 15). Exchange theorists argue that the desire for rewards is the motivator of all behavior, including management of one's public impression and conformity to the desires of others. Currently, ideas from exchange theory permeate much of sociology, and social psychologists have developed a strong tradition of laboratory experimentation on exchange.

Symbolic Interactionism

Cooley, Charles Horton
  1922 Human Nature and the Social Order. New York: Scribner's.

At the time that Cooley wrote, many scientists and intellectuals believed that the chief factors shaping a person's behavior were individual genetic inheritance and the biological nature shared by all human beings. Cooley did not disagree that these were important factors, but he asserted that social influence was equally significant. Although we talk about the individual separately from society, and society separately from individuals, really they are the same thing, what Cooley calls *Human Life*. Without society, no individual human being could exist, and without individuals there would be no society. It is not just that each individual relies upon society for food and other material necessities, but that an infant could not mature into a person without the formal and informal education provided by society. Society is the *collective* aspect of Human Life, and individuals are the *distributive* aspect.

If humans are the product of biological inheritance and social influence, do they have the capacity to choose, what is often called "free will"? Or is human behavior essentially automatic? True, human creativity always consists of a fresh arrangement of existing ideas and memories, but when the influences and alternatives are very complex, it makes sense to refer to human choice and volition. For individuals, then, choice is enhanced by elaborate mental processes, and for society, by complex social relations. The increasing complexity of modern society has magnified choice, as has the extreme diversity of American democracy.

Cooley's theory of Human Life emphasizes the way that sociability creates ideas in our minds that represent other individuals, and the way that others give us impressions of ourselves. A friend exists in our mind as a system of thoughts and symbols, representing how that person acts, sounds, looks, and responds to us. Society exists in our mind as the collection of ideas we have about specific other individuals. Cooley stresses that the solid facts of sociology are the imaginations that individuals have of each other. Thus the proper focus of sociological study is the thoughts that people have in their minds.

The individual *self* is simply what a person means when he or she says "I," "me," "my," or "mine." Part of it is a special feeling—Cooley calls it the *my-feeling*—rooted in biological instincts, which is hard to describe in words but everybody understands. Although we have this feeling about our own bodies, Cooley says that the social and psychological aspects of self are far more important to us. The *social self* is the set of ideas the individual has about himself or herself, which are derived from communication with other people. An important part of the social self is our impression of how other people view us. Since we cannot see into their minds directly, we learn about their picture of us by observing how they respond to us, almost as a mirror might reflect our image back to us. Cooley calls this the *looking-glass self*, a term widely quoted by later sociologists. It has three main parts: (1) how we imagine we appear to the other person, (2) how we think that person judges us, and (3) how we react to that judgment, whether with pride or shame.

The metaphor of a looking-glass fits when the social environment is especially stable, like the solid reflecting surface of a mirror. But Cooley recognizes that sometimes the social environment is highly unstable, and the reflection is distorted as if by rushing waters. Every human being, Cooley says, needs self-expression, appreciation from others, and a reasonable degree of security. When these needs are thwarted, the person becomes pathological; Cooley believes this is the source of nearly all social discontent. Powerless workers, exploited immigrants, and members of disvalued ethnic groups are sociological examples of people who are denied the chance to satisfy these needs. Human beings have an instinct to demand rules, which guide and reconcile their impulses, and they are comfortable with habits of thought and action. Thus when a stable and benign society provides ethical rules for its members, these are not experienced as an imposition but as a comfortable harmony between individual and group.

In a group, the individual develops a larger social self, using words like "we," "our," and "us." Elsewhere, Cooley calls this the *we-feeling*, an expanded version of the my-feeling. A fan of a sports team may exclaim, "We won!" without ever being at the game, and citizens who never served in the military may feel a sense of victory when "we" win a war. Often, however, a person develops a wider self through identifying not with the group but with a singular individual, the hero or leader. The person uses the leader as a moral guide, asking what the leader would do under the given circumstances before taking action. Sometimes that guide is a distant friend, and we imagine what he or she might say, or it could be our fanciful image of an ideal person we have never met, such as a national hero or a religious personage. But during unsettled times, like twentieth-century America, even the face of God may be blurred, like the sun reflected from troubled waters.

Blumer, Herbert
  1969 *Symbolic Interactionism: Perspective and Method.* Englewood Cliffs,
    New Jersey: Prentice-Hall.

Blumer seeks to define *symbolic interactionism* and to criticize other perspectives for ignoring its key insights. Symbolic interactionism is based on three premises:

1. Human beings act toward things on the basis of the meaning those things have for them.
2. The meaning of things arises from social interaction.
3. Meanings are handled and modified through interpretation by the person.

Thus, meanings are created socially yet interpreted actively by the individual, and they are central to human action. People must learn meanings from others, and an object does not simply have a fixed meaning. Rather, meanings change as people redefine objects. For example, the stars in the sky had very different meaning for ancient people than they have for us today, now that we consider them to be distant suns. Perhaps the most significant object for any person is the self, how he or she understands himself or herself. The self is the key factor in determining the person's actions. Like other objects, each self is created through social interaction, and we see ourselves from the perspective of other people. Because all objects are constantly being redefined, human society and behavior are constantly transformed by human creativity. Society itself is the result of symbolic interaction.

In any society there are recurrent patterns of joint action that follow somewhat stable principles, because people share meanings and know what behavior is expected of them. Sociologists have studied many of these varied patterns, such as families, boys' gangs, industrial corporations, and political parties. Some sociologists say that their stability is maintained by norms and values, but Blumer says the opposite is true: norms and values are created and upheld by the social processes of group life. Joint action consists of very complex networks of actions by diverse people who are linked together. The societal institutions that arise from this joint action are not stable entities in their own right but result from the interrelated actions of many individuals, as they define the varied situations in which they find themselves. Although human beings are constantly redefining objects and actions in the present, every social situation has a long history and cannot be understood correctly without examining the processes that shaped it in the past.

Blumer is highly critical of sociologists who employ other perspectives that assume the objectivity of such concepts as *attitudes* and *variables*. The concept of attitude assumes that a person has some kind of fixed tendency to act in a particular way that can be distinguished from the person's other characteristics (such as feelings, ideas, opinions, and decisions) and from the actions themselves. Symbolic interactionists think people do not possess a set of automatic responses but constantly respond to new demands and possibilities in a creative manner by sizing up situations and by developing fresh definitions through social interaction. Rather than misguidedly trying to measure a person's fixed attitudes, sociologists should study the dynamic process by which the person and the group define actions and mobilize for collective action.

In a similar manner, Blumer is critical of sociologists who rely too heavily upon measurement and statistical analysis of variables. A variable supposedly is a well-defined entity, like the tendency to vote Republican or having a college education, that varies from person to person. Blumer notes that quantitative sociologists select variables haphazardly, and that few of them represent abstract scientific concepts. Many sociologists wrongly assume that a variable has a stable meaning. Rather, it is constantly changing as people socially redefine it. For example, the Republican Party is not the same thing today that it was last year. Thus, meanings change over time, and respondents to a questionnaire will interpret the questions in different ways. Many sociologists claim that variations in the independent variables of a research study determine variations in the dependent variables. But this is wrong. For instance, a research study that merely correlated the introduction of a birth control program with the birth rate would be highly incomplete. It would need to employ symbolic interactionism to examine how birth control enters into the lives of the people, through the meanings they assign to it.

Goffman, Erving
1959 *The Presentation of Self in Everyday Life*. New York: Anchor.

Goffman analyzes the ways that people manage the public impressions they make, using metaphors taken from the theater and from subcultures that emphasize deception. He illustrates his ideas with examples taken from some of his own research in the Shetland Islands, from books about occupations and settings where people are apt to deceive each other, and from observations reported in unpublished dissertations and papers by members of the sociology department at the University of Chicago, where Goffman himself was a student. Sociologists had long spoken of the roles that people play, but Goffman shifted the emphasis in sociological understanding of role playing in two ways. First, he described people as very active shapers of their own roles, rather than merely accepting the roles society scripted for them. Second, he developed a language for talking about roles, partly derived from the theater, that he called the *dramaturgical* approach.

In the theater, some people called the *actors* play roles on stage that fit together into a particular drama. Other people play a very different role and belong to a group called the *audience,* which exists only in relationship to the actors but is excluded from much inside information that the actors possess. The actors on stage impose a *definition of the situation* on the audience, for example asserting that this is not a stage filled with actors but the castle of MacBeth populated with Scottish nobles and servants. Similarly, in the "real world" outside the theater, people attempt to impose upon others a definition of the situation that attributes to themselves characteristics that they may not really possess. Goffman does not seek to test whether this theory is true, or to determine statistically how often it is true. Rather, using this dramaturgical perspective, he identifies a number of roles, dramatic techniques, and role-playing contexts, describing their dynamics and assigning them names.

Performances vary in the degree of sincerity with which the actor plays them, but insincerity is not necessarily undesirable. A shoe clerk sells a customer a shoe that fits well, and lies when saying that it is the size the customer requested. Carried off well, this performance satisfies the customer not only with physically comfortable feet but also with the pride that his or her feet are not too fat. Little "white lies" commonly serve the needs of the audience as well as those of the actors, but often it is possible to use innuendo, strategic ambiguity, and crucial omisions to achieve a successful performance without actually lying. Goffman asserts that all legitimate vocations and relationships require the performer to conceal something, and thus all everyday performances are precarious. Social life is possible only because all ordinary human beings have some skill as actors.

The part of a performance that defines the situation for the audience is called *front*. This involves the setting, which includes furniture, decor, physical layout, and any items that serve as scenery or stage props for the performance. A doctor's office, with all its strange paraphernalia, is the setting that supports the role of physician. A routine performance of some importance for the society becomes idealized, in the sense that everybody shares standard expectations for it, and a good performance upholds the moral values of the community.

Goffman sees much to be learned from examination of the different performances that define the separate social classes, especially when a person from one social class acts like a member of another. In America, wealth is such a strong determinant of social class that people struggle to buy status symbols that will let them enter the next-highest class. In India, members of a moderately low caste may start practicing the rituals and food regulations of a higher caste to gain entry to it, despite formal prohibitions against caste switching. Sometimes people adopt the performances of lower classes, as when a Shetland farmer simulates being poor, with ragged clothes and a house in disrepair, in order to discourage the landowner from increasing the rents.

Actors often work in teams. A *performance team* is any set of people who cooperate in staging a given routine. Each teammate typically has the power to ruin the performance, and because the members of the team share inside knowledge about their joint performance they are unable to maintain its objectivity with each other. Teams are like secret societies, whose members cooperate to project a particular definition of the situation on their audience. They put on their performance in a *front region*, where the audience observes them, and they typically need a *back region* or *backstage* where the audience cannot go and where they can drop their burdensome roles.

The example to which Goffman continually returns is the hotel in the Shetland Islands where he stayed during his field research. In front of the guests, especially in the dining room, the staff of the hotel behaved in the dignified but respectful manner of middle-class professionals serving elite clients. In the backstage area of the kitchen, however, they relaxed, spoke disrespectfully of the guests, and resumed their rural habits of speech and manner. The presentation of food to the guests was a key element of the drama, and the kitchen staff understood well what the limits of play-acting were. The meat had to be reasonably fresh, because the guests understood how to judge it and tended to focus upon it. The soup, in contrast, could get by as a mixture of yesterday's brew, plus a little left over from the day before, with a few new ingredients. Perfectly good butter would return from the dining room in odd shapes, and it could be recycled simply by pressing it into nice patterns in the butter molds. When the staff was very busy, it would wipe the glasses rather than take the time to wash them, and the guests seemed happy at prompt service and unharmed by the dubious hygiene. Often, in social life, impressions count for more than does reality, if, indeed, there is any reality beyond the impression humans make upon each other.

Exchange Theory

Homans, George Caspar.
   1974 *Social Behavior: Its Elementary Forms.* New York: Harcourt Brace
   Jovanovich.

Homans seeks to set out a general theory of human social behavior, but before he can do this, he needs to state what a scientific theory is. Ideally, such a theory is a formal structure of *propositions*, which are statements about the relationship between properties of nature. Some of these propositions are very general, like the axioms in classical Greek geometry. Other propositions are derived from them through formal logic, like the theorems and corollaries of geometry. When sociologists discover a regular finding in their research, it should be stated as a proposition, and that proposition should be explained. To *explain* a proposition means to show that it follows as a matter of pure logic from other, more general propositions.

Homans offers five very general propositions, which he believes can explain much about human social behavior. Each is very much like an axiom from geometry, except that Homans believes it is rooted in human biological evolution rather than in the nature of lines and planes in space, as is the case for geometry. The five general propositions follow.

1. For all actions taken by persons, the more often a particular action of a person is rewarded, the more likely the person is to perform that action.
2. If in the past the occurrence of a particular stimulus, or set of stimuli, has been the occasion on which a person's action has been rewarded, then the more similar the present stimuli are to the past ones, the more likely the person is to perform the action, or some similar action, now.
3. The more valuable to a person is the result of his or her action, the more likely the person is to perform the action.
4. The more often in the recent past a person has received a particular reward, the less valuable any further unit of that reward becomes for that person.
5. This proposition is in two parts:

   a. When a person's action does not receive the reward he expected, or receives punishment he did not expect, he will be angry; he becomes more likely to perform aggressive behavior, and the results of such behavior will become more valuable to him.

b. When a person's action receives reward he expected, especially a greater reward than he expected, or does not receive punishment he expected, he will be pleased; he becomes more likely to perform approving behavior, and the results of such behavior become more valuable to him.

These propositions concern individual human beings, rather than large-scale phenomena such as society. Homans believed it would be possible to build sociological theory up from the individual level. The first proposition states that an individual's action is shaped by rewards. If a given action is rewarded, the person becomes more likely to perform it. Imagine that a fisherman has cast his line into a particular pool, and has caught a fish, which is rewarding to him. He will cast his line in the pool again. This proposition is taken from behavioral psychology, especially from the work of Homans's colleague at Harvard and close friend, B. F. Skinner.

The second proposition brings in stimuli, including new stimuli that may be more or less similar to old ones, and new actions. The fisherman may find that casting his line into dark pools has been rewarding, whereas light pools have not been. So he will discriminate dark pools from light ones, and be more likely to cast his line into dark ones. He can also generalize from the original stimuli and actions. He will try casting his line into many kinds of pool, and learn which are more rewarding, and he may even try hunting, which is the generalization of fishing from the water to the dry land. This proposition brings in the branch of psychology devoted to perception and cognition. Human beings are especially capable of learning complex judgments of similarity and dissimilarity compared with other animals studied by psychologists, such as pigeons and mice.

The third proposition concerns the value of results from a person's actions, which may be positive (rewards) or negative (punishments). Some values are innate, determined biologically by the gentic inheritence shared by all human beings. For example, hunger makes humans seek food. But some social values may also be innate. Humans evolved as social animals, living in groups that hunted and gathered food together, and the desire for social contact and such intimate actions as hugging may have been programmed into us by biological evolution, just as horses have been programmed to roam in herds. Values are not merely innate but can also be learned. For example, mothers may hug their children when they perform actions the mothers approve of, thus teaching children to value those actions as means of obtaining hugs. Social learning—developing a pattern of behavior because it is rewarded by other human being—is very important in Homans's theory, giving rise to the norms of groups and to the large sets of norms we call cultures.

The fourth proposition concerns satiation and deprivation. If we have just eaten a big meal, we are no longer hungry. Our hunger has been satiated, and thus the value of food has been reduced. But if we are deprived of food for a long time, our hunger will increase until no reward is more important to us than food. Surprisingly, this principle forms the very basis of social exchange. If a person, *A*, has much food, *A* will always be able to eat whenever he or she is even the least bit hungry. Thus the person will not value food very much, and is willing to part with it in return for some other reward that *A* lacks, for example warm clothing. If person *B* is hungry but has two warm coats, and the weather is cold, *A* may be willing to give *B* a lot of food in return for one coat. Person *B* is not much more satisfied by two coats than by one, so *B* is willing to make the exchange. Thus, the fact that people have different resources, and can be satisfied by a limited amount of each, allows both parties to exchange to profit.

The fifth proposition seems complicated, but both parts of it concern a person's reaction when he or she receives much less or much more than expected. The first part is a standard observation from psychology, that frustration often leads to aggression. If unexpected loss leads to angry aggression, Homans hypothesizes that unexpected gain should also lead to emotional behavior, in this case approval. In an exchange that frustrated one of the parties, aggression may force the other party to behave better in the future. Approval tells an exchange partner that some behavior was appreciated and should be continued.

On the basis of these five fundamental theoretical propositions, Homans seeks to build a structure that explains much human action. In office work, for example, a social relationship may develop out of repeated exchanges between two people in which one provides advice (the valuable reward of information) in exchange for approval (a purely social reward). Norms arise out of exchanges in groups. A norm defines expected behavior that will receive approval rather than punishing aggression. Using empirical studies by other social scientists for his illustrations, Homans develops explanations of conformity, stratification, and justice.

Blau, Peter
1964 *Exchange and Power in Social Life*. New York: Wiley.

Blau explains that the early chapters of his book are based to a great extent on Homans's *Social Behavior* (1961 edition), but he goes much further than Homans in developing a theory of how large-scale social structures are built out of social exchange between individuals. The key task of sociology, he says, is to analyze social associations, which are based on the fact that both parties to an exchange can often benefit. But this does not mean that the parties to an exchange benefit equally, that they have complete information about the exchange, or that each exchange occurs in a vacuum isolated from other commitments the parties may have. Often an individual is able to get more from an exchange than the other person does, because he or she has more power of one kind or another.

People are attracted to others if they expect exchanges with them to be rewarding, and they need to become attractive to the others in order to develop an enduring association. Often a person wants something from another but has nothing to give in return that the other wants. A person in this uncomfortable situation has four basic alternatives. First, it may be possible to force the other person to give the desired item, perhaps by threat of violence or outright theft. Second, it may be possible to find another person who can provide the item. Third, the person who wants the item can simply learn to live without it. And fourth, the person may subordinate himself or herself to the person who has the item, giving that person power. Thus, in the course of a large number of social exchanges, some individuals come to have power over others.

Looking at these four alternatives from a slightly different perspective, Blau examines what factors give a person independence from the power of others or power over others, and how these factors create large-scale social structures. He summarizes his theory in a chart (p. 124):

Alternatives to Compliance	Conditions of Independence	Requirements of Power	Structural Implications
1. Supply inducements	Strategic resources	Indifference to what others want	Exchange and distribution of resources
2. Obtain elsewhere	Available alternatives	Monopoly over what others need	Competition and exchange rates
3. Take by force	Coercive force	Law and order	Organization and differentiation
4. Do without	Ideals lessening needs	Materialistic and other relevant values	Ideology formation

If person A desires reward X possessed by person B, A can offer some valuable resource Y to B in return for X. Thus, A can be independent of B's power because A possesses Y. But B can assert power by being indifferent to Y. If B wants Y, then A and B exchange their resources and the beginnings of a distribution system for rewards emerges.

If alternative sources of X are available (people C and D, for example), then B cannot have power over A, because A can simply go to one of the other sources for X. However, if B can acquire a monopoly over X, being the only available supplier, then B has power. When there are multiple potential sources of a reward, then there is competition, and B, C, and D vie with each other in offering A favorable terms for the exchange.

If A has the capacity to exercise coercive force, then A might take X from B against B's will. Person B in collusion with C and D can create a system of law and order that prevents the use of naked force. This produces complex social organizations based on law and upholding order, and a variety of such organizations produce a differentiated social system.

Person A may be able to do without X, especially if A can adopt philosophical ideals that lessen the feeling of needing X. Person B can counter these ideals with materialistic values or other ideals that increase A's need for X. The result is the formation of ideology. In a large collection of people having different resources, many exchanges will therefore produce a complex social system, consisting of institutions that distribute rewards, competition between individuals and between groups, a structure of differentiated organizations, and ideologies.

Once the beginnings of such a system emerge, the dynamics of power change. Collective approval legitimates power, and legitimate authority forms the basis of organization. Persons A and B do not merely negotiate with each other, but also turn to others for support. If B can get C and D to agree that B has legitimate authority, then B's power over A is considerably strengthened. A value consensus may emerge in the society, convincing even poor A that B's authority is just. Norms develop that define the terms of fair exchange and justice. Even if A does not agree with the consensus, the agreement of the other members of the society imposes it upon A. Successful leaders command the willing compliance of many subordinates, who in turn impose the leader's power upon anyone who does not comply. A successful leader, therefore, cannot simply be a dictator but must offer sufficient rewards to the subordinates to be socially attractive to them. Thus legitimacy tends to limit an individual's power, even as it creates a powerful social system.

3
GROUPS AND SOCIAL NETWORKS

WORKS AT A GLANCE

The Invention of Sociometry

Who Shall Survive? by Jacob L. Moreno (1934)

Small Group Theory

The Human Group by George Caspar Homans (1950)

Diffusion of Influence

Personal Influence by Elihu Katz and Paul Lazarsfeld (1955)

The Shape of Social Networks

"Urban Families: Conjugal Roles and Social Networks"
  by Elizabeth Bott (1955)
"The Strength of Weak Ties" by Mark Granovetter (1973)
"Network Exchange Outcomes: Limits of Predictability"
  by Barry Markovsky (1992)

Interaction between human beings creates social units that surround the individual and are larger than the two-person *dyad*, but smaller than entire societies or societal institutions. A *group* is a more-or-less exclusive set of individuals who have relatively stable and extensive relations among themselves and who possess a sense of group identity or purpose. A *network* is a structure of relationships linking a number of individuals directly or indirectly. Its members usually lack a special awareness of themselves as a distinct social entity, and the web of relationships may extend far and wide through the society, including people of diverse identities and purposes. Clearly the concepts of group and network overlap, and sociologists have often debated whether a particular small-scale social phenomenon is better understood as one or the other. Underlying the works described in this chapter is the belief that network is the more fundamental concept, and a group is a relatively closed portion of a social network whose members have achieved a degree of unity in goals and perceptions.

In the 1920s, Jacob Moreno developed methods for measuring the social structure of groups and networks, which he called *sociometry*. By the middle of the twentieth century, when George Homans wrote his classic study of small groups, researchers had used a variety of techniques to examine how individual human beings cooperate to form groups. Findings from this research were significant for several applied areas. For example, the performance of industrial work teams could be improved, based on small group research done in factories. Scientific understanding of group dynamics could help society respond to the challenges to law and order presented by delinquent gangs. On a more intellectual level, Homans showed that the same theoretical principles could illuminate the cultures of pre-industrial societies and the historical transformation of modern communities.

In the 1940s, research in the related fields of advertising and politics showed that mass media communications have little effect upon most individuals, unless their influence is backed up by intimate personal relationships. Paul Lazarsfeld, a pioneer of questionnaire election research, collaborated with Elihu Katz in a comprehensive examination of personal influence that showed how the individual was bound into the community through an extended network of such relationships that serves as the informal communication system by which innovations spread throughout the society.

The second half of the twentieth century saw steady development of network theory and a series of research studies that tested and extended its ideas. Elizabeth Bott suggested that the structure of social relationships around a married couple could have profound effects on their roles and the extent to which they share their feelings with each other. Mark Granovetter pointed out that strong interpersonal ties could isolate the individual from the larger society, and he showed that weak ties could reach further across an extended social network to carry important communications. Barry Markovsky explained that small differences in the structure of social networks could sometimes have tremendous effects on the power of individuals, thus making social life chaotic and unpredictable.

The sociological writings discussed below demonstrate the fundamental importance of networks and groups by the great variety of social phenomena they consider: social influence in a reform school and in a typical American town, an industrial work team and the informal networks for getting jobs, the structures of schools and families. The concepts introduced in this chapter reappear in one form or another throughout the following chapters, because networks and groups are the building blocks for all larger social structures, from cities to social movements, churches to political parties.

The Invention of Sociometry

Moreno, Jacob L.
  1934 *Who Shall Survive?* Washington, D.C., Nervous and Mental Disease
    Publishing Co.

Moreno was a tremendously influential and creative man, but he was also controversial. He pioneered group psychotherapy and invented a therapeutic technique called *psychodrama,* in which group therapy clients improvised the roles of their parents or other people significant to them. Late in his life Moreno claimed to receive novel revelations directly from God, and many professional colleagues judged that his delusions of grandeur had finally gotten the better of him. Yet a scientific journal he founded is still published by the American Sociological Association; currently called *Social Psychology Quarterly*, it was originally named *Sociometry.*

Moreno presented the new science of sociometry in his dramatically named book, saying it was a tool for doing psychotherapy on the social group rather than on the individual. Like many intellectuals who had lived through the First World War, Moreno was appalled at the madness into which European societies had descended and judged that a new science of society was needed to prevent a further episode of world-wide insanity. The key would be a powerful tool for research into the structure of society and thus into its very nature. *Sociometry* means "measuring society," and it is carried out through observations or questionnaires that determine the pattern of relationships that link individuals.

In school research, Moreno reminded the students that they had been assigned classroom seats by their teacher. Then he asked them to imagine they could select which other students would sit beside them. Each was supposed to look around the class, then write down the name of the student he or she would best like to have sit in the next seat. Then the students did this again for the students they liked second best. Despite Moreno's grand aims, he was very good at collecting data about people's actual feelings, sticking to the concrete realities of the social setting in which the people found themselves. In settings other than school, he employed other questions that were better adapted to those environments.

Once he had sociometric data from a number of groups, Moreno explored the various ways these data could be analyzed. For example, he tabulated what percentage of boys chose girls, and girls chose boys, in different grade school age groups. The results showed clearly how the two sexes tended to separate socially for a number of years before adolescence would bring them back together. He also looked at how often two people chose each other, what he called *mutual pairs*, and how often a given individual was not chosen by anybody else, what he called *isolated* and today we call *social isolates*. He compared teachers' judgments of which children were popular or isolated with sociometric data from the children themselves, and he explored the factors connected with popularity. With his simple sociometric tests, Moreno had opened a window on an entire new world of research, one in which many social scientists are still active today and which has not yet revealed all its secrets.

As a tool for visualizing sociometric data, Moreno invented the *sociogram*. This is a chart that represents people as little shapes and relationships as lines connecting them. Following the conventions of some anthropologists in drawing family trees, he represented girls by circles and boys by triangles. If one of the boys chose a girl to sit beside him, Moreno would draw an arrow from the triangle representing the boy to the circle representing the girl. The diagrams in his book get quite complicated, with red arrows representing attraction and black arrows representing repulsion between people.

These sociograms communicated far more information than most people could extract from tables of numbers, and they revealed much about a group. It was immediately obvious that a school class was a *social network*, perhaps with a good deal of separation between boys and girls, and with some *cliques* in which the students mostly chose each other. Sociometric tests could be done repeatedly over time, and the resulting sociograms formed a kind of motion picture of the group's evolution. A sociogram of a fraternity revealed that one member was chosen by many others, and not surprisingly he turned out to be its president. But sociometry readily revealed informal leadership that otherwise might have been invisible. A sociogram showing both attraction (liking) and repulsion (disliking), with one individual at the center of the chart and all the others in a ring around that person, instantly showed the balance of friendships and hostility that surrounded him or her.

Moreno undertook a massive study of a reform school in New York State, administering sociometric tests to 505 girls living in 15 institutional cottages. Within this vast social network, he discovered many instances of small-scale structures, such as three girls who were all friends with each other, or more rarely three who were locked in hostile competition with each other. He also observed the girls' behavior with each other and analyzed what they had to say about their relations. The staff of the institution totaled just 80 individuals, and it was impossible for them to have warm, supportive relationships with all of the inmates. Yet positive social relationships could be among the most therapeutic of factors, helping these troubled girls find their way to happy adulthoods. Thus, many of the girls would have to become instruments of therapy for the others, transmitting through their social network the positive influence of the staff.

Moreno believed that sociometry provided the information necessary to re-organize groups to the benefit of all members. Social isolates could be brought into contact with people who would become their friends. Those individuals with hostile relations toward each other could be separated. When a new community is being planned, individuals who want to live in it could be given a population test to determine their sociological suitability. Migration from one town to another could be guided rather than haphazard, to create healthy communities. Publishing in the very year when Hitler gained control over Germany, Moreno believed that sociometry could be used to understand re-lations between Germans and Jews, and perhaps to create more favorable bonds between German Jews and the society surrounding them. Moreno's dream that his techniques could cure society of its pathologies never became reality—but sociometry has become an essential tool of sociological research.

Small Group Theory

Homans, George Caspar
   1950 *The Human Group.* New York: Harcourt, Brace and World.

Homans develops a general theory of group behavior through analyzing five different human groups reported in scientific publications by other social scientists: a work team in a telephone equipment manufacturing plant studied by Fritz Rothlisberger and William Dickson, a gang of young Italian-American men observed by William Foote White (see Chapter 7), inhabitants of a Polynesian island described by Raymond Firth, a community in Massachusetts called "Hilltown" (actually Hubbardston) investigated historically by D. L. Hatch, and an electrical equipment company examined by Homans's friend C. M. Arensberg with D. Macgregor.

To focus his analysis, Homans defines three elements of human social be-havior: activity, interaction, and sentiment. *Activity* refers to the things people do, such as planting potatoes, walking, or doing a particular kind of work. *Interaction* concerns episodes in which the activity of one person influences and is influenced by the activity of another person. *Sentiment* is a mental state of the individual, perhaps an emotion, such as affection for a particular other person, antagonism, and hunger. In some respects, Homans preferred activity and interaction, which a sociologist could observe directly, rather than sentiments, which must be inferred from a person's words or deeds. But sen-timents can be studied indirectly, for example in questionnaire surveys of attitudes or in sociometric studies of how people feel about each other.

Homans devotes four chapters of his book to a close analysis of data collected by Rothlisberger and Dickson in the Bank Wiring Observation Room, a special production facility set up at the Hawthorne factory of the Western Electric Company. Here, fourteen men assembled banks of terminals for telephone switching equipment. Nine of them were "wiremen" who put together plastic terminal blocks and attached wires to the appropriate contacts. Three solderman then applied metal solder to hold the wires in place. Finally, two inspectors checked these assemblies. The nine wiremen were divided into three soldering units, one for each solderman, and they were also divided into two inspection units, one for each inspector. As the men labored together for months, a team of social scientists collected many kinds of data about them and observed all phases of their work and social life within the factory.

The corporation that hired these men paid them according to a group piecework system that was based on the productivity of the team as a whole, thus encouraging them to cooperate as well as to work hard as individuals. The company assumed the men would labor up to the limit of fatigue, because only thus could they maximize their earnings. However, the men did not behave as expected. Somehow they set their own norm for how much work should be done, about two completed sets of equipment per wireman per day. They would work very hard in the morning, then ease up in the afternoon, leaving time for special chores, conversation, and games. Management agreed the output level was good, but would have preferred that the men produce more.

If a man did work harder than the norm set by his fellow workers, they would ridicule him as a "rate buster," and a man who did too little work was shamed as a "chiseler." One of the games played by the men illustrates the informal means they employed to enforce their norms. In "binging," one man would come up to another and playfully punch him on the upper arm. The other would respond by binging the first man back. The aim was to see who could hit harder, but naturally the men held their punches to some extent, knowing that each blow would be returned. But a man who worked either too hard or too little would get binged by several other men, each of whom could endure the few blows he gave each of them, while he had to suffer many blows.

The men did differ somewhat in output rates, however. Tests of intelligence and of manual dexterity failed to explain this variation. Among the data collected by the social scientists were several measures of relations among the men: who helped whom, who occasionally exchanged jobs, who played games together, who were friends with each other, and who were antagonistic. Sociometric analysis revealed that most of the men belonged to one of two *cliques* within the room, somewhat distinct social groups that had dense social relations inside but few social relations across cliques. It turned out that the two cliques differed in the average output of their men, and much of the variation across individuals could be explained by clique membership. That is, the entire room had set a rough norm of how much productivity was proper, but each clique had set its own norm noticeably different from that of the other. This discovery not only explains individual variations in output, but also illustrates the principle that norms tend to be set most precisely by the people closest to a given individual in his or her social network.

Homans found it useful to distinguish two aspects of the social system of a group: the external system and the internal system. The *external system* consists of those activities, interactions, and sentiments of a group that are intended to help it cope with its environment. For example, the men in the Bank Wiring Room worked together to satisfy the factory managers and earn paychecks. Homans says that human groups exist only to help individuals survive and extract things they need from the environment, so the external system is the essential behavior of a group that brings it into being. But once the group exists, and the external system is functioning reasonably well, the behavior of members becomes elaborated, and they begin to have activities, interactions, and sentiments that are related solely to each other, what Homans calls the *internal system*. Homans explains this development in terms of a short set of formal theoretical propositions:

1. Persons who interact frequently with each other tend to like one another.
2. If the frequency of interaction between two or more persons increases, the degree of their liking for one another will increase, and vice versa.
3. If the interactions between the members of a group are frequent in the external system, sentiments of liking will grow up between them, and these sentiments will lead in turn to further interactions, over and above the interactions of the external system.

Homans employs this approach to theory-building throughout his book, examining a particular situation and seeking to extract general principles from it that can be stated formally and connected logically with other general principles.

Diffusion of Influence

Katz, Elihu, and Paul Lazarsfeld
  1955 *Personal Influence*. New York: Free Press.

This book is the culmination of twenty years of research by social scientists on how social relationships shape the impact of mass media on individuals. The development of radio and then of television, along with the growth of advertising and political propaganda, gave rise to a concept of *mass society*. In such a society, the mass media communicate directly with individuals, informing them or deceiving them in a new and powerful manner. Research soon showed that four variables intervene between the media and the masses, either facilitating or blocking the flow of communications. First, *exposure* to the communication varies, because of variations in technology (e.g.,

TV has not yet been introduced into the country), politics (e.g., totalitarian countries forbid reception of some TV), economics (e.g., some families cannot afford sets), and the voluntary decision of people whether to listen to the message or not. Second, the *characters of the media* themselves are a factor, and radio, TV, and other mass media vary in how well they carry a particular kind of message. Third, the communication's *manner of presentation* is important, with techniques like repetition and appeal to respected authorities increasing its power. Fourth, the *psychology of the audience* can be decisive, with prejudiced people rejecting a message no matter how it is presented.

Many research studies, however, discovered that a fifth factor, *social relationships* among the members of the audience, was crucial. A two-step model of media influence emerged from some of these research projects. First, the communication goes to a small number of individuals who serve as *opinion leaders* for their communities. Second, if they are convinced, they transmit the message to other members of the population who play a more passive role. Katz and Lazarsfeld say that these opinion leaders are not a distinct kind of person, but rather they are group members who play a key role in communications. The interpersonal relationships among members of the group anchor its opinions, attitudes, habits, and values. Thus, no major change can occur unless it works through the relationships. Furthermore, the crucial communication occurs through interpersonal networks that relay the message and may reinforce it.

The centerpiece of the Katz and Lazarsfeld book is a study of personal influence carried out in Decatur, Illinois, in 1945. It began with a June survey of 800 women, focusing on four areas of decision-making: marketing, fashions, public affairs, and movie-going. The researchers not only asked the respondents about their own behavior and attitudes, but also inquired about the people who influenced them and whom they influenced. In August, interviewers returned to the women with the same set of questions. Whenever a respondent said something different in this second survey from what she had answered two months earlier, the interviewer would ask whether she had talked with someone about this issue in the meantime, and whether this person had played a role in changing her response. Questions also focused on how respondents might discuss with friends the things they had heard on the radio or read in newspapers. The researchers also interviewed 337 of the people these respondents said had influenced them (*influentials*) and 297 of those the respondents claimed to have influenced (*influencees*).

Although the respondents' everyday contacts tended to be with family members, more than half the people who influenced them were outside their families. About half of the influentials and influencees acknowledged they had played the role claimed by the original interviewee; many of the rest could not remember or described the conversation in terms of a more equal exchange of views. Influentials were more likely to acknowledge their role than were influencees. Several survey questions measured the impact that different forms of communication had, and personal contacts scored ahead of radio advertising, newspapers, magazines, and salespersons.

The Shape of Social Networks

Bott, Elizabeth
1955 "Urban Families: Conjugal Roles and Social Networks," *Human Relations* 8:345–384.

Elizabeth Bott studied twenty London families through intensive interviews, exploring many aspects of their lives to develop theories about the factors that determined the ways they played the roles of wife and husband. Some couples made relatively little distinction between the duties of husband and wife and played their roles in a *joint* manner, whereas some other couples had very different expectations for men and women in marriage and played the roles in a *segregated* manner. The key question was how the roles of wife and husband fit together, what Bott calls the *role-relationship*, and since these are roles in marriage, this is a *conjugal* role-relationship. When a husband and wife share the responsibilities together, both doing pretty much the same family tasks and spending their leisure time together, they have a *joint conjugal role-relationship*. When a couple divides the responsibilities along traditional lines—the husband having some tasks, and the wife having very different ones—and the two mostly spend leisure time apart, the couple has a *segregated conjugal role-relationship*.

In a couple with segregated roles, the man would be the exclusive breadwinner, and the woman would have responsibility for cooking, cleaning, and childcare. Such wives would spend much time with their extended families and depend heavily upon their mothers, while their husbands spent spare time away from home with their friends. When the roles were joint, there was a possibility the wife would have her own paying job, or at least be contemplating one, while the husband took care of some of the housekeeping and upbringing of children. When it was time for recreation, such couples would go out together, and they were more likely than couples playing segregated roles to share their thoughts and feelings with each other.

Bott examined her data to see if the difference in the two family styles was simply the result of social class. There was a tendency for middle class couples to follow the joint role approach, and for working class couples to play segregated roles. But several couples did not fit this pattern. Another possible explanation was that the joint role was a reaction to living in a neighborhood with highly varied kinds of people and a high rate of mobility, and that the segregated role was a reaction to a stable, homogeneous neighborhood. Again, the data showed a tendency in this direction, but the fit was not perfect. Then Bott tried to explain the conjugal role-relationship in terms of the shape of the social network surrounding the couple.

Each family lived in the midst of a social network, rather than an organized group. Some of each couple's friends were friends of each other, but other friends were strangers to each other. Although all twenty couples had social networks, these networks differed significantly in how dispersed versus connected they were. In a highly *dispersed* network, the couple's friends tend not to be friends of each other, and the friends tend to live in different neighborhoods. By contrast, in a highly *connected* network, friends of the couple tend to be friends of each other as well. Bott found that couples with a joint role-relationship had dispersed networks, whereas couples with a segregated role relationship had highly connected networks. Couples whose role relationships fell between the joint and segregated extremes had moderately connected networks. Thus the shape of a couple's social network predicted almost perfectly the kind of role the husband and wife would play.

A dispersed social network lacks the power to control the behavior of the couple and thus cannot enforce traditional conjugal norms, but it also cannot provide the moral support and material aid available in a highly connected network, so the husband and wife must depend upon each other. Growing up in the same neighborhood and remaining there in adulthood tended to give a couple a highly connected social network, while moving frequently would produce a dispersed network with friends living in different places, as well as taking the couple away from other family members. Social class and neighborhood type matter only to the extent that they shape the couple's social network. Among the people Bott studied, working class neighborhoods were stable and homogeneous, thus producing relatively connected networks that segregated the conjugal role-relationship. Middle class neighborhoods, in contrast, were more varied and fluid, giving rise to dispersed networks that in turn led to a joint conjugal role-relationship.

Granovetter, Mark
  1973 "The Strength of Weak Ties," *American Journal of Sociology*
    78:1360–1380.

Granovetter suggests we examine the different implications for the structure and dynamics of social networks of strong interpersonal ties versus weak ties. Intuitively, a strong tie between people who are not members of the same family is a close friendship, although some other kinds of relationship might also qualify. Sociologists could measure the strength of a tie by the amount of time the two people spend together, the intensity of the emotions they share or have toward each other, the extent to which they confide in each other or otherwise are intimate, and the services they perform for each other.

Strong ties are very important for the indviduals involved, but it would be wrong to assume that in all respects strong ties are more important than weak ties. Consider the structure of the social network around two people, call them *A* and *B,* who share a strong tie. If *C* is a friend of *A,* he or she is likely to be a friend of *B* as well. Parties to a strong tie spend much time together, so *A* and B are likely to be together when either of them is with C. The stronger a tie between two people, the more similar they are in many respects, so they will tend to have similar relationships with each of the other people they know. Parties to a strong tie influence each other, so if A is friends with C, A is likely to influence B to become friends with C also. The same logic follows for person D, who is a friend of C. Other things being equal, a strong tie will tend to be part of a network of strong ties linking the members of a cohesive social group to each other.

Granovetter argues that these deductions have real implications for the flow of information through a social network. Suppose A has some information, and person Z does not have it. The information flows from A to B to C to D, but since D now has strong ties to A and B, the information would tend to flow back to them, where it is not needed. Strong ties tend to produce clusters of people who are connected to each other but who lack many ties to other cohesive groups. The information can flow all the way to Z if there are relationships that form bridges between groups, and many of these bridging ties will be weak. Because strong ties tend to kink up the network into relatively closed groups, information flows best across chains of weak ties that are cool friendships or cordial acquaintanceships. Removal of an acquaintanceship from a large network can do more harm, paradoxically, than loss of an intimate friendship, where the transmission of information and thus the functioning of the total network are concerned.

After this theoretical discussion, Granovetter notes that much sociometric research failed to take account of the importance of weak ties, and thus neglected to collect data about them, concentrating instead on best friend relationships. One study of 851 high school students, however, asked each one to list his or her eight best friends. When the researchers traced out the social network from each individual, they found that tracing through the best friends reached fewer other students than tracing through the lower-ranked friends. This supports Granovetter's prediction that information can travel faster and farther through weaker rather than stronger ties.

Granovetter did his own study of adults in a Boston suburb who recently changed jobs. Many earlier studies had found that people often get jobs through their friendship networks. The question is whether they more often get jobs through strong ties, perhaps because a close friend is highly motivated to help them, or through weak ties, perhaps because chains of acquaintances extend more quickly across the network and thus more efficiently bring in information about job opportunities. Among the people Granovetter interviewed, relatively few of the job contacts came through friends the person saw often, and more through friends or acquaintances he or she saw seldom. Granovetter suggests that many social processes may occur more rapidly in social networks that are marked by many weak ties, rather than by few strong ones. For example, a social movement may spread along these weak ties, recruiting fresh individuals rapidly, but if it encounters a nest of strong ties it may have difficulty getting past them. Granovetter argues that proper attention to the characteristics of social networks requires not only awareness of the importance of weak ties but also the application of often complex mathematical techniques to analyze their geometry and dynamics.

Markovsky, Barry
  1992 "Network Exchange Outcomes: Limits of Predictability," *Social Networks* 14:267–286.

Collaborating with a variety of other researchers, Markovsky has created new theories of how the structure of a social network shapes the relative power of individuals, and he has done laboratory experiments to test these ideas. For example, an experiment might have four people play a bargaining game with each other, in which one of the people can choose to exchange with any one of the other three, whereas they are prevented from exchanging with each other. This gives the one player more power than the other three. A relatively new way of analyzing the power inherent in various positions in a social network is to create a computer program that simulates people interacting according to the rules of the experiment and to the principles of one of the sociological theories that seeks to explain network power. When the networks are small, results tend to be highly regular and predictable. But Markovsky found that larger networks often become highly sensitive to very minor differences in the power of one of the positions. Results can become unpredictable. Thus, complex computer simulations are often chaotic, leading to unexpected outcomes. Markovsky suggests that the behavior of social networks in the real world may be predictable only if they are small and operate for a short period of time. Large-scale social behavior, however, may be chaotic, sometimes fitting into neat patterns, and at other times diverging to quite unanticipated consequences.

4
FAMILY

WORKS AT A GLANCE

The Family as a Social System

The Changing Family in Modern Society

Great debates surround the family in modern societies, concerning the viability of this traditional institution, its relationship to the community, and the changing roles played by wives and husbands. Many textbooks have claimed that traditional societies possessed *extended families*, linking members of three or more generations and many relatives of the same generation. In contrast, it was said, modern societies focus on the *nuclear family*, consisting just of a married couple and their children. Some writers claim that even this small, nuclear family is currently breaking down. The sociological works described in this chapter assess these claims, examining the changes and continuities of families as social systems in the modern world.

Michael Young and Peter Willmott found that extended families were still the mainstay of the community in the Bethnal Green section of London, England. The parents of a newly married couple help the husband find a job and the wife find an apartment. In emergencies, the family is a crucial source of help. Through the family, each individual is linked into the wider social system. Glenn H. Elder's research focused on the way that this system provides mates, in a marriage market where individuals compete for the most desirable members of the opposite sex, and members of one social class may seek or accept a spouse from another class.

Rising divorce rates seem to indicate, however, that the family is eroding as an institution. Andrew Cherlin charts the changing rates of marriage, birth, and divorce in twentieth-century America, seeking explanations for the variations and trends he finds. Especially perplexing is the baby boom that followed the Second World War, interrupting a long declining trend in the birth rate. Alice Rossi examines the changing gender roles in marriage, a profound cultural trend that may be connected to the declining birth rate. She raises difficult questions about the degree to which innate biological characteristics may prevent the roles played by women and men from becoming identical. Sara McLanahan considers whether the problems often faced by female-headed families stem from the lack of a husband and father, or are primarily caused by poverty. Toby Parcel and Elizabeth Menaghan do a similar analysis of the effect of a mother's work on the development of her children. Martin Whyte surveys women of various ages to learn if dating patterns and the meaning of marriage have really changed over the decades.

From the extended families of East London, documented by Young and Willmott, to the traditional marriages of Detroit described by Whyte, sociologists have found that the family retains great strength as an institution. Changing sexual norms and gender roles certainly mean change, but whether this transformation of the norms for women and men will give the family fresh strength in new forms, or also will be a form of erosion, we cannot yet tell.

The Family as a Social System

Young, Michael, and Peter Willmott
1957 *Family and Kinship in East London*. Baltimore: Penguin.

In 1953–1955, Young and Willmott studied family life in two contrasting urban environments, Bethnal Green, a working class borough of East London, and "Greenleigh," a "housing estate" (what Americans would call a development) on the outskirts of the city, to which many residents of Bethnal Green moved. The research was based chiefly on interview surveys of three groups of people: (1) a random sample of 933 adults living in Bethnal Green, (2) 45 married couples in Bethnal Green who were studied more intensively, and (3) 47 married couples in Greenleigh who had come from Bethnal Green. Contrary to what many sociologists expected, Young and Willmott discovered that the extended family was alive and well in Bethnal Green.

Contrary to popular stereotypes of urban working-class families, husbands and wives in Bethnal Green seemed highly supportive of each other. Divorce was rare, and the historically declining death rate meant that the incidence of broken homes actually had been decreasing for several years, rather than increasing as one might expect in a major industrial city. Married couples were close to their parents, physically as well as emotionally. Among 369 married adults whose parents were still alive, fully 54 percent had parents who also lived in Bethnal Green, and the parents of a further 17 percent lived in an adjacent borough. Among the 45 Bethnal Green couples who were interviewed intensively, only four lacked close relatives in the borough (not counting parents or cousins). Fully 33 couples had at least five close relatives other than parents, and five couples had more than 30 each.

The extended family centers on the mother ("Mum"). It tends to gather in her home, and she receives great honor from the crucial role that she plays. Mothers perform many important functions for their daughters: providing knowledge on how to make a home, assisting with the practical challenges of childbirth, offering aid and advice during emergencies, and helping her negotiate her relationship with her husband. Because a young wife has such a close relationship with Mum, a certain amount of tension necessarily exists between her mother and her husband. Typically, the husband becomes reconciled with his mother-in-law, and he is absorbed into her extended family.

Mothers who have good records in paying their own rent can often find a home for their daughters, and fathers with a good record on the job can find employment for their sons. The jobs available tend to be manual labor with no opportunity for promotion, so the chief economic issue for the family is the husband getting a decent job and holding it, rather than upward social mobility. Thus, the extended family in Bethnal Green does not cut the individual off from the wider community, but ties him or her into it.

In 1931, about 108,000 people lived in Bethnal Green, but by 1955 it contained only 53,860. During this period, 11,000 families with more than 40,000 members were moved to municipal housing developments established by the London County Council. Greenleigh consists of nearly identical little houses, with fenced yards containing flower and vegetable gardens, lined up along concrete roads. Young and Willmott think it is possible that couples who moved out of Bethnal Green may have had somewhat weaker family ties than those who stayed, but the chief decision on who moved was made by the London County Council, who allocated the nice new homes on the basis of a master list.

Data from the interviews with couples who moved to Greenleigh reveal the tremendous influence residence has on family relations. Before leaving Bethnal Green, the wives had an average of 17.2 contacts with parents or siblings each week. In 1953, soon after moving to Greenleigh, the average had dropped to 3.0, and two years later it had dropped still further to 2.4. For husbands, the numbers were 15.0, 3.8, and 3.3. Husbands were slightly more able to maintain contact with the extended families than were wives, because a few of them worked with family members. Modern transportation allowed workers in Greenleigh to commute to distant jobs, but the twenty miles to Bethnal Green discouraged mothers from helping their daughters, even in times of illness or childbirth.

All aspects of community life are weaker in Greenleigh than in Bethnal Green. For example, in Bethnal Green there is one pub for every 400 residents, whereas in Greenleigh there is one for every 5,000. Television sets were twice as common in the development as back in the borough, an indication that people were struggling to compensate for the loss of family social life that moving away from Mum had inflicted upon them. Relations with neighbors were incapable of making up for diminished kinship relations, and the nuclear families of Greenleigh tended to keep to themselves. In Bethnal Green, people receive status from their family ties and are known for their personal characteristics. In Greenleigh, people rely much more upon status symbols like their cars to express who they are, given the anonymity of the housing development. Young and Willmott say that modern social services, pensions, and longevity should strengthen the extended family, but other modern trends like suburban developments apparently weaken it.

Elder, Glen H.
   1969 "Appearance and Education in Marriage Mobility," *American Sociological Review* 34:519–533.

People tend to marry others from their own social class, a phenomenon known as *class endogamy*, but some individuals marry people from a higher social class, thereby achieving upward social mobility. Elder evaluated factors that contributed to mobility among 76 women who had been studied both in 1932, when they were fifth and sixth grade children, and as late as 1958, after they had married. This was a period when the social class of a couple was largely determined by the occupation of the husband, so Elder focused on the characteristics of these women that determined the social class of the husbands they gained.

Hypergamy is marriage by a lower status woman to a higher status man. Elder suggests it is obvious why a woman might want to do this, because she gains status. But the man loses status unless the woman has exceptional qualities that make the match a good deal for him as well as for her. Elder conceptualizes their choices in terms of a *marriage market* where individuals seek to gain advantages from the individuals with whom they pair up, and in which individuals of the same sex are in competition with each other for the most desirable members of the opposite sex.

Studies had shown that American men rank physical attractiveness near the top in the qualities they want in a wife, so a beautiful woman from the lower classes may convince a higher class man to marry her. Ambitious women, like ambitious men, may seek to rise in individual social status by getting good educations. But a woman may also gain from education because it brings her into contact with high-status men, for example fellow students at college, one of whom may marry her. Thus it make sense to examine both beauty and education as determinants of a woman's chances of achieving hypergamy.

Back in the 1930s, the girls had participated in the Oakland [California] Growth Study, which collected a great variety of data about them. Each girl was rated for physical attractiveness by two members of the research staff, and these ratings showed high levels of agreement. A series of tests measured their status aspirations and their intelligence. The girls from middle-class backgrounds tended to be rated higher on attractiveness, perhaps because their standards of grooming were higher, as well as to have slightly higher intelligence scores. The classes did not differ in the extent to which the girls possessed aspirations to attain high status. Over the years data on occupation, education, and marital status were collected. Elder compared the occupational status of their fathers and husbands to measure social mobility.

Attractiveness was indeed an asset that favored upward social mobility, especially among the women from working class origins. Intelligence was only mildly favorable, but higher education did apparently help and was a way that women from higher class families were able to find similar husbands. Within each social class, high status aspirations did correlate with obtaining higher status husbands. Thus, whatever their social origins, women who strongly wanted upward social mobility through marriage could often achieve it.

The Changing Family in
Modern Society

Cherlin, Andrew
  1981 *Marriage, Divorce and Remarriage.* Cambridge, Massachusetts:
  Harvard University Press.

This book links the sociology of the family to *demography,* the study of human population (Chapter 16). The birth of children takes place in families, and birth is one of the three key processes of demography, the others being migration and death. Demographic trends such as changing birth and death rates produce the age and sex distributions that shape marriage and divorce. Cherlin examines changing rates of marriage, birth, and divorce in the twentieth century, finding they are a combination of gradual long-term trends and relatively short-term deviations from these trends that must be explained in terms of historical events and sociological processes.

The most striking feature of childbearing trends was the *baby boom* that immediately followed the Second World War, which Cherlin says that demographers had not expected. For many decades, the birth rate had been gradually declining, but in retrospect we see that the rates were unusually low during the Great Depression.

Two competing theories have been offered to explain the baby boom that followed, one stressing family values, and the other economics. Sociologist Glen H. Elder studied children born in Oakland, California at the beginning of the 1920s. When the Depression hit, many boys and girls took on adult responsibilities at a younger age, and were deprived of happy childhoods and close relationships with their overstressed parents. They also learned that strong families were a valuable practical resource during hard times. When they reached adulthood, during or shortly after the war, they quickly married and showed every evidence of being unusually family-oriented, including having more children than young adults had produced in the 1930s.

The second theory was proposed by economist Richard A. Easterlin. Birth rates were low in the Depression because of the poor economic conditions. After the war, this meant that a relatively small number of young men were competing for the jobs that were available. Because this was a period of great economic growth, many of them were able to get good jobs with high pay. But the deprivations of the Depression had taught them to get along without many luxuries, so they had ample money to raise several children. There is no reason why both theories could not be true, each identifying a slightly different set of social-psychological mechanisms by which the deprivations of the 1930s and early 1940s produced a baby boom when good times returned. In the 1960s, birth rates returned to their long-term downward trend.

Annual divorce rates gradually increased from about 1 per 1,000 married women per year in 1860 to about 5 in 1915, then there was a surge to 8 right after World War I, a dip at the beginning of the Great Depression back to 6, then a great leap after World War II to 18, followed by a drop below 10 in the 1950s, and a rapid surge in the 1960s and 1970s to 22. Cherlin observes that the divorce rate apparently reacted to the Depression and the prosperity after World War II, just as the birth rate had. But the trend in divorce in the 1960s and 1970s goes above the long-term trend, and apparently signals a fundamental change in attitudes about marriage and divorce. Divorce laws were liberalized considerably across the nation in the 1970s, and opinion surveys showed that the public accepted this. However, Cherlin notes that the attitudes changed only after the divorce rate had begun to increase rapidly, and divorce rates in states with liberal laws did not differ from those in states that lacked them. He suggests that rapidly increasing employment of married women, earning increasing wages, may have permitted many of them to support themselves and thus encouraged them to leave unhappy marriages.

Easterlin has extended his economic theory of the baby boom to the marital behavior of those babies when they reached adulthood. Raised in prosperous households, the baby boomers found competition very stiff when they became adults, both because economic growth had stagnated and because there were so many other people their age to compete with. So, they married later, and struggled to maintain a high standard of living. Thus they did not feel they could afford many children, and they experienced marital stresses that often led to divorce.

Most people who get divorced—something like five out of every six divorced men and three out of four divorced women—will eventually remarry. Cherlin says the rates of remarriage for divorced or widowed women aged fourteen to fifty-four held steady from 1920 to 1940, with about 10 percent remarrying each year. This rate increased to 15 percent in the late 1960s but then dropped below 14 percent a decade later. Divorced people who do marry tend to do so fairly soon after divorce, half of them within three years. The risk of divorce of second marriages is somewhat higher than for first marriages. Excluding marriages that ended in death, 30 percent of first marriages and 39 percent of all remarriages end in divorce, according to 1975 rates. One consequence was an increase in the proportion of children experiencing the trauma of divorce and growing up in single-parent households. Cherlin surveys the wide variety of problems faced by families experiencing divorce or remarriage, and notes that the society is learning new norms to cope with the significantly changed nature of the family.

Rossi, Alice S.
1984 "Gender and Parenthood," *American Sociological Review* 49:1–16.

In the lecture she gave to the American Sociological Association when she was its president, Alice Rossi chides sociology for ignoring the biological roots of parenting behavior. Many sociologists of the family might hope that the differences between the ways mothers and fathers treat small children are the result of socialization to cultural roles or male political dominance. But Rossi argues that women and men are biologically different in ways that affect the development and functioning of their brains, rather than just their reproductive organs. Humans resemble their close relatives in the animal kingdom, apes and mammals more generally, in exhibiting *sexual dimorphism*, a significant difference in the biological natures of the two genders manifested in behavior as well as in physical appearance.

Drawing on a large body of scientific literature, most of it outside sociology, Rossi sketches the innate behavioral differences between women and men, which may be significant in four areas: (1) sensory sensitivity, (2) aggression or activity level, (3) cognitive skills, and (4) parenting behavior. With respect to parenting, women tend to have more empathy, stronger bonds to other people, greater sensitivity to nonverbal communication, and more fully developed social interaction. In contrast, men emphasize mastery of skills, individual autonomy, and achievement in mental tasks. Thus, women are far more interested in infants and devote more loving care to them. Men tend to become really interested in children and devote appropriate care to them once the children have reached the age of eighteen months. This means that it may be unwise to expect the sexes to assume identical parenting roles in future generations.

Rossi's analysis of biology takes on special significance in the context of information she offers about social change. Lifespans have increased in modern societies, as have divorce rates. Paradoxically, males are more fragile than females, and if women are not burdened by the high mortality rates from childbirth found in pre-industrial societies, women tend to live significantly longer. A longer life gives a man more opportunities to produce children, but beyond about age 45, this is not true for women. Men tend to marry women somewhat younger than themselves, and this is especially true for second marriages after divorce. Women tend to have fewer children than in earlier generations, in part because they have them later in life. Out-of-wedlock births appear to be on the rise. Mothers, disproportionately, find themselves in the role of single parent, and the relative contribution of fathers to parenting seems to be decreasing significantly. These factors combine to produce a situation in which parenting is being separated from marriage.

Detached from the family, isolated males increase the dangers of crime and violence for society. On the other hand, the changes in family structure appear to socialize children to more egalitarian sex roles that would support equal rights for women. Thus, our society faces great challenges reconciling cultural change with sexual dimorphism. Rossi doubts that biology will permit humans to create a sex-blind culture. But creative work in all sectors of society may benefit from a blending of the natural qualities of women and men.

McLanahan, Sara
   1985 "Family Structure and the Reproduction of Poverty," *American Journal of Sociology* 90:873–901.

   Increasing rates of divorce, illegitimacy, and female-headed families have raised great concern that the American family is disintegrating and that this decline of traditional family forms is aggravating poverty and other social problems such as crime and drug abuse. Households consisting of a mother and her children, but with no husband and father, have often been called "broken homes" and blamed for raising children poorly. But it is equally possible that children from female-headed families suffer only because they tend to be poor, and most of their problems would be solved simply by providing adequate income to their mothers. McLanahan sets out to test competing theories concerning the connection between coming from a female-headed family and being poor or failing to graduate from high school. From the extensive scientific literature on these issues, McLanahan draws four competing hypotheses:

1. **No Effects.** Children from female-headed families tend to be poor, but only because female-headed families are far more common among people who are already poor. The lack of a father in the household is not a problem in itself, but merely reflects the conditions of poverty in America.
2. **Economic Deprivation.** The lack of a father is a disadvantage only because it deprives the family of the income he would bring in, and this economic deprivation traps many of the children in poverty even after they become adults. Without his income, the mother must work and cannot supervise her children properly, adolescent children are forced to leave school early and take low-paying jobs, and the family may become permanently dependent upon public welfare.
3. **Father Absence.** Without a father in the home, boys lack an adult male role model and children of both sexes receive incomplete socialization, which limits them psychologically and socially. The absence of the father is especially harmful in early childhood, when his children's personalities are largely formed.
4. **Family Stress.** The breakup of a marriage inflicts great psychological tension upon children, causing antisocial behavior and a loss of self-esteem. The negative effects of separation and divorce are most severe at the time they are happening, and the mother and children may adjust successfully to their situation over a few years.

   McLanahan says it is extremely difficult to test these theories, in part because the necessary data would include information on a large number of families over a considerable period of time. Past studies were based on highly inadequate data sets. McLanahan employs information from the Panel Study of Income Dynamics (PSID), a survey that had followed 5,000 American families over the eleven years 1968–1978. (This project has continued up to the present time and has now followed the families and their offspring for well over a generation.) The PSID combines a random sample of American households with a special sample that is representative of poor families, so there were sufficient numbers of poor families in the data for McLanahan's purposes. She focused on 3,289 offspring who were aged 17–27 in 1978, 1,730 whites and 1,559 blacks, and one of her key variables was whether the respondent was still in school at age 17. Of these, 48 lived with mothers who had never married, 242 lived with mothers whose husbands had died, 342 lived with mothers who had separated from their husbands but not formally divorced, and 290 lived with divorced mothers.

Children from female-headed families were indeed worse off, poorer and less likely to graduate from high school, than those from families with fathers. Statistical controls for the socio-economic backgrounds of the families did not erase this big difference, so the first hypothesis is false. The poverty of female-headed families is more than just the result of a poor background. The second hypothesis was strongly supported. The lack of money that a father would have brought in increased the chances that a child would leave school early and that he or she would be poor in early adulthood. The picture was somewhat complicated, however, and being on welfare seemed to have negative consequences for whites, but positive ones for blacks. The evidence about the effect of father-absence on child socialization was mixed but did not give clear support to the theory that lack of a father in itself prevented children from growing up properly. Somewhat stronger evidence supported the theory that divorce-related stress was bad for children, but the effect of this stress seemed to last for years rather than fading as the mother and children adjusted to their situation. McLanahan concluded that public policies aimed simply to raise the incomes of female-headed families would significantly improve their children's futures.

Parcel, Toby L., and Elizabeth G. Menaghan
  1994 "Early Parental Work, Family Social Capital, and Early Childhood Outcomes," *American Journal of Sociology* 99:972–1009.

Parcel and Menaghan use questionnaire data from the National Longitudinal Survey of Youth to illuminate the public debates about the effect on young children when their mothers hold jobs. Earlier studies had given inconsistent results, possibly because the effect of work on children might vary depending upon their age and upon other conditions in the family. Therefore, Parcel and Menaghan performed a complex analysis, comparing children whose mothers worked at different points in their childhood, examining the effect of father's work as well as mother's, and looking at two kinds of outcomes. *Cognitive outcomes* are the child's mental abilities as measured by standardized tests. *Social outcomes* are the extent to which people around the child report that he or she has behavior problems. A mother's current work affects cognitive outcomes in complex ways depending upon how many hours she works. Social outcomes were affected by father's work early in the child's life, and long-lasting problems often resulted if he had not worked full time. Mother's employment during the child's infancy harms the child's cognition only if the mother is trapped in bad jobs. The chief lesson of this study is that mother's employment need not hurt her child, and it is harmful only under unfavorable conditions.

Whyte, Martin King
   1990 *Dating, Mating and Marriage*. New York: Aldine de Gruyter.

To learn if American marriage was an institution "in trouble," Whyte's research team administered face-to-face interviews to 459 women aged 18–75 in the greater Detroit metropolitan area who had been married at least once. Items in the interview questionnaire examined the process of mate choice and the marital relations experienced by these women. His most general finding was that many aspects of marriage had remained the same over decades, but there had been a decline in social conventions surrounding marriage, and the factors that used to predict how well a marriage would do had lost much of their predictive power.

   In the latter part of the nineteenth century and the early twentieth century, America developed a dating culture, in which it was assumed that young people should pair off, without adult supervision, as a step toward marriage, and in which the young people could judge for themselves how good a mate their dating partner would be. The chief change in this dating culture is that sexual intercourse has become common among the activities shared by a dating couple, whereas decades ago it was prohibited and the few young women who permitted it were disparaged for doing so. Additionally, cohabitation by an unmarried couple has become more common, and even many of their parents consider it like a trial marriage. There are competing theories about the effect that extensive dating has on eventual success in marriage. Some people feel that dating is both a learning process and a selection process that gets a woman ready for marriage and helps her find the right mate. Others worry that dates are selected because they give the woman status with her peers, rather than rating men as potential husbands, or that early heavy dating causes a woman to marry before she is ready, or that too much premarital experience spoils marriage by making it no longer special and thus easy to abandon.

   For much of his analysis, Whyte divided his respondents into three groups, those who married in 1925–1944, those who married in the baby boom years of 1945–1964, and those who married in 1965–1984 after the "sexual revolution" had begun. There was no tendency for women from the later marriage cohorts to begin dating earlier, and the average age for all three groups was 16. However, the later cohorts dated a larger number of men before marriage; women in the 1925–1944 cohort tended to date 4–7 males compared to 12–15 for the women in the 1965–1984 cohort. Whyte estimates that 76 percent of the 1925–1944 cohort were virgins at marriage, compared with only 28 percent of those married in 1965–1984. Indeed, premarital sexual activity was continuing to increase even in the latest period, and only 12 percent of women married in 1980–1984 were virgins. Whyte thinks this is not just a change in sexual norms, but a greater emphasis on intimacy both psychological and physical. He emphasizes that we should be cautious in extrapolating such trends far into the future. Historians have shown that there was a great increase in premarital sexual activity around the year 1800, but the culture moved back toward premarital chastity at the end of the nineteenth century.

There is no sign that women are either quicker or slower to marry now than earlier. Those who married in 1925–1944 had dated their future husbands an average of 2.5 years, compared with an almost identical 2.6 years for those who married in 1965–1984. The cohort in the middle, during the baby boom, had married somewhat sooner, after an average of just 2.2 years of dating their future husbands. Similarly, there has been no decline in the importance of the wedding ceremony. Perhaps because of increasing affluence, bridal showers and bachelor parties are far more common in connection with recent marriages. The overwhelming majority of weddings in all periods were religious ceremonies rather than civil ones.

Among women who married recently, very few traditional factors explained the kinds of dating experiences they would have. Despite the Catholic Church's conservative attitude toward premarital sex, being Catholic did not delay a young woman's experience of intercourse, for example. The influence of parents appears to be extremely weak, as well. The intimacy revolution is affecting young women of all social classes and subgroups in the population. At the same time, traditional values concerning marriage itself have not changed. In fact, Whyte finds that premarital sexual activity has no consistent effect on the quality or durability of marriages. Thus, the revolution in dating practices has had little discernible effect on marriage, which remains in most respects quite traditional.

5
DEVIANCE AND CONTROL

WORKS AT A GLANCE

Social Disorganization Theory (Control Theory)

The Gang by Frederic M. Thrasher (1927)
Mental Disorders in Urban Areas by Robert E. L. Faris and
   H. Warren Dunham (1939)

Structural Strain Theory

"Social Structure and Anomie" by Robert K. Merton (1938)
Delinquency and Opportunity by Richard A. Cloward and
   Lloyd E. Ohlin (1960)

Subcultural Deviance Theory

Principles of Criminology by Edwin H. Sutherland (1947)

A Study Comparing the Theories

Causes of Delinquency by Travis Hirschi (1969)

Sociologists have studied crime and other kinds of deviant behavior from many perspectives, including some viewpoints that belong more properly to other disciplines, such as psychology, biology, and economics. The distinctively sociological theories of deviance boil down to just four competing ways of explaining deviance:

1. social disorganization theory (today generally called control theory)
2. structural strain theory
3. subcultural deviance theory
4. labeling theory (also called societal reaction theory)

The first three of these theories have long histories in sociology, and they share some of the same assumptions. In particular, they take for granted that certain actions are criminal or deviant, and they accept the standard criminal law and informal customs of the society. In other respects, they compete directly with each other in trying to explain deviant behavior. Therefore it makes sense to consider them together, as we shall do in this chapter. The fourth theory is more radical, raising the question of why a given act is labeled deviant in the first place, and suggesting that the society may often perversely force a person to play the role of deviant person. Thus it makes sense to consider labeling theory in the next chapter, along with related perspectives on how human beings construct reality.

Frederic Thrasher, Robert Faris, and H. Warren Dunham were members of "The Chicago School," the tremendously influential group of sociologists centered at the University of Chicago who concentrated on urban life and problems (see Chapter 7). They conceptualized the city as a collection of distinct areas or neighborhoods, each with its own characteristics that impressed themselves upon the individuals living in it. In socially disorganized areas, individuals would lack the social control required to enforce normality. Some would become criminals, and others would become mentally ill.

Beginning in the Great Depression of the 1930s, other sociologists shifted the focus from disorganized urban areas to poverty and to social influence. Robert Merton, Richard Cloward, and Lloyd Ohlin argued that deviance resulted when social strains prevented a person from achieving a satisfactory life by following the norms of the society. Edwin H. Sutherland stressed the ways that individuals learned deviant patterns of behavior through communication with members of deviant subcultures.

Travis Hirschi's study employed survey research methods to test the three competing theories. Three decades of subsequent research have not fully answered the questions he raised, however, and all three classic theories thrive within the sociology of deviance. Most likely, all three theories are true under certain conditions. One or another may explain a particular kind of deviance in a particular social setting. Often two theories must be combined, or even all three, to provide a full explanation. A person who lacks social bonds, who is frustrated by very low social status, and who comes into contact with members of an existing deviant subculture, is more likely than anyone else to violate the norms of society. But in every social class and kind of community, there will be individuals for whom just one or two factors are sufficient to cause deviant behavior. Thus care must be used in applying these theories, and we cannot be confident in any one theory unless properly designed research studies of the particular setting and kind of deviance have confirmed that it is the correct explanation.

Social Disorganization Theory (Control Theory)

Thrasher, Frederic M.
  1927 *The Gang*. Chicago: University of Chicago Press.

Thrasher says his book was based on data about 1,313 gangs in Chicago, but his exact methods of research are unclear. Probably, he got information about most of the gangs from newspapers, social workers, youth-oriented organizations, and law enforcement officials. But he apparently did extensive field observational research himself, as evidenced by the many photographs he took that were included in the book.

Gangs were found disproportionately in *Gangland*, a ring of dilapidated residential buildings and factories that surrounded the central business district of Chicago. Gangland was a slum. It was not merely a physically run-down place where many poor people lived, however, but an area that was poorly integrated into the social life of the rest of the city. Thrasher said gangland was *interstitial*, meaning a space that filled the gap between other things.

An inordinately large number of children were crammed into this disorganized part of the city. With little to organize their activities, the children constantly formed spontaneous play groups that could readily evolve into gangs. The stimulus for this evolution was the almost inevitable conflict that arose between play groups, as they competed for territory, loot, and relationships to the other unstable groups in gangland. Surrounded by a hostile environment, the members of a play group came to depend upon each other in the struggle with other groups. They became committed to each other and developed what Charles Horton Cooley called the "we" feeling that marks all high-solidarity groups (see Chapter 2). Thus the play group becomes a gang.

The gang is a primitive society that the boys create for themselves because the larger society is unable to meet their needs. In gangland, the standard institutions of society have broken down. Families disintegrate. Slum schools offer little of interest. The churches are too formal and remote. Local politics is corrupt. Low wages and high unemployment prevent the boys from finding much of value at places of work. Importantly, there are few opportunities for wholesome recreation in well-structured activities.

Thrasher offers many stories about various gangs to illustrate these ideas and to show the different ways that a gang may evolve. The most rudimentary gangs stress adventure and excitement, which often become sexual in gangs of older boys. Over time, successful gangs tend to develop very strong bonds linking the members to the group, going through three stages that Thrasher calls *diffuse, solidified,* and *conventionalized.* The typical conventionalized gang is an athletic club, which often achieves respectability and contributes to the social organization of the city. Sometimes, however, a gang fails to become conventionalized as the members grow older, and it remains outside the structure of the community. Then it may become an adult criminal gang.

In Thrasher's theory, the gang has its origins in the social disorganization of the surrounding neighborhood. The individual's delinquent behavior has its origin in the fact that a boy in a disorganized neighborhood is under far weaker social control than he would be in another community. Thrasher frequently compares gangland with an ancient feudal society, divided up into a number of warring clans or tribes. Within a high-solidarity gang, the members may follow a strict set of norms. But these are norms that support the survival and other goals of the gang itself, and they often conflict with the norms of the surrounding society. Thus, gangs are deviant subcultures.

Faris, Robert E. L., and H. Warren Dunham
  1939 *Mental Disorders in Urban Areas.* Chicago: University of Chicago Press [1967].

Robert E. L. Faris was the son of sociologist Ellsworth Faris, and was practically born and raised in the Chicago tradition. The leading figures of the Chicago sociology department were Robert E. Park and Ernest W. Burgess (see Chapter 7 for their work in urban sociology), who had a tremendous influence on the graduate students and thus on American sociology more generally. Already, two Chicago students, Ruth Shonle Cavan and Calvin F. Schmid, had done research on how social disorganization might be responsible for suicide, so it was not surprising that the younger Faris decided to do his doctoral dissertation on the connection between disorganization and serious mental illness. Shortly later Dunham became involved in the project, for his master's thesis, and their joint book is an excellent example of the fully developed Chicago approach to deviance.

Faris and Dunham begin with a geographic survey of Chicago, arguing that some areas are far more disorganized than others. The first of their many maps of the city is identical to the one that Thrasher published, except that they did not highlight gangland as he had done. Other maps show the distributions of various measures of disorganization, such as the proportion of housing that is in rooming houses or tenements, and the percent of residents who were foreign-born immigrants. A neighborhood with a lot of rooming houses must have a transient population, and where residents are constantly moving in and out there is not the stable community membership required to support a high level of organization. Similarly, areas with many immigrants may often be chaotic places with the added disorganizing feature that the inhabitants may have come from so many different cultures that there is no consensus in norms and values.

Faris and Dunham obtained data on 28,763 cases of mental illness from the 1922–1934 records of the Cook County Psychopathic Hospital, which screened all mental patients before they were admitted to other public institutions. They sought two key pieces of information about each case: the nature of the psychiatric diagnosis and which of the 120 subcommunities of the city the person had lived in. When they had tabulated this information, they were able to calculate rates of mental illness for all the subcommunities. The highest rate was in the central business district, where 1,757 out of every 100,000 residents had been hospitalized for mental illness during the period. The lowest rate, just 110 per 100,000, was in a high-class residential area. A map showed that the highest rates tended to be near the center of the city, in those areas identified as socially disorganized. Data from private hospitals did not show the same geographic pattern as those for the public hospitals, but Faris and Dunham argued that private cases were few enough that they could not change the results significantly.

The next step was to separate the cases by diagnosis, to see if different kinds of mental illness had different social origins. A total of 10,575 individuals were admitted to Chicago hospitals with a diagnosis of schizophrenia, compared with 2,311 cases of manic-depressive psychosis. Schizophrenia is marked by lack of contact with reality, delusions or hallucinations, impaired judgment, and the idiosyncratic ideas called autistic thinking. By contrast, manic-depressive psychosis is marked by moods that were either far too low (depression) or far too high (mania) for the person's real circumstances. Definitions today are slightly different, but the distinction fits a familiar division between two kinds of mental activity. Thoughts are generally considered to be different from feelings. Schizophrenia seems to involve disordered or deviant thoughts, whereas manic-depressive psychosis is a disorder of the person's moods. Faris and Dunham discovered that the geographic pattern for schizophrenia matches social disorganization, but the geographic pattern for manic-depressive psychosis appears to be random.

In their concluding theoretical analysis, Faris and Dunham argue that the human mind is based on the biology of the brain but is created through social interaction. To be mentally normal, a person requires successful interaction with other people over a long period of time. Even when interaction exists, if it is inconsistent it cannot provide the intellectual order required for mental normality. If a person is cut off from social interaction, or receives only very chaotic interaction, over time he or she will drift away from conventional ways of thinking. As Faris and Dunham (p. 174) say, such a person "is completely freed from the social control which enforces normality in other people." Thus, social disorganization will cause schizophrenia. Put another way, the individual mental disorganization we call schizophrenia is merely a reflection of social disorganization. In contrast, manic-depressive psychosis shows a different social pattern and thus must have other causes.

Structural Strain Theory

Merton, Robert K.
  1938 "Social Structure and Anomie." Pp. 185–214 in *Social Theory and Social Structure*. New York: Free Press [1968].

Merton begins his theoretical essay with an analysis of how the norms and values of a society ideally relate to each other. First, he argues that human beings receive many of their goals from society, rather than from biological instincts. The values of a society are the goals that most individual members are supposed to strive for in their lives. Second, the institutions of a society provide means for achieving those goals. The norms of these institutions regulate the ways that individuals are supposed to strive for the goals. Thus, the culture of the society ideally contains values and norms that are well integrated with each other. The norms allow people to achieve the values, and the values give meaning to the norms.

In a society where norms actually do allow people to reach the values, most people will be motivated to conform to these norms, and there will be relatively little deviant behavior. But in a society where following the institutional norms fails to bring many people to the culturally-defined goals, many people will be driven to deviate, perhaps through crime or in other ways. The United States exemplifies such a society, because American culture stresses the importance of gaining individual wealth and status, but the realities of life for the poor and disadvantaged prevent many from succeeding.

Merton says this situation is the state of normlessness that Emile Durkheim called *anomie* (see Chapter 1), although many different social processes might produce anomie, and sociologists have offered a variety of definitions for this word. Anomie afflicts the individual person, but it is really a condition of the surrounding society. Thus, in Merton's theory, the responsibility for crime and other troublesome deviant acts rests with the society, not with the individual.

At this point in his analysis, Merton introduces a chart of five different ways that people may respond to the values and norms of their society. People may either accept the values of the society or reject them. Similarly, they may either accept or reject the norms. In the chart, shown below, Merton places a plus sign (+) when the person accepts values or norms, and a minus sign (–) when he or she rejects them. In the last row of the table, a plus-and-minus (±) means that the person has rejected the prevailing values and norms, replacing them with a new set. There are four possible combinations of plus and minus, and Merton adds a fifth alternative characterized by ±/±, so the chart shows five modes of adaptation that different people may take in a society with a significant level of anomie.

Modes of Adaptation	VALUES Culture Goals	NORMS Institutionalized Means
1. Conformity	+	+
2. Innovation	+	−
3. Ritualism	−	+
4. Retreatism	−	−
5. Rebellion	±	±

+ means acceptance; − means rejection;
± means replacing standard values and norms with new ones

In a society with well-integrated values and norms, people will tend to conform. In a society with much anomie, many individuals will still be able to achieve the culturally defined goals by the institutional means, so they will conform also. In Merton's table, *conformity* is marked by acceptance of both values and norms, or + and +. He comments that a country where few people conform could hardly be called a society, and sociologists of his period were indeed coming to a consensus that every viable society was organized around a coherent set of values and norms, assumptions that were not widely questioned for nearly three decades after Merton wrote.

In American society, however, poor people with limited educations can seldom climb the legitimate ladders of success to wealth and status. Many of them have been socialized to accept the values of the society, or else they might become resigned to their deprived state. But precisely because they accept the values, they are forced to reject the norms. In pursuit of conventional goals that they cannot attain by conventional means, they violate the norms and seek new routes to wealth and status, such as crime. Merton calls this *innovation*, because the people following this mode of adaptation must find a new or different way of behaving, marked by acceptance of values but rejection of norms, or + and −. Interestingly, Merton wrote much about art and science in other parts of his career, and this analysis could be applied to the forces that encourage people to innovate in these socially-approved fields. A new scientific discovery, or a new style of art, can catapult an otherwise deprived person to wealth and status. But it is chiefly in connection with crime that Merton's concept of innovation is remembered.

The logical opposite of innovation is what Merton calls *ritualism*. A person has given up on ever achieving the values of the society, but he or she persists in following the norms, almost like the gestures of a meaningless ritual. Perhaps the individual has been so thoroughly socialized that he or she simply cannot violate the norms, but the lack of social or educational advantages makes it impossible to reach the society's goals. Merton says that innovation will be especially common among lower class people, whereas ritualism is common in the lower middle class. In contrast, the upper middle class is populated by successful conformists.

A fourth logical possibility is rejection of both the values and the norms. This mode of adaptation is called *retreatism*, because the people who follow it have retreated from the society. They wind up dropping out of the social class system, and are "psychotics, autists, pariahs, outcasts, vagrants, vagabonds, tramps, chronic drunkards and drug addicts" (Merton, p. 207). Like innovation, this is a category of deviance.

Merton might have ended his analysis here, but the existence of political deviance required him to go further. The first four modes of adaptation assume that there are no competing societies, either actual other nations or imagined future states, that offer comparable but different integrated sets of values and norms. When Merton published his essay in 1938, the world was filled with alternatives to western capitalist democracy. Traditional monarchies and pre-industrial societies existed in many corners of the globe, and fascism was threatening to engulf Europe. In just two decades of existence, the Soviet Union had convinced some western intellectuals that it was leading the way toward a socialist paradise. Thus, it was easy to imagine well-disciplined, responsible people who might reject American norms and values but substitute a different set, such as using political means to create a society in which all people would be equal. This Merton called *rebellion*.

Cloward, Richard A., and Lloyd E. Ohlin
   1960 *Delinquency and Opportunity*. New York: Free Press.

Like Thrasher, Cloward and Ohlin argued that there was more than one kind of delinquent gang, and they identified three. First was the type they called a *criminal subculture*, dedicated to stealing, extorting, and other illegal ways of getting money. Second, in the *conflict subculture* youth sought status through violence, often directed against each other. And third, members of a *retreatist subculture* chiefly consumed drugs. Each of these three subcultures expects members to violate some norms of the larger society, and each is a response to structural strain or anomie imposed by the society upon the members.

Cloward and Ohlin explicitly follow Merton's analysis of deviance, including his modes of adaptation to anomie. They argue that many boys in poor neighborhoods aspire to the same kinds of success as do the more fortunate youngsters in prosperous neighborhoods. However, several barriers block their access to opportunity. Children of immigrants may belong to cultures that are ill-adapted to the American economic system. The needs of a poor family force its children to leave school early to take jobs, thus preventing them from following a chief avenue of upward social mobility. Schools in poor neighborhoods may be lower in quality than those in wealthier communities, and poor families cannot pay for private school or college. As Merton explained, if people cannot achieve the standard success goals by conforming to the norms of the society, they will seek alternative avenues to reach them.

A *criminal* gang illustrates Merton's innovation mode of adaptation. Unable to achieve society's goals by legitimate means, the members of the subculture turn to illegitimate means, such as theft. For this strategy to work, they must have the personal characteristics needed to steal without quickly getting caught. If much of their loot consists of valuable things rather than cash, the surrounding community must contain adult institutions that mediate between the criminal and conventional worlds. A "fence" or a pawn shop that is not too particular where it gets its merchandise can give the boys money for the stolen objects. In the absence of these advantages, the boys may fail in their attempts at crime, and innovation will not be a successful mode of adaptation for them, any more than conformity was.

One response is the *conflict* gang, which illustrates rebellion in Merton's scheme. Unable to achieve conventional values either by conventional means or by unconventional means, the boys in these gangs are forced to find new goals. Typically they try to establish their status and honor by winning over other gangs in a violent contest for territory ("our neighborhood") and in pitched battles where they triumph physically over other boys. Thus they employ new violent means to achieve a new goal, status with respect to other conflict gangs. Naturally, boys who are physically weak, easily intimidated, or incapable of developing mutually-supportive relationships with other tough boys will fail in any attempt to gain status through conflict.

The final response is the *retreatist* subculture, named after Merton's retreatism mode of adaptation. In a sense, the boys in this category suffer three doses of anomie. First, they cannot achieve society's values by legitimate means. Second, they cannot do so with illegitimate means, either. And third, they cannot use violence to achieve the new value of status in a conflict system. For them, drug use is the ultimate defeat.

The individual boy does not need to discover his own mode of adaptation, because all three kinds of gang exist in many poor neighborhoods. Therefore, the existence of these delinquent subcultures produces a higher rate of deviant behavior than if each individual had to develop patterns of delinquency on his own.

Subcultural Deviance Theory

Sutherland, Edwin H.
  1947 *Principles of Criminology*. Philadelphia: Lippincott.

Working at the same time as Thrasher, Edwin H. Sutherland developed a theoretical explanation of criminal behavior that rejected the emphasis upon social disorganization that was popular at the time in criminology. Sutherland took for granted the existence of deviant subcultures and sought to understand how they could influence the behavior of individuals. Because rates of immigration to the United States were very high prior to the exclusionary laws of the 1920s, sociologists naturally traced many features of American life to the

often discordant cultures that immigrants brought with them. Whether populated by immigrants or by native-born citizens, adult criminal gangs had existed for a long time and were sustained by recruitment of young men who
were thereby turned into criminals. To explain this process, Sutherland developed a nine-step model he called *differential association theory*:

1. Criminal behavior is learned...
2. In interaction with other persons in a process of communication...
3. Principally within intimate personal groups.
4. The learning includes:
   a. techniques of committing the crime, and
   b. the specific direction of motives, drives, rationalizations, and
   attitudes.
5. The specific direction of motives and drives is learned from definitions
   of the legal code as favorable or unfavorable.
6. A person becomes delinquent because of an excess of definitions favorable to violation of law over definitions unfavorable to violation of law.
7. Differential associations may vary in frequency, duration, priority, and
   intensity.
8. The process of learning criminal behavior by association with criminal
   and anti-criminal patterns involves all of the mechanisms that are involved in any other learning.
9. While criminal behavior is an expression of general needs and values, it
   is not explained by those general needs and values, since non-criminal
   behavior is an expression of the same needs and values.

The first three steps of the model simply assert that criminal behavior is
learned, rather than being a result of the person's biological inheritance, and
that this happens in intimate communication with other people. The fourth
step of the model says that the future criminal learns two things. First, many
kinds of crime require information and skills, for example how to crack a safe
or pick a pocket. Second, the person must want to commit crimes and feel it
is proper to do so ("specific direction of motives, drives, rationalizations, and
attitudes"). The fifth step says that the crucial attitudes concern rejection of the
legal system ("definitions of the legal code as...unfavorable").

The somewhat obscure language in the model, especially the references to
definitions, comes from the general theoretical perspective called *symbolic interactionism* (Chapter 2). This approach emphasizes the messages that human
beings communicate to each other. People come to define a situation in a particular way, for instance defining the legal system as unjust or irrelevant. They
then communicate this definition to others. An individual receives a variety of
messages from different sources. If most of the messages favor criminal behavior, then the person will become a criminal. If most of the messages favor
obeying the law, then the person will become law-abiding. This is the point
made in step six of the model.

In recent decades, many sociologists have tended to read a somewhat different idea into step 6 of Sutherland's model. They interpret the word *associations* in step 7 to mean *social relationships*. Thus, a person will become criminal if most of his or her friends (associates) are already criminals. But the psychology of Sutherland's day employed the term *association* also for mental connections between ideas, essentially synonymous with *definition*. Thus, Sutherland himself originally seems to have meant the differential strength of definitions received by the person, rather than social relationships. A tribute to the fruitfulness of differential association theory is the fact that it works, whichever interpretation is used.

Step seven of the model notes that the messages a person receives do not all have the same impact on him or her. A pro-crime definition outweighs an anti-crime definition if the person hears it many times (frequency), it is stated at length (duration), it comes first such as in early adolescence (priority), and it is expressed more strongly (intensity). Similarly, we tend to be more influenced by the friends we see frequently, for a long time, early in life, and with whom we have very intense relationships.

The eighth and ninth steps in the model say there is nothing special about the learning of criminal behavior. It depends on the same social mechanisms and individual motives as any other kind of behavior. The distinguishing feature of criminal behavior is that it is learned from criminals, and anyone might become a criminal if he or she were more strongly influenced by the criminal subculture than by conventional society.

A Study Comparing the Theories

Hirschi, Travis
  1969 *Causes of Delinquency*. Berkeley: University of California Press.

In 1965, Travis Hirschi evaluated the relative validity of the three theories by administering a large questionnaire to 4,077 junior and senior high school students in western Contra Costa County, California, not far from San Francisco. In addition to items that related to the theories, the survey asked whether respondents had committed any of a list of delinquent acts, including theft, vandalism, and battery. Not wanting to rely entirely upon what the students said about themselves, Hirschi also obtained school records and information from the police about which of the students had gotten into trouble.

Hirschi preferred control theory, which he defined as the view "that delinquent acts result when an individual's bond to society is weak or broken" (p. 16). That bond has four parts. First there is *attachment* to people, such as close relationships with one's parents, which makes a person sensitive to the wishes of others. Second there is *commitment*, which means investing time and energy in a conventional line of activity, such as getting a good education, where the investment would be endangered by delinquent behavior. Third comes *involvement*, having no opportunity to deviate because all one's time and energy is monopolized by conventional activities such as extracurricular activities and other adult-supervised recreation. Fourth is *belief*, the conviction that the norms of society are just and should be obeyed. Hirschi's data provided ample supportive evidence for the first three of these four. For example, teenagers who shared much time with their parents and were heavily involved in school were less likely than other youngsters to commit delinquent acts.

Strain theory did poorly in Hirschi's analysis. Among 1,121 white boys, there was little correlation between low social class and commission of delinquent acts. Whereas 38 percent of the sons of unskilled laborers admitted engaging in some kind of delinquency, 39 percent of the sons of men with professional and executive jobs did so. There was a tendency for more lower class boys to be habitual delinquents, committing many such acts, compared with upper middle class boys. Hirschi tried elaborate analyses looking more directly at the frustrations that motivate deviance in strain theory, but he did not find evidence in favor of it. Some later writers have argued that Hirschi's measures of delinquency were not serious enough to provide a good test of strain theory. In their view, the frustrations of very low social class lead to lives of crime that were far more intense than found among many of Hirschi's decent school children.

Subcultural deviance theory was partly supported by the data, although Hirschi argued that it did less well than control theory. Delinquent teenagers tended to have other delinquents for friends, which is what subcultural deviance theory would predict. But they did not seem to value or trust these friends very much, so it may be that they became friends after becoming delinquent, when no one but another delinquent would tolerate them. However, the high schools Hirschi studied may simply have lacked the strong delinquent subcultures found in major cities. In addition, his questionnaire did not measure some kinds of deviance, notably illegal drug use, that are usually attributed by sociologists to a subculture. Thus Hirschi's work was an important step in the evaluation of the three competing theories, but many questions remain unanswered.

6
LABELING AND SOCIAL CONSTRUCTION

WORKS AT A GLANCE

The Deviant as Victim of Labeling

"Paranoia and the Dynamics of Exclusion" by Edwin Lemert (1962)
Being Mentally Ill by Thomas Scheff (1966)
Deviance and Medicalization by Peter Conrad and Joseph W. Schneider
(1980, 1992)

The Deviant as Active Labeler

"Techniques of Neutralization" by Gresham Sykes and David Matza (1957)

Social Construction of
Multiple Realities

"On Multiple Realities" by Alfred Schutz (1945)
The Social Construction of Reality by Peter L. Berger and
Thomas Luckman (1966)

Drawing upon symbolic interactionism and other traditional approaches, in the middle of the twentieth century a number of sociologists began describing deviance as a socially-constructed category. This meant that judgments of deviance or conventionality were somewhat arbitrary, and societies had great latitude concerning which kinds of behavior they would accept. Some of these sociologists aggressively claimed that there was no substance at all to such notions as *mental illness*, whereas others offered more modest analyses that examined the significant effect of social definitions in shaping the fates of individuals who were labeled deviant.

All conceptions of individual behavior are cultural creations, not images of deviance alone. However, everyone understands that we may use a variety of languages to describe the world of phenomena; the question is the extent to which labels distort or create realities, rather than merely naming them. Edwin Lemert suggested that one particular label, "paranoia," described the outcome of a process of social exclusion, rather than being a form of disease that existed within certain people. Thomas Scheff applied the same logic to schizophrenia, arguing that schizophrenics were otherwise normal people who had been railroaded into the mental hospital and compelled to play the role of insane person.

Peter Conrad and Joseph Schneider have examined "hyperkinesis," the alleged condition of children who are "too active" in school, suggesting that sometimes the power of a particular group in society can define ambiguous problems to its own advantage. Gresham Sykes and David Matza, in contrast, show that at other times deviant individuals themselves can take advantage of labeling. Philosophically-oriented writers like Alfred Schutz, Peter Berger, and Thomas Luckman place such issues in an intellectual context that is both broader and deeper, as special examples of the general principles of the social construction of reality.

The Deviant as Victim of Labeling

Lemert, Edwin
    1962 "Paranoia and the Dynamics of Exclusion." Pp. 246–264 in *Human Deviance, Social Problems and Social Control*. Englewood Cliffs, New Jersey: Prentice-Hall [1967].

Throughout the 1950s, Lemert collected data on the social processes that determined the fates of people who were labeled mentally ill. At the end of the decade, he concentrated on an intensive study of eight individuals who had been diagnosed as *paranoid*. Clinically, this word was reserved for people with *delusions of grandeur and persecution*. That is, they were people with unreasonably high estimations of their own importance, and who incorrectly felt that other people conspired to harm them. None of these people were intellectually impaired or experienced hallucinations, and they ranged from hospitalized mental patients to troublesome characters who were free to bother other people.

Lemert avoided simply accepting the psychiatric notion that there was something wrong with these individuals. Instead, he examined the paranoid relationship that existed between them and others. The paranoid was disloyal to the norms of the groups to which he belonged, and he posed a real threat to them because he was liable to expose informal power arrangements that people had labored long to create. At the same time, communications from other people lacked genuineness, and they really did conspire to avoid him. Thus the battle between the paranoid and the surrounding world was not a delusion at all, but was very real. And paranoia was not a disease of the individual but a relationship that resulted from a process of social exclusion.

The process always seemed to begin with a threat to the person's social status. For example, a teacher might lose his or her certificate, which would prevent him or her from ever teaching again. Or a business person might fail to get a regular promotion, which he or she would expect to get at that career stage. Or a person might experience physical disfigurement. This negative event would threaten the person's status with family, work associates, or the community. From this first step, it is possible to outline Lemert's argument as a nine-step model of how an individual might be taken from a satisfactory life and placed in the role of a paranoid:

1. Persistent interpersonal difficulties threaten loss of social status to the person.
2. The person makes an awkward attempt to defend the status, becoming arrogant, haughty, and exploitative of others to enhance his or her own status.
3. Members of the person's group come to perceive the person as untrustworthy and unlikeable.
4. Interaction becomes spurious, as people cease behaving genuinely with the person, and instead patronize, humor, and fail to respond normally to him or her.
5. This spurious interaction stops the flow of information to the person, creates discrepancies in the thoughts and feelings of people the person interacts with, and makes the situation highly ambiguous for the person.
6. The person is excluded from the group while still in it, as a coalition begins to form that is a rudimentary conspiracy against the person.
7. The person loses the feedback needed to correct his or her behavior and understanding of the social relationships in the group.
8. The emerging paranoid "delusion" is reinforced when police and other authorities fail to help the person and seem to take the side of the group against him or her.
9. The role of the paranoid becomes a way of life.

After this process of exclusion, the person has a private sense of being a very important person. Why else would everyone gang up against him or her?

The paranoid person indeed seems to have special insights into the conspiratorial nature of the group, and thus may feel very intelligent and knowledgeable. To give up the "delusion" of persecution would be to give up the only remaining proof of being a special person, and thus surrender to the complete loss of social status. On occasion, a "paranoid" person actually functions as the spokesperson for disadvantaged and politically unrepresented members of the population, or can take on the function of scapegoat for the group as a whole. Although the model begins with a small measure of original deviation (whatever failure provokes the original threatened loss of status), the paranoia itself is almost entirely the result of the process of social exclusion.

Scheff, Thomas
1966 *Being Mentally Ill.* Chicago: Aldine.

This book rejects conventional psychiatric explanations of severe mental illness in favor of one based on labeling and social expulsion. Scheff focuses on schizophrenia, a common psychiatric diagnosis applied to people whose thought processes seem seriously disordered and who may experience hallucinations. He summarizes five decades of psychiatric research on schizophrenia, and five thousand scientific publications, in five words: "no headway has been made." Scheff observed mental patients in hospitals and studied psychiatric commitment proceedings in courts. By his own standards of judgment, he found that some of the people judged mentally ill seemed to be quite sane, and he collected a good deal of evidence that the judgments of professional psychiatrists and judges are arbitrary. This work led him to propose a model of how schizophrenia might merely be the result of a process of social labeling.

As the intellectual groundwork for his model, Scheff asks us to imagine we have written a list of all the actions that human beings perform that violate societal norms. Once we have this long list, we should go through checking off all the forms of deviation that have explicit names. Erratic behavior under the influence of alcohol is "drunkenness," so we check that off. Taking something without permission that belongs to someone else is "theft," and so on. When we have gone through the list, checking off explicitly-named forms of deviant behavior, we will be left with a number of actions that are the *residue* of this categorization process. (These might be things like muttering to an unseen companion, crouching in the corner of the room, or moving in unusual and apparently purposeless ways.) Scheff calls these acts *residual deviance.* They violate norms that are so taken-for-granted that we do not explicitly talk about them or give them formal names. Yet modern society does gather them up under an overarching label, and that is *mental illness.*

Scheff's theory of residual deviance parallel's Lemert's theory of paranoia in many respects. It consists of six ideas that explain how a normal, ordinary person might be caught up in a process of labeling and made to play the role of schizophrenic.

1. Residual rule-breaking arises from a wide variety of sources, and in itself is not an illness.
2. Practically everybody engages in residual rule-breaking from time to time, and this form of deviance is far more common than is the "mental illness" diagnosed and treated by psychiatrists.
3. Most of the time, people ignore occasional residual rule-breaking, but societal reaction can turn it into a persistent pattern of behavior.
4. Crucial factors in shaping this process are the cultural stereotypes of mental illness people learn early in childhood.
5. These stereotypes are reinforced during adulthood by the mass media and by ordinary social interaction.
6. People who play the role of mentally ill person, fulfilling these stereotypes, may be rewarded for doing so, for example because they support the psychiatrists' own positive image of themselves.

Thus, Scheff viewed schizophrenia as the result of a *deviance-amplifying system* that magnified some cases of residual-rule breaking until they fit into the cultural stereotypes and psychiatric institutions of the society. In the years since Scheff wrote this influential book, conventional psychiatry has moved even further from his position. Schizophrenia is believed to be a chemical or structural disorder involving the neurotransmitter chemicals by which nerves in the brain function, and many psychiatrists give sociology no role to play in explaining this disorder. The fact remains, however, that diagnosis of schizophrenia is often problematic, and doctors frequently disagree about whether to apply this particular label to a patient. Over the past two centuries of psychiatry, physiological theories have been popular in some decades, and social-psychological explanations have been popular in others. Thus it is quite possible that the current medical consensus gives too much emphasis to physical causes, but too little to social ones, and in some form Scheff's insights still have some measure of validity.

Conrad, Peter, and Joseph W. Schneider
   1980 *Deviance and Medicalization: From Badness to Sickness.*
      Philadelphia: Temple University Press [1992].

Conrad and Schneider critique the gradual transformation of American culture, from a time when deviant behavior was either ignored or labeled sin, to a time when deviance was defined as a medical problem requiring treatment. Among the kinds of behavior often treated as medical problems today, which alternatively could be either accepted or criminalized, are heavy alcohol use, indulgence in ecstasy-producing drugs, and high levels of activity in school children. Under the guise of helping people who often are said to be incapable of understanding their own needs, medical "science" has become a new instrument of punishment and social control. Conrad and Schneider stress that *deviance* is not necessarily bad or sick, but merely is behavior that the society defines negatively and condemns. They list five principles of a sociological theory of deviance.

1. In every society some individuals deviate from the accepted standards of behavior, but there are few if any acts that are defined as deviant in all societies.
2. Deviance is socially defined, rather than being an objective characteristic of any behavior or status.
3. Social groups make rules and impose definitions through the specific acts of judging and sanctioning deviant individuals.
4. Within a particular society, an act becomes deviant only in certain contexts, and if performed under other circumstances or by a different category of person might not be deviant at all.
5. Defining and sanctioning deviance requires power, and powerful groups are able to establish standards of morality and definitions of deviance that serve their purposes.

In the first half of the nineteenth century, the flimsy profession of medicine collapsed in the United States, and throughout much of the country anyone could claim to be a doctor and treat patients without any special education or licensing. However, in the middle of the century the profession began to consolidate, and the founding of the American Medical Association in 1847 was a landmark. Ironically much of the progress in American health throughout the century was the result of improved hygiene and nutrition, rather than of medical treatment, yet the prestige of doctors steadily grew. Medical licensing became progressively more strict, and objective advances in surgery demanded thorough training. Even before the invention of antibiotics, medical understanding of the nature of bacterial infections led to effective methods of prevention and treatment. A standard cultural model of disease emerged, in which each illness had a specific cause that disrupted the proper functioning of the body, and that could be countered by a suitable treatment. Religion lost some of its power to enforce norms, and the very complexity of modern society left a power vacuum into which the profession of medicine could expand, as it promised to solve an ever greater number of human problems.

One challenging example is the recently "discovered" ailment called *hyperactivity* or *hyperkinesis*, which "causes" 3 to 10 percent of school boys (plus a much smaller percentage of girls) to have problems in school. Conrad and Schneider say we cannot understand hyperkinesis without first examining the gradual evolution of our culture's conception of children over the past several centuries. Every society recognizes that infants are different from adults, and every culture has imposed somewhat different expectations on different age groups. But the notion of childhood is a modern invention. In many societies, including our own until perhaps three centuries ago, children above about age seven were treated as little adults. According to Conrad and

Schneider, many children worked, swore, engaged in some kinds of sexual activity, frequented taverns, and never saw the inside of a school. Perhaps the high rates of mortality among children prevented their parents from lavishing care on them, and economic need forced them into apprenticeship or manual labor if they survived. Only gradually did the idea emerge that childhood should be a special period, during which tender young personalities should be protected from the harshness of adult life and should submit to the authority of adults who understood better than they what they needed. Throughout the nineteenth and twentieth centuries, a sequence of "child saver" social movements developed concepts like *juvenile delinquency* (as distinct from simply *crime*) and built the set of distinctive institutions and formal practices to deal with deviant youth that only modern society possesses.

Thus, both the growth of power of the medical profession, and the development of a concept of childhood, set the stage for a medical approach to children's misbehavior in school. Some children, mostly boys, find it difficult to keep quiet, to focus their attention on one activity for long periods of time, and to sustain the same moderate mood throughout the school day. Unwilling to conclude that school itself was at fault, harried teachers were receptive to a definition of such children that would reduce blame and offer a way of controlling them. In 1937, a medical researcher named Charles Bradley observed that amphetamine drugs calmed some children. This was a paradoxical finding because amphetamines generally agitate people rather than subduing them, a fact reflected in the drug's popular name, "speed." Two decades later, this paradoxical discovery legitimated using amphetamine-type drugs to treat highly active children, and the practice soon became widespread in the American school system. True, the medication changes the behavior in a way that would be hard to explain if something were not wrong with the individual. But a diagnosis of hyperkinesis depends entirely upon observing that the child violates the norms that schoolteachers wish to impose upon him or her. Compared with doctors and schoolteachers, children are powerless. In a tremendous advertising campaign, pharmaceutical companies sold the public on the medicalization of "excessive" youthful activity.

The Deviant as Active Labeler

Sykes, Gresham, and David Matza
  1957 "Techniques of Neutralization: A Theory of Delinquency," *American Sociological Review* 22:664–670.

Sykes and Matza argue that juvenile delinquents accept the norms of the surrounding society to a significant degree, and they would not violate these norms unless they had justifications or rationalizations that they themselves found somewhat plausible. In other words, juvenile delinquents find a way of defining their actions, at least in their own minds, so they feel the norms do

not apply. Sykes and Matza identified five major categories of such rationalizations that juvenile delinquents commonly use.

In *denial of responsibility*, the delinquent claims that he or she could not
help violating the norm. Perhaps the deviant act was an accident, or uncon-
trollable forces were at work, such as bad companions or poverty. Highly sophisticated delinquents may even explain their actions in terms of sociological theories that blame social conditions and thus absolve the delinquent of
individual responsibility.

Denial of injury says that no real harm was done by the deviant deed.
Vandalism may be defined as a harmless prank that the victim can easily afford, and gang violence may be considered a fair fight between two willing
parties.

Denial of the victim acknowledges that someone was hurt but says that under the circumstances the harm was justified. The victim may really have "had
it coming," and the delinquent's deed was appropriate punishment for something the victim had done.

Condemnation of the condemners shifts attention for the delinquent's action to those who criticize him or her for it. These condemners are spiteful
hypocrites who have no warrant for their moral judgment. In this view, a
teacher who rewards some students and punishes others is just showing fa-
voritism, and successful people are either lucky or secretly corrupt.

Appeal to higher loyalties regrets that it was necessary to violate the norm,
but the welfare of the gang, friendship group, or family required it. Norms like
"always help a friend" and "never squeal on a buddy" take precedence over
the norms of teachers and the police.

This theory of norm neutralization rests on the symbolic interactionist observation that it matters how we define a situation, and the labels we attach
to actions shape how we will behave. In contrast to the other labeling studies
above, Sykes and Matza show that the deviant is an active party in labeling.

Social Construction of
Multiple Realities

Schutz, Alfred
  1945 "On Multiple Realities." Pp. 207–259 in *Collected Papers*, Volume I.
    The Hague: Nijhoff [1971].

Schutz considers how our sense of reality may vary. In everyday life, every
sane person takes the reality and meaning of familiar things entirely for
granted. This unquestioning sense of reality Schutz calls the *natural attitude*,
and he says that the world of everyday life is the *paramount reality*. Here we
act, and our actions have consequences. We work with objects that offer re-
sistance to our actions. Yet this paramount reality of everyday life is not the
only reality. There exist several other *finite provinces of meaning* that could

be called other realities, each with its own distinctive experiences, structure, and attitude. Among these multiple realities are dreams, art, religious experience, the play world of children, the realm of scientific theory, and the distinctly other reality inhabited by severely insane people.

Time is the crucial dimension of all our experience. Meaning does not exist in our experiences themselves; rather we invest past experiences with meaning from the perspective of the present, and we set meaningful goals to achieve in the future. However, when we imagine the future, we really see it as a kind of past, as if future deeds had already been accomplished. And there is more than one kind of time. One is *inner time*, that is, your own private feeling of the passage of events and experiences. Another is the objective or *cosmic time* of the world of objects. The paramount reality of everyday life is the one reality in which people share time by interacting with each other.

A person cannot move smoothly from one of these worlds to another. Rather, a person's consciousness must leap across, and the transition from one reality to another is always a mental shock. Compared with the paramount reality of everyday life, these finite provinces of meaning lack coherent social interaction. The experience of time is different, perhaps utterly so, and we cannot share time coherently with another person. Objects are not stable, and the results of our actions typically vanish. Schutz considers the worlds of *phantasms* (fiction, fantasies, myths, jokes, and the like), dreams, and scientific theory, finding each distinctly different from and yet connected to the world of everyday life.

Except for his passing references to insanity, Schutz does not directly connect this analysis to deviant behavior. Yet within sociology, and even to some extent in wider modern culture, the concept of multiple realities has taken on a broader meaning. Different sets of norms and beliefs—what sociologists usually call subcultures—are sometimes referred to as realities, implying that each one is just as genuine as the others. Thus deviant religion, schizophrenia, lethal violence, or political extremism get defined rather blandly as alternative realities. For Schutz, the reality of everyday life is not only paramount but unified, and only in this reality is social life fully possible.

Berger, Peter L., and Thomas Luckman
  1966 *The Social Construction of Reality*. Garden City, New York:
    Doubleday.

This is a treatise in the sociology of knowledge, although some readers might prefer words like "ideology" or "mythology" instead of "knowledge." For Berger and Luckman, knowledge is whatever passes for knowledge in society, whether or not we, ourselves, believe it. *Knowledge* is the feeling of certainty that a particular phenomenon is real and possesses familiar characteristics. *Reality* is the quality phenomena have that the individual cannot simply ignore them or wish them out of existence, whether these phenomena are physical, social, or psychological. In the sociology of knowledge, the word *construction* has a double meaning. It can refer to something that people build or create. Or it can refer more modestly to the act of construing, interpreting, or explaining. Every sociologist would agree that human cultures provide ways of interpreting reality, but radical sociologists of knowledge assert that many phenomena (perhaps all) do not exist until a society imagines them.

Berger and Luckman note that the traditional sociology of knowledge was based in the work of Karl Marx and began with the assumption that a person's consciousness was a product of his or her social context. For example, a rich person "knows" that the surrounding social system is just, even though a poor person might feel it is unjust. Knowledge that serves the interests of a particular social class is a self-serving ideology. Often the dominant social class is able to foist its ideology on the other classes, making them accept it as true, even though their own social class might be far better served by a different ideology. When a class accepts the wrong ideology, typically one suited to the interests of a different class, it suffers from false consciousness. Berger and Luckman do not deny that many valid sociological insights can be derived from the Marxian sociology of knowledge, but they offer a new departure that does not focus so much on the class interests that are served by particular systems of knowledge. Instead of Marx, they draw much of their inspiration from the work of Alfred Schutz, blended with symbolic interactionism.

Schutz distinguished the paramount reality of everyday life from a variety of multiple realities. He noted that it is a shared reality through which individuals interact, and this is the quality Berger and Luckman call *intersubjectivity*. A given individual experiences much of the world routinely, taking for granted the meanings given to its elements by language. The system of words that defines a taken-for-granted reality and places all its parts in a coherent order is a *typification scheme*. Each thing we encounter in this world belongs to a type, which was socially created in the past, and we associate particular characteristics with each such type. Our aims are pragmatic, to attain some goal in this world. Therefore, much of the social stock of knowledge is recipe knowledge, telling us what actions to perform with which objects to attain our goal. Berger and Luckman look more closely at the structure of that paramount reality than Schutz did, stressing that it is divided into a large number of alternative sectors, some of which are compatible with each other, and others that are incompatible.

To show how the stresses and strains of human interaction produce knowledge, Berger and Luckman frequently return to a whimsical, hypothetical example. They imagine a tiny society consisting of just three people, *A, B,* and *C.* Person *A* is a male heterosexual; *B* is a female bisexual; and *C* is a female homosexual. Person *A* has sex with *B, B* has sex with *C,* and *A* and *C* share the hobby of flower arranging. Berger and Luckman argue that human instincts, such as the sexual drive, are extremely pliable. So if *A, B,* and *C* define their relationships as normal, then they are normal. But the three will have to invest considerable energy constructing their tiny social order, naming all the roles and acts they share with each other, and creating whatever institutions are required to make them feel legitimate and coherent. For example, Berger and Luckman note that real societies have incest taboos, prohibiting sex between close relatives, but these taboos have no meaning outside each particular society's system of kinship relations, which define which relations are incestuous and which are not.

Very elaborate systems of typification and symbolism may arise to support such a system, and they come into being through the meaning-creating actions of people. For example, *A* may feel that *C* spends too much time making love to *B*, and she does not devote enough attention to flower-arranging with him. What's worse, if the relationships among the three become unbalanced, their tiny social system may fall apart. Therefore *A* invents a new religion to explain why all three relationships are crucially important. In this mythology, a god and goddess sexually produced the land; the goddess and her sister sexually produced the sea, and the great flower dance of the god and the sister-goddess produced life. Relations among *A, B,* and *C* merely reflect the relations among the deities, so they must never stray from this sacred, objective pattern.

In all stable societies, Berger and Luckman say, the institutional order becomes *objectivated*; that is, people come to believe that its socially-constructed meanings are really objective and could not be otherwise. Perhaps the biggest symbolic challenge faced by society is making death meaningful. All societies are constructions of humanly-created order in the face of chaos, and the loss of socially-constructed meaning thrusts the individual into anomie, where he or she will be exposed alone to unspeakable terrors.

Because social reality is both essential and precarious, societies fiercely combat symbolic threats to their existence, such as deviant behavior. For example, Berger and Luckman ask us to imagine a militaristic homosexual society, in which warriors are emotionally tied to each other by powerful romantic bonds and who thus are willing to endure danger to rescue each other on the battlefield. (Ancient Sparta, in Greece, may actually have been like this.) Such a society would react negatively to a heterosexual, saying that failure to react erotically to members of the same sex was abnormal, immoral, perhaps a form of mental illness that required scientific treatment, or a crime that demanded dire punishment. Modern society, however, is not a unified world, but is divided into many subuniverses (competing subcultures as well as compatible roles). Intellectuals, such as sociologists, make it their business to be worldless to some extent, doubting the mythologies of the society that surrounds them and relying upon the support of an intellectual subculture as they analyze the ways that all people, including themselves, creatively construct reality and then treat it as objective.

LARGE-SCALE SOCIAL STRUCTURES

7
COMMUNITY AND URBAN

WORKS AT A GLANCE

The Chicago School of Urban Sociology

The City by Robert E. Park, Ernest W. Burgess, Roderick D. McKenzie, and Louis Wirth (1925)
The Hobo by Nels Anderson (1923)

Culture and Social Organization

Middletown: A Study in American Culture by Robert S. Lynd and Helen Merrell Lynd (1929)
Street Corner Society by William Foote Whyte (1943)
"Family Neighbors" by John R. Logan and Glenna D. Spitze (1994)

Contemporary Urban Theory

"Toward a Subcultural Theory of Urbanism" by Claude S. Fischer (1975)
Urban Fortunes: The Political Economy of Place by John R. Logan and Harvey L. Molotch (1987)

Among the central issues for urban sociology is the process that causes every city to differentiate into a number of neighborhoods, each with its own distinctive characteristics. This can be studied either by examining the city as a whole, perhaps by collecting statistics to compare its parts with each other, or by intensively studying the life of a particular neighborhood. Both approaches were pioneered by sociologists at the University of Chicago early in the twentieth century, who developed a unified perspective on cities called *The Chicago School* (see Chapter 5). Robert Park and his associates conceptualized the city as a dynamic competition between individuals and groups that produced neighborhoods that were distinctive social environments. Other Chicago School writers such as Nels Anderson recognized that some people suffered from the machinations of capitalist economies, notably migrant workers.

Robert and Helen Lynd took a more anthropological approach when they studied Muncie, Indiana, stressing detailed description of urban life without overarching theories. William Foote Whyte drew on both approaches in research on Boston's Italian North End, living in the neighborhood himself to gain access to the residents and to learn how they experienced city life. John Logan and Glenna Spitze used modern survey research methods to learn how family and friendship relationships sustained communities in Albany, New York.

Drawing on ideas from the old Chicago School, Claude Fischer developed a theory of how the sheer population size of urban environments could support many distinctive subcultures. John Logan and Harvey Molotch argue that some of these groups compete intensely with each other. Much urban ethnography, such as the studies of Muncie and Boston, optimistically hoped that economic growth would eventually allow most groups to participate in the prosperous mainstream of American life. But Logan and Molotch fear that local groups of capitalists are so intent upon making profits that they ruin neighborhoods, causing cities to be dismal places of poverty and suffering.

The Chicago School of Urban Sociology

Park, Robert E., Ernest W. Burgess, Roderick D. McKenzie, and Louis Wirth
    1925 *The City*. Chicago: University of Chicago Press.

This is a collection of ten essays, six of them by Park, two by Burgess, one by McKenzie, and one in the form of an annotated bibliography by Wirth. Despite their diversity of topic and authorship, these chapters are based in a unified perspective on city life called *The Chicago School*. It was centered at the University of Chicago, where Park and his colleagues and students dominated American sociology from about 1915 to 1940.

Members of the Chicago School adopted a *concentric zone* model of the geographic development of cities. A normal city takes on the form of an archery target. The bull's eye at the center is the downtown business district (called the Loop in Chicago), where land values are at their peak and relatively few people live. Around that is a ring of factories and decaying residential buildings called the *zone of transition*. Another ring contains cheap but respectable working-class homes, conveniently within reach of, but not overshadowed by, the transition-zone factories where the men work. Still farther out is a ring called the *residential zone,* marked by comfortable homes. The *commuters' zone* extends outward to the fringes of the urban area. Each of these zones has its own characteristics and contributes to the nature of the city as a whole. The shape of the zones is the result of history, as a growing city allowed the innermost residential neighborhoods to be invaded by factories and commercial enterprises, while building new and often better residential neighborhood farther out. Thus the city is a dynamic balance between processes of concentration and decentralization.

Within the zones, cities consist of neighborhoods in which people are tied together by intimate personal relationships. Neighborhoods emerge and dissolve as the city evolves, and they generally lack formal organization. Some neighborhoods tend to consist of a single immigrant ethnic group, and these may develop high internal solidarity along with a considerable degree of isolation from the wider city. Each neighborhood becomes a somewhat distinct *moral region* with its own norms and culture, and some are dominated by special facilities like a race track or opera house that set the tone of the district. Neighborhoods in the zone of transition may take on highly deviant characteristics, such as *Gangland,* where social life is dominated by gangs, or *Hobohemia,* where the population consists of constantly shifting migrant workers.

The Chicago School drew much of its intellectual inspiration from recent developments in biology called *ecology.* The scientific discipline of ecology studies plants and animals as they exist in nature, with great attention to their interdependence and their relation to the environment. When a forest develops, one set of plant species will be succeeded by another, and it in turn will be succeeded by another, until the forest is mature. So, too, the concentric zones of a city are the residue of a process of ecological succession. The neighborhoods of a city are *natural areas* with distinctive environments created by the interactions among the kinds of individuals and institutions found within them. The ecology of a city tends to stabilize over time, until some event such as the introduction of a new industry disturbs the equilibrium. Although the residents of a city are interdependent, a key fact about human ecology is that individuals are always in competition with other individuals.

Competition in large cities forces people to specialize and to acquire special skills that improve their chances of success, thus producing a very high diversity of interests and tasks. This in turn breaks down the traditional organization of society based on family, local associations, and culture, and produces a new but incomplete organization based on vocation. No longer is there a solidarity based on sentiment and habit, but one based on shared interests. Charles Horton Cooley suggested the term *primary group* for a set of relations characterized by intimate, face-to-face interaction and enduring cooperation. But in the modern city primary relations are largely replaced by *secondary relations,* which are more fragmentary and indirect. The breakdown of primary groups greatly weakens informal social control, so the cities experience high rates of vice and crime. In response, cities emphasize rational law and formal organizations of social control such as courts. When an area of the city stabilizes economically and culturally, competition becomes less ruthless and rules of social control provide a measure of strength to the community.

A community is more than simply a collection of individuals. More importantly, it is a collection of institutions such as churches, schools, and businesses. No urban community is completely isolated, but is always part of a larger community such as the city or nation. Each community that develops a distinct character will have a center and a circumference. Within its borders, populations and institutions will group themselves in a characteristic pattern that may be called the ecological organization of the community. Within this ecological organization an economic organization based on the division of labor arises, in which people take on different jobs in economic competition with each other. A mature community also has cultural and political organization, which limit competition and impose restraints on individuals. In principle, sociology can contribute to the solution of city problems through scientifically-informed social work and public policy, but the authors of this book admit that sociology had not yet done much to improve communities at the time they wrote.

Anderson, Nels
 1923 *The Hobo.* Chicago: University of Chicago Press.

Anderson himself had experienced the life of a migrant worker (or "hobo"), so under the direction of Park and his associates he was able to carry out an extremely detailed ethnography of their section of Chicago, Hobohemia. Around 1920, this area contained from 30,000 to 75,000 itinerent workers, and nearly half a million of them passed through the city each year on their way to construction and agricultural jobs all across the nation. Chicago was the railway center of the country, and therefore it had become a vast labor exchange, centered on the employment agencies of West Madison Street, which were called "the slave market."

Every large city had a similar district where homeless people collected, called the "stem," or the "main drag." Despite its economic significance as the migrant labor hub, it was an extremely disorganized part of the city, overrun with many kinds of deviance: bootleggers, dope peddlers, professional gamblers, pickpockets, jack rollers (who rob poor men in their sleep), drunks, cripples, beggars, and old broken men, worn out by the trials of life. Hardly any children could be found in Hobohemia, and the few women either worked in religious missions or were the poorest kind of prostitute.

A night's lodging in a single room in one of the cheap hotels cost fifty cents; a space on the floor of a "flop house" could be rented for a dime. For less than fifty cents a man could buy enough coffee and bread to make it through the day. Long-term survival could be achieved for a dollar a day. Many of the men were unable to work, but others merely pretended to be. A beggar who feigned deafness was called "dummy," pretend paralysis was "stiffy," and any kind of faked affliction was "jiggers." Hobos often rode on freight trains without permission. One who lost a foot doing this was "peg," and one who lost a leg was "sticks." A "straight crip" was honestly disabled, whereas a "phoney crip" was either faking or had inflicted a real injury on himself in order to gain sympathy while begging.

Few of the hobos were beggars or petty criminals, and they sought the same kind of self-respect enjoyed by more prosperous citizens. But the realities of migrant work beat them down, sooner or later. They lived from hand to mouth, and could not readily establish themselves in stable communities. They were the victims of the economic forces of industrial society, and financial depression or simply the passage of time would degrade most migratory workers from economic independence to abject poverty.

Culture and Social Organization

Lynd, Robert S., and Helen Merrell Lynd
  1929 *Middletown: A Study in American Culture.* New York: Harcourt, Brace and Company.

In 1924 and 1925, a team of social scientists led by the Lynds studied the way of life of Muncie, Indiana, much as anthropologists might study an exotic tribe. They were trying to understand a typical American city as a whole, rather than to test any particular theory. However, their research needed focus, so a central theme was understanding the present by examining the past, especially the year 1890. Further intellectual structure was provided by an emphasis on six main kinds of activity carried out by citizens of Muncie: (1) getting a living, (2) making a home, (3) raising children, (4) using leisure, (5) engaging in religious practices, and (6) participating in the community.

The team collected data by a variety of labor-intensive means. They participated in Muncie's life, attending churches, school meetings, court sessions, political rallies, labor gatherings, cultural events, card parties, and numerous dinners both public and private. In such settings they would take unobtrusive notes if possible, or they would write down their observations immediately afterward. They examined public documents of every conceivable kind, such as census records, daily newspapers, and the meeting minutes of diverse organizations. The team compiled statistics on such things as church membership, automobile ownership, and employment wages. They carried out many inter-views, including formal interrogations of nearly two hundred families. Questionnaires collected data from four hundred clubs, and from twice that number of high school children.

In 1890, Muncie had about 11,000 residents, and by 1924 the population had risen above 38,000. Over this time, it evolved from the hub of an agri-cultural area into an industrial center concentrating on manufacture of glass or metal products and automobile components. The discovery of natural gas deposits in 1886 launched the industrial development, but it continued long after the gas ran out. Few non-whites or foreign-born people lived in Muncie, but in many respects it was typical of small cities throughout the heartland of America. Of every 100 residents, 43 were employed outside the home, 23 were homemakers, 19 attended school, and 15 were either too young or too old to engage in these activities.

All aspects of Muncie's life depended on the work people did to earn a liv-ing. Four out of five employed persons were male, and a man would lose sta-tus if he did not have a job. Women were not culturally expected to have jobs, but their involvement in the labor force had increased from one in ten in 1890, to one in six in 1920. Muncie's industries attracted workers from the sur-rounding farm land, so many in the working class had moved from the rural to urban environment. In both 1890 and 1924, a chief product of Muncie was glass jars, but the method of producing them had changed completely. Originally, it had taken 24 highly skilled men and 24 boy helpers to blow 19,200 jars per day, but later just 8 men running machines could produce 79,200 in the same time. Everything had been mechanized over this period, from making ice cream to manufacture of fence wire. Working-class men faced the challenge of unsteady employment as the economy fluctuated up and down, and there was little chance of promotion up into the middle class. The men worked hard, but most earned less than the $1,921 annual estimated mimimum cost of living for a family of five.

The people of Muncie lived in 9,200 homes, 86 percent of which were single-family dwellings. Most homes were wood, and the modest dwellings of the working class contained only two to four rooms divided by partitions. In 1890, only one house in eight had running water, but by 1925 the proportion had reached three fourths. Almost all houses had electricity, but not quite half possessed telephones. Women married relatively early and devoted them-selves to homemaking and motherhood. Both divorce and birth control were rarely resorted to, and both were opposed by the prevailing culture. However, family culture was gradually changing in many ways. Families tended to be smaller than in the past, teenage girls and boys were more free to experience romance, and young people were finding greater opportunity for social life outside the home. Family life still centered around the dinner table, but food preparation at home was declining; for example, the bread was bought rather than being baked in private kitchens.

When compulsory education began in 1897, school was required only twelve weeks a year for children aged eight to fourteen. By 1924, 70 percent of residents aged six through twenty-one were attending school. High school graduation had become common, and a significant minority went on to college. Average class size was 58 in 1890, and 30 in 1924. School curricula had become more diverse, but the aim of education continued to be the instilling of conventional values and attitudes, as well as useful skills. About 80 percent of teachers were women, most of them relatively young and unmarried. The majority had been educated in the state, and policies tried to discourage teachers from other regions who might bring in unfamiliar ideas.

Over the years, leisure time and the variety of ways to spend it had increased. On average, a Muncie resident took more than six books out of the public library in 1924, compared with fewer than one in 1890. In 1924, more than a tenth of the 9,200 families subscribed to each of the following periodicals: *American Magazine, Saturday Evening Post, Delineator, Ladies' Home Journal, McCall's, Physical Culture, True Story,* and *Woman's Home Companion.* Muncie's first phonograph arrived in 1890, and by 1924 radios were found in 6 percent of working class homes and 12 percent of business class homes.

The abundant religious life of the community revolved around traditional Christianity. Among junior and senior high school students, 82 percent of the boys and 92 percent of the girls agreed with a questionnaire item that said, "Christianity is the one true religion and all peoples should be converted to it." The Lynds suspected that the influence of religion was gradually weakening, but their evidence indicated it remained strong.

Many community institutions were stable and conservative, such as the Republican party, which dominated Muncie's political life. Progress was notable in medicine, and charity was becoming progressively more organized, in both private and public forms. The newspapers of 1924 emphasized local events, thus replacing the neighborly gossip of 1890. Civic pride harmonized with a pervasive dislike of people who deviated from the somewhat bland norms of Muncie.

Although it did not settle any theoretical questions, the research by Robert and Helen Lynd provided rich descriptions of a representative middle-American city. It set the standard for a whole series of later Middletown studies and similar projects in other urban areas, such as the "Yankee City" studies of Newburyport, Massachusetts, by Lloyd Warner, Paul Lunt, and their collaborators, which in turn influenced William Foote White in his study of a Boston ethnic slum.

Whyte, William Foote
  1943 *Street Corner Society.* Chicago: University of Chicago Press.

This widely-read book describes the social structure of an Italian "slum," which White called Cornerville but was actually the Italian "North End" of

Boston. Whyte assigned fictitious names to all the people and organizations in the book to protect their privacy. To immerse himself in the community, Whyte resided there from early 1937 until the middle of 1940, the first 18 months of which were spent living with an Italian family. His research data consist of extremely detailed observations of the actions and interactions of small groups of young men who were constantly competing with each other in the attempt to lead small informal groups and club organizations. Whyte was a *participant observer*, acting almost like a member of the group, but the men were aware that he was writing a book.

Whyte begins with the "Nortons," a social gang of men in their twenties organized by "Doc" in the early spring of 1937. Born in 1908, Doc had grown up in the area, and as a boy he collected around him a group of friends, including Nutsy and Danny who later became his lieutenants in the Nortons. Except for six months when he ran a small community center, Doc was unemployed for the period of Whyte's research, and one of the great challenges was finding a little cash to support the gang's recreational activities. The men took their relationships with each other very seriously, and they were keenly conscious of the status hierarchy in their small group. Whyte published a sociogram of the 13 members, showing Doc had highest status, Danny and Mike were in second place, Long John a little to the side with ties to the three top men, with Nutsy and the others arranged in columns under the leaders.

Bowling and other games were extremely important media in which the men acted out their status roles. In several bowling contests, Whyte observed that men achieved status by playing well, but also subtle social pressures would be brought to bear on a low-status man to keep him from winning. The fact that the men were largely unemployed prevented them from using occupational accomplishment or money to gain prestige, so the games were a very serious arena for competition and alliance. In 1938, Doc ran for a position in the Massachusetts state legislature, and he was able to attract a number of local supporters. But before the election he dropped out, explaining he simply did not have the money to run a credible campaign. He lost confidence and was unable to exploit his status in the Nortons to gain position in the larger society.

For a time, Doc and other Nortons belonged to the Italian Community Club organized by another young man, whom Whyte called "Chick Morelli." The club was an arena for status competition not only among individual men but also between two factions, the *corner boys* (like Doc) and the *college boys* (like Chick). College boys were dedicated to upward social mobility, and high education was a means toward this goal. They saved their money and they avoided tying themselves to close friends who would make demands incompatible with personal achievement. Corner boys were committed to their local community. They spent their money, not because they lacked financial discipline, but to invest in social activities that gave them status in their immediate group of friends. The difference between college boys and corner boys was not primarily intelligence, because Doc and some of his group were smart, but social aggressiveness. College boys were ready to sacrifice today's local friendships for future status in the larger world, whereas the corner boys were trapped in the present by their solidarity with their friends. Because they were interested in individual advancement, the college boys had difficulty developing the warm social relationships that could make a club function well, and they overemphasized formal regulations like club by-laws. Because of Chick's extreme ambition, the Italian Community Club broke apart and failed. But it provided Chick some valuable lessons in leadership, and he went on to law school and a successful career, while Doc limped from year to year without getting anywhere.

Outsiders believed the North End was chaotic and disorganized, but in fact it possessed a considerable degree of social organization. Many of the immigrant men had known each other in Italy, and those who came from the same town became a cohesive group. The second generation grew up as a coherent community linked by friendship relationships that became formalized in adulthood by social and political groups. The neighborhood's problem was that its organization did not mesh with that of the surrounding city. The Italian political and racket organizations, especially, clashed with the institutions of Irish and Old New England communities that dominated Boston. During the period of the Great Depression, the conventional routes for social mobility had become blocked for the recent immigrants and their children. Thus the Italians had to build up their own business, political, and racket hierarchies, which became major focuses of social structure.

Logan, John R. and Glenna D. Spitze
1994 "Family Neighbors," *American Journal of Sociology* 100:453–476.

Many sociologists have argued that both the family and the neighborhood community have declined in recent years, so the link between family and neighborhood is very much in doubt. Logan and Spitze interviewed 1,200 people in the Albany, New York, area, aged forty or older. Their questions focused on the interactions respondents had with family members and neighbors, asking how often they talked with them and what help they received from them. Few respondents had close family members who lived in another home in the same neighborhood, but these "family neighbors" proved to be very influential. Just 15 percent had an adult child in the same neighborhood, and 7 percent had a parent, but these provided far more interaction and help than did non-family neighbors. People with family neighbors tended to become especially involved in their neighborhoods. Thus, family relationships continue to be an important factor creating and sustaining communities.

Contemporary Urban Theory

Fischer, Claude S.
 1975 "Toward a Subcultural Theory of Urbanism," *American Journal of Sociology* 80:1319–1341.

The traditional view of cities, as presented in the works of Emile Durkheim or members of the Chicago School such as Louis Wirth, was that urban conditions generated anomie or social disorganization, which in turn produced deviant behavior of many kinds. Supposedly, the mobs of people from many different ethnic backgrounds eroded social relationships and prevented consensus in norms and values. However, more recent research like that of William Foote Whyte showed that cities were not, by and large, anomic. Fischer argues that this finding presents a challenge for theorists, because it is still true that rates of many kinds of deviance are higher in cities than in areas where the population is less concentrated. He then offers a four-step theory that seeks to derive the deviance of cities directly from their population density, without relying upon anomie.

1. The more urban a place, the greater its subcultural variety.
2. The more urban a place, the more intense its subcultures.
3. The more urban a place, the more numerous the sources of diffusion and the greater the diffusion into a subculture.
4. The more urban a place, the higher its rates of unconventionality.

The larger a city, the more readily competition among individuals can produce complex social systems, and the more diverse the geographical area from which it will draw immigrants. In large cities, there are enough people of every kind to support intense social relations within each subculture and conflict between subcultures. With so many diverse and intense subcultures, there are ample opportunities for cultural practices to spread from one to another, the process called *diffusion,* thus producing novel combinations of beliefs and practices. The great variety of subcultures in a large city implies directly that some are likely to be unconventional, from the standpoint of the surrounding society. The intensity of subcultures, and the creation of cultural innovations by diffusion, also produce deviance. All of these processes work together, and many of the subcultures are ethnic or tied to particular professions, rather than being inherently deviant. Thus, the population size of large cities produces unconventional behavior through a complex dynamic among groups that themselves are not anomic and can be internally quite well organized.

Logan, John R., and Harvey L. Molotch
  1987 Urban Fortunes: The Political Economy of Place. Berkeley,
    California: University of California Press.

Logan and Molotch survey a vast literature on urban economic development, arguing that its causes and consequences are far less benign than proponents of city growth claim. Real estate can be said to have two kinds of value: use value and exchange value. A home has *use value*, for example, to the people who live in it and enjoy the neighborhood in which it is situated. *Exchange value* is the money that an owner can gain from selling or renting the property. Economists tend to focus on exchange value, because it is readily expressed in dollars, but it is hard to place a dollar value on the use that a family has for its home, especially if the family has neither the money nor the political power to prevent urban development from taking its home or destroying its neighborhood. Relatively poor people may pay what the landlord demands because they value their home's location, and prosperous people may employ a variety of political means to maintain the use value of their property. In consequence, places become stratified just as social classes are stratified, and the place a person lives in has great consequences for his or her life chances.

People for whom the exchange value of a place is most important, such as the owners of rental property or real estate speculators, have an interest in cooperating with each other to promote "growth." In the relatively free market of American real estate, this often produces a local *growth machine*, a sociopolitical arrangement that unites business and government groups in favor of policies of economic growth, for example, building industrial parks, convention centers, sports arenas, and shopping malls. Often, government will give tax concessions, exempt projects from environmental regulations, provide transportation and other services, confiscate ownership of some key properties, and even invest public money in order to assist business in "developing" a particular area of the city. This is done under the doctrine of *value-free development*, the claim that everybody will benefit as the city advances economically. But, Logan and Molotch say, this doctrine is false. Frequently these development projects fail to achieve all their objectives, and at best they tend to move jobs from one place to another, rather than creating new jobs. On balance, the large-scale landlords ("rentier capitalists") benefit, but the average family does not, because rents go up without counterbalancing increases in wages, and the use value of a neighborhood is harmed.

Local business elites are extremely influential in urban politics, often essentially buying the mayor and city council through campaign contributions or investment opportunities. However, a city's elites have good reason to defend their own neighborhoods against the growth machine they have created. They do this through zoning regulations, control of the newspapers, civil associations, and by using their political influence to make sure that profitable development occurs in areas of the city that will not harm the use value of their own private property. To a lesser extent, middle class groups can also employ these means to protect their neighborhoods, but the poor are unable to do so, so the growth machine becomes yet another mechanism by which the rich exploit the poor.

The stratification of places, which has long occurred within each city, now reaches around the world. In the modern global economy, capitalists can invest wherever the profits are high. World-wide competition severely erodes the ability even of some elite groups to defend use values against the unrestrained hunger of capitalists for exchange values. In the future, Logan and Molotch assert, cities may play one of five roles, and their residents will have little if any control over their fate:

1. **Headquarters.** The elite locations where capital markets and the home offices of major trans-national corporations rule the world.
2. **Innovation centers.** Metropolitan areas (e.g., "Silicon Valley" in California or "Route 128" around Boston) where educational institutions and corporate research and development laboratories create new technology.
3. **Module production places.** Industrial cities, often polluted but possessing a favorable mixture of natural resources and cheap labor, that manufacture components of industrial goods such as automobiles.
4. **Third world entrepôt.** Border metropolises that are centers of trade and transportation in poor countries, linking them to the world economic system.
5. **Retirement centers.** Places with good climates but poor housing and high taxes that contain the increasing numbers of elderly people, who struggle to get by on pitifully small incomes.

Thus, Logan and Molotch agree with the writers of the classic Chicago School that the city was shaped by competition between individuals and groups, but they reject the classic assumption that the results are beneficial.

8
WORK, OCCUPATIONS, AND PROFESSIONS

WORKS AT A GLANCE

Ideologies of Labor

Work and Authority in Industry: Ideologies of Management in the Course of Industrialization by Reinhard Bendix (1956)

"The Soviet Transition from Socialism to Capitalism: Worker Control and Economic Bargaining in the Wood Industry" by Michael Burawoy and Pavel Krotov (1992)

Systems of Control

"Social Control of Occupations and Work" by Richard L. Simpson (1985)

"On the Degradation of Skills," by William Form (1987)

Consequences of Work for the Individual

"Job Conditions and Personality: A Longitudinal Assessment of Their Reciprocal Effects" by Melvin L. Kohn and Carmi Schooler (1982)

"National Comparisons of Occupational Prestige" by Alex Inkeles and Peter H. Rossi (1956)

Sociologists have approached the study of work from many perspectives. Often the goal is to understand how to increase productivity of workers, or how to give them greater satisfaction, or how to accomplish both of these aims at once. A central concern for sociologists, however, has always been the ways that power is generated and exercised by some people over other people. Thus, a prime research question has been the nature of authority in work organizations and the consequences for workers of having more or less control over their own labor. Reinhard Bendix has examined the ways that vastly different ideologies about authority evolved in the histories of the English-speaking nations and Russia. Bendix argued that the old authoritarian system of the czars was continued under the Soviet Union. Michael Burawoy and Pavel Krotov doubt that Russia after the demise of the Soviet Union is ready to adopt the English and American system.

Richard Simpson suggests that there are five principal ways in which work is controlled in the United States: simple, technical, bureaucratic, occupational, and worker self-control. William Form surveys the research on whether workers have lost autonomy over the decades as their jobs have been rationalized to reduce the need for skill. Melvin Kohn and Carmi Schooler explore the effect that working conditions may have on workers' personalities and thus on their behavior away from the job. If all the world is adopting a similar form of industrialism, then the system of occupational prestige may become uniform, a question examined by Alex Inkeles and Peter Rossi.

In modern industrial societies, organized work is the fundamental basis of the economy, much of the social structure, and many dimensions of social stratification. Those who are in control of influential, bureaucratic organizations wield power and command high salaries. Professionals can sometimes compete with them in terms of salary, and their prestige may be higher, but their power is more narrowly limited to their dealings with their clients. People whose work is controlled by others, or who are mere cogs in huge bureaucratic machines, lack power, and this powerlessness may carry over into their private lives, shaping their personalities in decisive ways. Across all modern societies, the nature of the work a person does and the way it is organized largely determine the person's socio-economic status.

Ideologies of Labor

Bendix, Reinhard
   1956 *Work and Authority in Industry: Ideologies of Management in the Course of Industrialization*. New York: Wiley.

This historical study examines the ideologies that have been used to justify the subordination of large numbers of workers to factory discipline and to the authority of managers. Bendix says the question, "How can many people be convinced to obey a few?" is a fundamental question in sociology. The book contrasts the situation in four societies: England and Russia when they were in the process of becoming industrial, compared with the United States and Soviet-controlled East Germany, where many large-scale economic enterprises already existed. Another important comparison is between the two of these societies where entrepreneurs and managers formed an autonomous class with considerable independence from outside control (England and the United States) versus the two societies in which entrepreneurs and managers were subordinate to government control (Russia and East Germany).

In the hundred years centered around 1800, English industrial entrepreneurs were struggling to build up their manufacturing enterprises despite the fact that much in the surrounding culture and social structure worked against them. They were not members of the aristocracy, which still depended largely upon the income from farm land for its wealth, but came from relatively modest family backgrounds. Thus they had to overcome the dominant aristocratic ideology, which held commerce and industry in some contempt. They also had to cope with workers who were very traditional in their outlook, lacking the habits of sustained factory labor and expecting the factory owners to show a paternalistic feeling of responsibility for their welfare like that which some aristocrats showed for the farmers who tended their land. Facing formidable problems concerning their own survival, early British industrial entrepreneurs were ruthless in exploiting the labor of men, women, and even children, and few of them accepted any responsibility for the welfare of the workers.

Many of these entrepreneurs lacked a coherent set of shared values and beliefs concerning the proper organization of work, and they merely took advantage of their situations in a thoroughly expedient manner. However, a set of mutually supportive ideologies arose that pretended to explain why some people got to be bosses, whereas others were subordinate to them. Some ideologists for the entrepreneurs believed that workers must be kept poor because hunger was one of the most effective motivators of hard labor. More widely, impoverished workers were considered to be degraded, lazy, improvident, and vice-ridden. Entrepreneurs thought of themselves as paragons of virtue who deserved to be counted as a "higher class" beside the old aristocracy. Evangelistic religion sanctified the success of the entrepreneurs and gave them a tool for inculcating values of thrift, chastity, and industriousness into the workers.

In Russia, the power of the czar was much greater than that of the King of England, because the Mongol occupation from 1237–1452 and the constant, subsequent wars had concentrated authority in the central military apparatus that belonged to him. Many of the population were serfs, essentially slaves who worked the land under an aristocracy that was itself subservient to the czar, and who in 1649 were legally forbidden to leave the particular tract of land to which they belonged. No groups in Russian society could operate independently, so it was practically impossible for private entrepreneurs to start modern industries. Economic development depended upon the czar, and Peter the Great (1689-1725) ordered his government to develop industry. After

Peter's death, the aristocracy increased its influence, thereby reducing the independence of merchants and industrial entrepreneurs. Factories on aristocratic estates forced serfs to work for very low wages, thereby giving the small, independent middle class such severe competition that it could hardly develop capital to invest in modern enterprises. The modest industrialization that did occur only increased class differences, rather than reducing them as in England.

In some respects the ideology was similar to that in England, in that Russian leaders believed workers were lazy and stubborn. But the Russian management ideology asserted that only brutal force could make workers obey. Any rights the workers enjoyed were a gift from the czar that he could take back at any moment. A serf who insulted his master would be beaten with rods until the master was satisfied, whereas a master could kill a serf and often escape punishment of any kind. The factory bosses commonly believed that paying workers regularly would only give them bad habits, and they frequently violated their formal contracts with workers. The ideology held that the fundamental principle of society was the sovereign will of the czar, and government agents were given the duty of controlling both managers and workers in the factories. Bendix says that the Bolshevik Revolution in 1917–1918 preserved the fundamental autocratic principle of czarist Russia, but put the Communist Party in the dictatorial position formerly held by the czar.

In the United States, the industrial entrepreneurs did not have to fight for social recognition against a well-entrenched landed aristocracy, as in England, but the ideologies of early industrialism were comparably unflattering to workers. Life was viewed as a struggle for survival, in which the best men would succeed in becoming leaders, and the worst would be forced to be mere laborers. Thus, workers should accept the authority of the better men who held management positions, although the door was open for some workers to prove their worth by becoming successful in their own right.

American industry, however, became progressively bureaucratized, which gave less emphasis to individual entrepreneurial risk taking and more to smooth functioning of large-scale social organizations run by bureaucrats. For example, the Swift meat company went from 50,000 workers with 500 executives in 1923 to 75,000 workers managed by 2,150 executives thirty years later. The labor movement achieved some success, and the necessities of modern bureaucratic employment also served to change management ideology. By the middle of the twentieth century, American management had adopted "scientific" techniques for testing and managing workers that cloaked their authority in the supposedly objective mantle of science. The belief that all people needed self-fulfillment, workers as well as management, served to moderate the power of bosses at the same time it limited the capacity of workers to develop a counter-ideology that might have threatened the bosses's considerable remaining power.

Communist leader Lenin believed that Russian workers would not labor hard or well unless management had complete, dictatorial control over them.

Soviet ideology held that the Communist Party was the vanguard of the working class, and understood the worker's real needs much better than most of them did, so the party would run everything in every detail from centralized institutions. In 1945, the Soviet Union seized East Germany in the last days of the Second World War, and proceeded to set up a fairly mature form of the system that had been developed in Russia over the preceding decades. The Communist Party sought to dominate the lives and minds of its members totally, and its ideology supposedly provided a basis for making every management decision. Bendix analyzes the complex hierarchy of planning agencies in East Germany in 1953, from the Soviet Control Commission at the top, down through the centralized State Planning Commission, to the ministries that ran various industries. Orders came down from the top, without the managers (let alone the workers) having anything to say about them. To make sure that management at every level followed orders, there were two parallel and sometimes competing systems of control. One was the hierarchy of industrial management, and the other was the Communist Party, which had party functionaries at every level, spying on both workers and management. The Party limited the power of a factory's Director in some respects, but by supposedly being the only legitimate representative of the workers (seldom actually listening to the workers themselves), it also strengthened the Director's power. The collapse of East German communism came fully a third of a century after Bendix published his book, but his account of the wave of worker discontent that swept East Germany in 1953 indicated that the Communist ideology was not effective.

Looking back on the histories of industrial authority in the four societies he studied, Bendix concludes that management ideologies can be valuable tools for holding and wielding power. He is not convinced that workers are always influenced directly by the ideologies, but having a firm set of beliefs strengthens an elite group in its competition with other elites. Societies that were influenced by the Soviet Union have had a long struggle working their way out from under an ideology that claimed to serve the working class through an authoritarian system rooted in czarist imperialism. And nations like England and the United States are still influenced by the early-industrial ideology that believed that degraded workers must obey superior managers.

Burawoy, Michael, and Pavel Krotov
  1992 "The Soviet Transition from Socialism to Capitalism: Worker Control and Economic Bargaining in the Wood Industry," *American Sociological Review*, 57:16–38.

Burawoy worked for several weeks inside a Russian factory manufacturing wooden furniture, and both authors draw upon extensive information about the organization of Russian industry before and immediately after the collapse of the Soviet Union in 1991. The Soviet economy began to decline in the early 1970s, but the conditions twenty years later were not merely the result of economic crisis. They also reflected the Soviet economic system. In capitalist societies, Burawoy and Krotov argue, managers can plan how employees do their work, but the market that surrounds their corporations is unplanned anarchy in which they can never be sure of selling their products. In state socialist societies like the Soviet Union, the reverse was true. The national economy was planned on the large scale, but managers were almost powerless to control their workers. The essential work of Russian managers took place outside their factories, as they developed special relationships with other organizations in order to get the scarce raw materials and machinery needed by their factories to carry out production. With the collapse of the Soviet Union, national planning fell apart. This left Russia prey to *merchant capitalism*, which is anarchy on every level as entrepreneurial hustlers try to get rich selling or bartering whatever valuable things they can get their hands on, and where nobody systematically works to produce industrial wealth. This study doubts that Russia can quickly become an industrial capitalist nation.

Systems of Control

Simpson, Richard L.
  1985 "Social Control of Occupations and Work," *Annual Review of Sociology* 11:415–436.

On the basis of an extensive review of the literature, Simpson suggests that there are five principal ways in which work is controlled:

1. *Simple control* means that a boss gives orders that the worker must carry out, and the boss is not constrained to any great extent by formal rules, being free even to control the worker in an arbitrary manner. Simple control exists in two forms, direct and hierarchical. In small offices and shops, the boss interacts closely with the worker, exercising direct control. If the organization is too large for the boss to supervise each worker directly, a hierarchy is set up, in which the boss gives orders to managers, who in turn give orders to the workers below them in the hierarchy.
2. *Technical control* exists when the technology of the work makes the chief demands on the worker. For example, a worker on an assembly line is controlled by the array of machines he or she works with. The line sets the pace and the sequence of actions the worker must perform.
3. *Bureaucratic control* often involves a hierarchy, but its chief feature is a set of formal rules and procedures that define how both workers and managers should behave. Bureaucratic control makes use of formal incentives and punishments, and it often employs formal techniques for monitoring the worker and measuring his or her output.
4. *Occupational control* is most often found in autonomous professions, such as medicine and law, where individuals are not under bosses but control each other by establishing a set of standards for professional

behavior and then developing methods for getting each other to adhere to them.

5. *Worker self-control* concerns workers who are not under one of the four other kinds of control. These are self-proprietor jobs, such as the operator of a one-person store or a self-employed piano tuner, or a freelance writer or taxi driver.

There can be mixed cases, and often the line dividing two of these categories is blurred. In modern factories, both technical control and bureaucratic control coexist. Government regulation of a profession adds bureaucracy to occupational control. In some group medical practices the individual doctors may have so much independence, and control by local medical associations may be so weak, that the doctors effectively have self-control.

Simpson gives special attention to occupational control in professional work. One of the chief ways in which professions control the nature of their work is by establishing monopolies in which only they can grant a license to practice the profession. Some professions have gained such power that they dominate related occupations. For example, the medical profession has influenced licensure laws to limit the scope of other health professions. Professions with great power can expand their scope to cover issues that might otherwise have been left to other professions, as in the case of medicalization of social problems (see Conrad and Schneider in Chapter 6).

Many social scientists have considered the factors that allow a field of work to become an autonomous profession with the ability to control its own work. If the work is easy for most people to understand, and uses ordinary language to describe its procedures, it is unlikely to be able to convince other people it deserves to rank as a profession. If the work has a very well-developed technical basis, so that it can be divided up into routine tasks, it is more likely to fall under bureaucratic control than become an autonomous profession. However, if the work is highly varied in nature and its techniques are poorly understood, the worker is likely to gain a fair degree of autonomy, and this may lead to development of a self-controlled occupation or profession. If the nature of the work changes, so, too, may the form of control. When computer programming was very new and arcane, programmers had considerable self-control. But as programming became systematized and broken up into modules that were handled as a matter of routine, it came under closer bureaucratic control.

A major debate in recent sociology has concerned which of two opposite trends dominates the other in modern economies. One trend is monopolization, in which occupational groups gain control over their type of work and become professions. This is most likely to happen if the occupation deals with clients who themselves are not especially powerful, and if the characteristics of the work allow its practitioners to develop prestige in the society. The other is proletarianization, in which professions become subject to bureaucratic controls and are transformed into ordinary workers lacking control over their own work. This is most likely to happen if a particular kind of work can be rationalized technically into a number of well-understood tasks. One aspect of this process is *deskilling,* a change in which the work comes to require less skill and therefore to provide the workers with less autonomy and fewer rewards of both money and satisfaction.

Form, William
1987 "On the Degradation of Skills," *Annual Review of Sociology* 13:29-47.

Prior to the industrial revolution, which began roughly two centuries ago in England, much manufacturing was done by highly skilled workmen who understood every aspect of their product. But the growth of factories and then assembly lines produced the same items with less skilled workers, each of whom may have mastered only a few of the steps required to make the product. This is the classic example of *deskilling* in which skills were degraded. Form notes that sociologists employ two somewhat different theories to explain why deskilling occurs, each stressing the decisions of the owners of the enterprise. First, owners like low-skill mass production because it is more efficient, allowing them to produce products at lower cost. Second, they like the increased power it gives them over workers, because low-skill workers are easily replaced and do not have the bargaining power of skilled workers.

Although there has been a fair amount of research in this area, Form notes that there are three problems that should raise doubts among sociologists whether either of these theories is true. First, social scientists disagree on how to define and measure skill, thus making it nearly impossible to do convincing comparative studies. Second, researchers have not contrasted industries in capitalist societies, where private owners presumably dominate industry, with state socialist societies where this was not the case. Third, historical studies focusing on particular points in time are not capable of determining trends. Form reviews the literature on the first and third of these points; there is essentially no literature on the second.

Scholars have defined skills in many ways. Some argue that a high-skill job requires a balance between mental and physical expertise, and that it makes the worker feel the job is highly meaningful to his entire personality. Others believe it is safe to assume that jobs that command high salaries must require high skill. Another group of scholars says that highly routine jobs require low skills. And yet another group associates high skill with jobs where the worker has great autonomy, improvising tasks and operating without very close supervision. Form finds problems with all these approaches and advocates a definition of skill that builds on ideas in more than one of them. Skill has several dimensions, he says. Complexity of the work and autonomy are among the most important, and studies show that these two correlate highly with each other. However, the disagreement about how to define and measure skill weakens research that intends to chart skill changes over time. In historical research, it is seldom possible to find exactly the best information and, reasonably enough, many researchers measure skill in terms of the level of education or amount of other preparation required to do a given job.

Acknowledging all these measurement problems, Form then examines the literature to see if there is consistent evidence of deskilling. Historical studies show that many early factory workers had high levels of skill, and the routine of factory work mainly changed the situation for unskilled laborers. Some skills declined, but new skills emerged, notably the technical knowledge required to maintain the machines that were replacing much semi-skilled labor. When labor unions emerged, apparently they resulted from the upgrading of education among unskilled labor more than an attempt by skilled workers to defend themselves against deskilling. By World War I, factory managers had centralized much production under their direct control, and this may have led to deskilling among the manufacturing crafts. However, new machines and production methods required new skills, and the people who gained them were comparable to craft workers. It is very difficult to determine whether the general level of skill rose or fell.

Form highlights fourteen studies that examined the skills of male manual workers in early American and European cities. Unskilled workers constituted between 25 to 50 percent of the labor force, whereas artisans and skilled workers constituted 25 to 54 percent. After taking account of low-skill employees who were not tabulated in some of these studies, Form concludes that the skill level was probably not very different from that found today. Studies examining trends in the occupational distributions of workers in the United States census seem to indicate that skill level has risen over the twentieth century. No one has been able to do a convincing study of the extent to which skills rise or fall when workers shift from farming to industry. It is possible to find particular occupations where skills definitely declined, and others where skills rose. But more generally, across the whole economy, it is impossible to demonstrate the existence of widespread deskilling.

Theorists have been undeterred by these uncertainties, and they have proposed a number of intriguing ideas that require study. Some say that the long-term trend is toward increased skills, and Daniel Bell (see Chapter 15) has argued we are moving into a post-industrial phase of society that will require high levels of intellectual training. Others believe that automation has reversed a deskilling trend; the introduction of factories reduced skills a century or two ago, but the introduction of computers and other information technologies is now increasing the skills required. Still others assert that information technologies are currently deskilling office work, turning many white-collar workers into essentially unskilled laborers, and that much of the new employment in the service sector is unskilled. Form believes these are important ideas that should be followed up in carefully-designed research studies. But he concludes on the basis of existing studies that deskilling has been limited to specific jobs at particular points in time, and a large number of factors determine whether skills will rise or fall as the nature of work changes.

Consequences of Work for the Individual

Kohn, Melvin L., and Carmi Schooler
  1982 "Job Conditions and Personality: A Longitudinal Assessment of Their Reciprocal Effects," *American Journal of Sociology* 87:1257–1286.

Melvin Kohn and several of his colleagues conducted a long series of studies on the ways that the nature of work and individual personality affected each other. This particular study analyzed data from 687 men who responded to a pair of questionnaires in 1964 and 1974. A study that collects data on the same subjects over a period of time is called *longitudinal*, and the men who responded at both points in time are a *panel* of respondents. With a single questionnaire it is possible to learn that two variables correlate with each other, but not to tell which one is the cause and which the effect. Because this study uses data from two points in time, it is possible to identify the causes.

Kohn and Schooler examined information about fourteen job conditions that ought to be significant for the workers' psychology, under four headings: the worker's place in the organization, the degree to which he has self-direction in his work, the pressures he works under, and the risks and rewards related to his job. They theorized that an especially important variable would be *occupational self-direction*, which is the extent to which the man uses his own initiative and independent judgment on the job, as opposed to doing exactly what a boss tells him. A particular job will require self-direction if it is intrinsically complex work, if the worker is not closely supervised, and if the work is not highly routine. High-status jobs tend to have this quality, as do many jobs in bureaucratic organizations and the work done by owners of businesses.

The psychological characteristic of greatest interest to Kohn and Schooler was *intellectual flexibility*. A person with this quality will weigh both sides in economic and social issues and give a mixture of responses to questionnaire agree-disagree items. Kohn and Schooler theorize that occupational self-direction and intellectual flexibility are related. Working with a high level of self-direction may increase a man's intellectual flexibility, whereas working under close supervision for many years may destroy flexibility. Also, people may be drawn to jobs that match their psychological characteristics, or people may transform the jobs they have so the work harmonizes with their personalities. A very complicated statistical analysis verified both that jobs shape personality in the expected manner, and that people enter jobs that fit their personalities, but little evidence appeared that the men were able to transform the nature of their work to match their personalities.

Kohn and Schooler believe that many of the differences found by sociologists between the middle class and the working (or lower) class may be the result of the different work experiences of people in these classes. In particular, the higher a person's social class the more likely he or she will have a job that permits or requires great self-direction. Jobs that are low in self-direction will produce workers who are fatalistic, anxious, and authoritarian off the job as well as on. In contrast, jobs high in self-direction will produce people who are morally responsible, confident, and creative.

Inkeles, Alex, and Peter H. Rossi
> 1956 "National Comparisons of Occupational Prestige," *American Journal of Sociology* 61:329–339.

Inkeles and Rossi contrast two competing theories about the prestige of different jobs. The *structuralist* theory says that industrial occupations in modern society form a highly coherent system that has essentially the same form in every society. Therefore a given factory-related job has the same prestige across all the societies in which it is found. In time, other occupations that are not directly related to the factory system will align themselves to the industrial prestige ranking and also come to have uniform prestige across societies. The *culturalist* theory says that the traditional cultures of different societies are highly varied and will endure long after factories have been introduced. Therefore each society will judge occupations in terms of its traditional values, and the prestige of a given occupation will tend to vary greatly across societies.

At the time that Inkeles and Rossi wrote, sociologists had not yet done extensive studies of prestige in many nations, using exactly the same methods and occupational definitions from country to country. But Inkeles and Rossi were able to obtain data on the prestige of comparable occupations from surveys administered in five nations: the United States, Great Britain, New Zealand, Japan, and Germany. A sixth study had collected a few prestige rankings from refugees from the Soviet Union. By current sociological standards, the data sets were of mediocre quality, because their respondents were not from random samples of the population, because the questions had not been standardized, and because the raw data themselves were not always available for analysis by Inkeles and Rossi. These problems would tend to exaggerate apparent differences in the prestige of each occupation across the nations, thus giving the culturalist theory an unfair advantage.

Inkeles and Rossi compared prestige rankings across the nations, finding that many occupations had about the same score in each country and that pairs of nations correlated highly in their rating scores. They suggest that this is strong evidence in favor of the structuralist theory, given the fact that errors in the research were biased against it. The six nations tend to agree highly about the prestige of most occupations. A few differences emerged, however. For example, in the United States ministers of religion rate much more highly than their equivalents (Buddhist priests) do in Japan. Inkeles and Rossi used statistical techniques to identify the occupations that showed the greatest or least prestige variation across nations, and they looked for patterns.

In line with structuralist theory, occupations that were directly related to factory work showed a high level of prestige agreement across nations. However, the very highest agreement was shown by professions (such as doctors) that are not directly related to industry. Service occupations (like chef or barber) showed the greatest variation across nations, and this may reflect cultural differences in how personal service is regarded. Considering all their findings, Inkeles and Rossi conclude that the evidence for culturalist theory is weak, evidence for structuralist theory is strong, but a complete explanation for national variations in occupational prestige would have to wait for future research.

9
ORGANIZATIONS

WORKS AT A GLANCE

Structure of Roles

"The Social Structure of the Restaurant," by William Foote Whyte (1949)

Commitment and Careers

Commitment and Community: Communes and Utopias in Sociological Perspective by Rosabeth Moss Kanter (1972)
Chains of Opportunity: System Models of Mobility in Organizations by Harrison C. White (1970)
"A Theory of Group Stability" by Kathleen Carley (1991)

Systems of Organizations

Rational, Natural, and Open Systems by W. Richard Scott (1981)
"The Population Ecology of Organizations" by Michael Hannan and John Freeman (1977)
"The Iron Cage Revisited: Institutional Isomorphism and Collective Rationality in Organizational Fields" by Paul J. DiMaggio and Walter W. Powell (1991)

An organization can be conceptualized as a structure of roles, performed by people with varying natures and needs, created to achieve some common goal. Thus, a crucial question is how organizations can motivate people to fulfill those roles. Another question is the way that roles and statuses fit together in the organization, maintaining some kind of structure even when individuals move from one position to another during their careers. Each organization is a system of interacting parts, and organizations relate to each other in a larger system characterized by cooperation, competition, and mutual influence.

An organization can be considered as a system of roles, commitments, positions, and information. After publishing a practical manual on human relations based on field research in the restaurant industry, William Foote Whyte wrote a conceptual article for a sociology journal, setting out theoretically-rich issues concerning the ways that roles in an organization conflict or support each other. Rosabeth Kanter examined six social-psychological mechanisms that might commit a person to any kind of organization, based on historical study of nineteenth-century American communes. Harrison White looked at the way that job openings travel through an organization in a chain, employing sophisticated mathematical analysis of data on clergy in religious denominations. Kathleen Carley used computer simulations to see how information affects the stability of social groups in an organization.

Any given organization exists in a larger system composed of many interacting organizations. Richard Scott says that sociologists study these systems at three different levels: the behavior of individuals, the social structure and processes within the organization, and relations between the organization and other organizations in the larger environment. He contrasts three different ways of conceptualizing systems: rational, natural, and open. Hannan and Freeman say that a system of organizations is like a biological population, in which it may be more important to understand the environment than the behavior of a single organization. Paul DiMaggio and Walter Powell stress that individual organizations influence each other, often becoming more similar than they objectively need to be in a given field.

Structure of Roles

Whyte, William Foote
    1949 "The Social Structure of the Restaurant," *American Journal of Sociology* 54: 302–310.

With a team of researchers, Whyte carried out interview and participant-observation studies of twelve restaurants in the Chicago area, on behalf of the National Restaurant Association. He begins by showing how restaurants of various sizes are social systems in which people playing more-or-less set roles interact in standardized ways with each other. In a particular establishment, the customer gives orders to the service employees (waiters and waitresses) and may also do so to the manager. A service employee gives orders to the kitchen staff and sometimes also to the dishwashers. The kitchen staff give orders to the dishwashers. And the manager gives orders to all three other kinds of worker at the restaurant. As orders flow in these directions, food and clean dishes flow along other paths. A change in any one of these flows will affect the others, and relations between any two roles or any two individuals have implications for all the others.

Expansion of a restaurant forces changes in the social structure and interactions. A restaurant faces problems in three areas: administration, relations with customers, and the flow of work. Large restaurants especially have difficulty connecting the line of authority with the flow of work, and a key question is who originates action for whom and at what rate. During a busy time of day, a perceptive manager will know to avoid giving orders to the service staff, suspending his or her usual authority until the pace of work calms down. In general, Whyte hypothesizes, relations are best when higher status persons are able to originate work for lower status ones, and relations will be problematic when low status persons originate work for high status ones. For example, Whyte observed relations between waitresses and countermen (who put together the food orders from the kitchen). The countermen liked to think they were superior to the waitresses, but the waitresses gave the customers' orders to the countermen. This violation of expected status relations caused blowups unless something was done to insulate the countermen from the waitresses, for example, using a high counter so they could hardly see each other, or having an impersonal system through which the countermen dealt with the order slips delivered by the waitresses.

Communication can be a serious problem, especially in very large restaurants. If the kitchen is remote from the dining area, the establishment may try to use electronic systems to communicate, but if the menu choices are complicated these messages may become garbled. Whyte observed the bizarre phenomenon of pantry supervisors rushing up and down stairs to transmit messages personally and in detail, thus invading the territory of other workers and increasing the social pressures to everybody's distress. During the rush hour, customers push waitresses who push pantry girls who push supply men who get excited and nervous. A supply man may then write "rush" on quite ordinary orders to the kitchen, or order up more supplies than he needs. The kitchen staff catch on to this, so they fail to hurry "rush" orders and they give the supply man less than he ordered. Communication deteriorates and everybody suffers.

Whyte identifies five areas where future sociological research is warranted. First, researchers should study the formal structure of establishments, with full awareness that informal structures might be different, because the formal structure sets limits on how the organization can operate. Second, quantitative research can systematically examine interaction in the social system of the restaurant. Third, to understand the reasons why interaction proceeds in a certain way, attention needs to be given to the symbols that act as incentives or inhibitors of interaction. Fourth, excellent methods exist for studying attitudes and the ways they change as interaction itself changes. Fifth, the physical layout and equipment, while not of sociological interest in themselves, have a powerful effect on the social system. Whyte advocates both qualitative case studies and hypothesis-testing quantitative studies.

Commitment and Careers

Kanter, Rosabeth Moss
  1972 *Commitment and Community: Communes and Utopias in Sociological Perspective.* Cambridge: Harvard University Press.

Kanter developed and tested a theory of how individuals become committed to the norms and goals of an organization, based on analysis of historical information about thirty American "utopian communities" of the nineteenth century. There were several varieties of these experimental communes. Perhaps the best-known was the Shaker religious sect, brought from England by Ann Lee and first established as a village in New York State in 1787. The Shakers farmed and manufactured such items as chairs and wooden boxes, living in big communal dormitories. They lasted two centuries, reaching a population of about 5,000 around 1850, by recruiting families and taking in orphans, because their celibacy prevented them from having children. Another example was Oneida, founded by John Humphrey Noyes, which practiced a form of "free love" in which many adults would have brief sexual relations using "male continence" birth control, reproducing according to a strict plan to breed spiritually advanced children. A number of immigrant German communes followed more conventional customs, including Harmony, Amana, Zoar, and Bethel. Apart from these religious communes, there were also non-religious experiments following the schemes of British industrialist Robert Owen and French socialist Charles Fourier. Although the thirty utopian communes were strikingly unusual social experiments, Kanter believed that general principles of organizational commitment would be revealed by close study of them.

Drawing on a wide range of sociological literature, Kanter developed a theory of six *commitment mechanisms*, institutional arrangements that function to bind the individual to the organization. The six commitment mechanisms come in three pairs, each pair relating to one dimension of a person's behavior: rewards, relationships, and identity. Organizations can control an individual's behavior by manipulating the *rewards* the person can get, whether they are money, security, or anything else that the person values. Social *relationships* can bind a person to the organization, and lack of relations outside the organization prevent the person from being pulled away from it. People's *identity* is their concept of who they are, and if the organization can shape personal identity it can also control behavior. One mechanism in each of the three pairs makes the person give something up, so it could be described as *negative*. The other mechanism in the pair is *positive*, giving the person something to replace that which was given up:

Dimension	Negative Mechanism	Positive Mechanism
Rewards	1. Sacrifice	2. Investment
Relationships	3. Renunciation	4. Communion
Identity	5. Mortification	6. Transcendence

Sacrifice requires giving up rewards, whereas *investment* holds out the hope of getting rewards. A person who sacrifices for the sake of the organization will therefore feel membership in it must be valuable, following the psychological principle that people need to feel their values and behavior are consistent. In many of the communes people were required to give up sex, alcohol, rich food, or luxurious living accommodations. Members find it costly to leave an organization if they would lose the value of the labor and resources they invested in it.

Renunciation means giving up social relationships that might disrupt commitment to the organization, and *communion* means gaining social bonds that tie the individual to the group. Among the relationships that threaten commitment to an organization are friendship ties to outsiders and romantic attachments within the group. Some communes, like the Shakers and Harmony, prohibited sexual relations of any kind. Oneida, in contrast, encouraged sex but discouraged romantic ties between individuals. In both cases, the organization prevented men and women from forming erotic couples, which might function as rudimentary love conspiracies eroding commitment to the group. Organizations can build commitment by stressing communion experiences that bind members together through group rituals, shared work, and simply living important parts of their lives together.

Mortification strips away a recruit's former individualistic identity, and *transcendence* provides a new identity as a committed member of the organization. Some religious organizations make people give up their original names, and others require them to wear uniforms, in both cases taking away intimate aspects of the person's identity. Highly demanding non-religious organizations follow some of the same mortification practices. For example, members of the armed forces wear uniforms, and radical political groups sometimes require code names. Another kind of mortification is close supervision of the person's behavior, including sessions in which individuals are expected to confess their misdeeds and submit to public criticism. Transcendence gives the person the feeling of participating in something much larger than himself or herself that provides meaning far beyond that which can be obtained in daily life. Religious beliefs and ceremonies instill awe, making the member feel involved in something supremely powerful, but ordinary business organizations can achieve a milder version of the same thing through pep rallies and all the hoopla of sales campaigns.

Kanter tested her theory by comparing the characteristics of the nine most successful communes, all of which lasted at least thirty-three years, with the twenty-one less successful ones. The long-lived communes made extensive use of most of the commitment mechanisms, but the shorter-lived ones did not. Thus, Kanter concluded, her six commitment mechanisms probably are ways that an organization can bind members to its norms and goals.

White, Harrison C.
  1970 *Chains of Opportunity: System Models of Mobility in Organizations.*
    Cambridge, Massachusetts: Harvard University Press.

Trained as a physicist as well as a sociologist, Harrison White adapted an idea from physics to create a new way of analyzing the movement of people from job to job in organizations. Beginning in the late 1940s, research on semiconductor materials led to the invention of the transistor and all the modern microelectronic devices that evolved from it, including the computer chip. Physicists traditionally analyzed the flow of electric current as a stream of tiny charged particles called electrons. But in semiconductors, an individual electron often moves only a short distance, making room in the lattice of atoms for another electron to take its place, which in turn makes room for another one, and so on for a very long chain of short electron jumps. For some purposes, physicists found it more convenient, therefore, to analyze these processes in terms of the movement of holes that go long distances in the opposite direction to that in which the individual electrons take short jumps. A hole is a position in the structure that could contain an electron but is currently empty. An electron that moves into this space leaves a vacancy where it came from, so one could say that a hole moved back in that direction.

White imagined that an organization, say a religious denomination, could be viewed in the same way that physicists analyzed semiconductors. Each minister was like an electron. Particular jobs were positions where an electron (minister) could fit. And as a person moved out of one job to take another, he or she left a hole (vacancy) behind. Suppose Father Ambrose is the priest of a major urban church, St. Anne's. Father Basil runs a good-sized suburban church in the same district and denomination, called St. Benedict's. And Father Calvin takes care of a small rural church, Chrysostom Chapel. In January, Ambrose is appointed bishop of the diocese, leaving a vacancy at St. Anne's. In May, that vacancy is filled when Basil moves to St. Anne's, leaving a vacancy at St. Benedict's. And in August, Calvin takes over at St. Benedict's, leaving a vacancy at Chrysostom Chapel. As clergy move from smaller churches to bigger ones, a vacancy moves from big ones to small ones. White called the series of open positions that were linked by the movement of individual people a *vacancy chain*.

To develop his new method of analysis, White took data on career moves in three Protestant religious denominations: Episcopalian, Methodist, and Presbyterian. Each of these denominations publishes an annual directory of clergy, often giving a good deal of information about each minister and saying who was minister in each church. Painstakingly, and without help from computers, White and his team of research assistants took data from many years of these directories, arranged so they could trace the movement of vacancies. The idea of vacancy chains is fairly simple. The hard part was developing the right tools for analyzing them, and that required mathematics.

One of the great questions about sociology is the extent to which it should be a science comparable to physics, requiring great mathematical talent to understand, or should be one of the humanities, relying more on the human sensitivity of students and professional sociologists. White happens to be very interested in the arts, and he would be the last to say that sociology should focus narrowly on only one kind of work. But his own work illustrates the fact that much modern sociology cannot be understood fully, let alone performed competently, without a solid mathematical background. *Chains of Opportunity* assumes that the reader knows calculus, probability theory, and some matrix algebra. It employs technical concepts such as "Markov chain" without providing any explanation of what they mean. Clearly, this is not a book for beginners, and it assumes that the system of sociological education somehow produces graduate students with the sufficient mathematical knowledge to follow its logic. At the same time, *Chains of Opportunity* illustrates the value of mathematical sociology and the importance of having at least a few experts in some universities capable of comprehending it.

Vacancy chain analysis can be used to understand many aspects of an organization that are not apparent if one looks only at jobs and job holders. For example, the average length of vacancy chains is a measure of how stratified the organization is, that is, how many promotion steps there are from the bottom to the top. Many organizations publish "organizational charts" diagramming how all their offices fit together into a hierarchy, but these seldom reflect the real levels of authority that exist, and vacancy chains can measure the size and number of the hierarchy levels directly. A geographic analysis, looking at how often vacancy chains cross regional boundaries, can determine how local versus national an organization is. Precisely because they are so abstract, vacancy chains can be used to compare types of organizations of very different kinds that have different names for their job positions and different pay scales. Vacancy chain analysis achieved a solid status within the sociology of organizations, and it illustrates the principle that on occasion sociology can benefit from becoming mathematical in the same way as physics.

Carley, Kathleen
1991 "A Theory of Group Stability," *American Sociological Review*
56: 331–354.

Carley conceptualizes groups as social mechanisms for processing information. With this perspective, she used mathematical computer simulations to
develop a theory of group stability based on three axioms:

1. Individuals are continuously engaged in acquiring and communicating
   information.
2. What individuals know influences their choices of interaction partners.
3. An individual's behavior is a function of his or her current knowledge.

A group is stable when each member knows everything that all the others
know and when no new information enters the group. If new information
does enter the group, people will share it through interaction. Individuals
are constantly learning new things that affect their behavior. People who are
similar to each other tend to interact. Thus culture (knowledge) and social
structure (patterns of interaction) tend to evolve together. Carley's computer
simulations of communication show that a group will endure within an organization, regardless of how big or small it is, if it has distinctive knowledge.
Thus, new ideas can contribute to social stability by making the group that
possesses them more different from other groups. In contrast, the addition of
new people to a group endangers its stability, because new recruits lack
knowledge possessed by long-time members, yet they share knowledge with
some non-members. These principles apply not only to a small group within
a formal organization, but also to the organization within the surrounding
society.

Systems of Organizations

Scott, W. Richard
1981 *Rational, Natural, and Open Systems.* Englewood Cliffs, New Jersey:
Prentice-Hall.

This textbook was so successful in synthesizing the literature on organizations, and putting it into a logical structure, that it has become an influential
theoretical treatise for the field. Scott notes the many kinds of organizations
sociologists study: hospitals, schools, police departments, insurance companies, banks, factories, museums, television stations, police departments, professional football teams, and many others. Most scholars conceive of organizations as social structures created by people to help them work together for
specific goals. However, organizations often devote much of their energy to
maintaining the organization itself, and the goals can be lost or even replaced
by new goals.

There are three different levels at which social scientists often examine organizations: (1) the behavior of individuals, (2) the social structure and processes within the organization, and (3) relations between the organization and other organizations in the larger environment. Researchers often focus on one or more of the five elements of an organization:

1. **Social structure:** the patterns of interaction and relationships among individuals.
2. **Participants:** the individuals themselves, with all the needs, skills, and characteristics they bring to the organization.
3. **Goals:** the purposes or desired ends for which the organization presumably exists, both formal and informal.
4. **Technology:** the techniques with which the organization does its work or pursues its goals, which range from the "hardware" of machines to the "software" of symbols with which participants communicate.
5. **Environment:** the physical, technological, cultural, and social world in which the organization operates and from which its external resources and challenges come.

As the title of Scott's books suggests, there are three chief theoretical perspectives on organizations. Although the three can be combined in various ways, they are so different that each has a different fundamental conception of what an organization is.

1. **Rational system.** "An organization is a collectivity oriented to the pursuit of relatively specific goals and exhibiting a relatively highly formalized social structure." The term "rational" refers to the logical, efficient structure and set of procedures a successful organization develops to achieve its goals. The goals themselves may be irrational, however. Over the past century, researchers invested much effort learning how to make the tasks of manufacturing and office work highly efficient, treating human beings as if they were machines. They sought to rationalize management as well as labor, following basic principles such as the following:

   a. The *scalar* principle: Everyone should be linked into a single hierarchy of authority in the form of a pyramid.
   b. The *unity of command* principle: Each person should receive orders from only one superior.
   c. The *span of control* principle: No superior should have more subordinates than he or she can effectively supervise.
   d. The *exception* principle: All routine business should be handled by subordinates according to a set of well-established rules, and superiors should concentrate on dealing with the exceptions that fall outside the routine.

2. **Natural system.** "An organization is a collectivity whose participants are little affected by the formal structure or official goals but who share a

common interest in the survival of the system and who engage in collective activities, informally structured, to secure this end." This perspective arose from criticisms of the rational system approach, and it stresses that organizations are, first of all, collectivities (social units) that share much with other kinds of human groups. The primary goal of an organization is survival, and much of the effort goes into maintaining the social group. Although an organization may have a formal hierarchy, many of the influential social relationships will exist outside it. It is possible to analyze many features of an organization in terms of the functions they perform in sustaining it, however irrelevant they may seem to the purposes it officially professes. Rationalizing the procedures and structures may not improve its functioning. Rather, attention should be given to building leadership, motivating workers, and strengthening human relations.

3. **Open system.** "An organization is a coalition of shifting interest groups that develop goals by negotiation; the structure of the coalition, its activities, and its outcomes are strongly influenced by environmental factors." This perspective views organizations as similar to complex biological and computer systems, in which information flows from one subunit to another. In contrast to many physical systems, the units of a social organization are only loosely coupled, which means they have much autonomy, and they influence each other in partial and complex ways. A living, biological cell is a good example of an open system. It maintains itself by taking resources from the environment. Like a cell, or a computerized data processing system, an organization has input (information and resources coming in from the environment), throughput (information and resources moving on the inside), and output (products and activities that affect the environment). Rather than setting a fixed course toward a goal, an open system uses feedback, monitoring its changing orientation toward the goal and adjusting its activity accordingly. Related to the open system approach is contingency theory, which says that there is no one best way to organize, and different forms of organization will work better in different environments.

Hannan, Michael and John Freeman
  1977 "The Population Ecology of Organizations," *American Journal of Sociology* 82:929–964.

Hannan and Freeman suggested that concepts from biology could illuminate the sociology of organizations, especially ideas from population ecology that examined evolutionary processes at the large-scale level of entire environments and their inhabitants, rather than at the small-scale level of individual organisms or organizations. Hannan and Freeman note that the sociology has tended to conceptualize change as the result of adaptation by individual organizations. Population ecology has tended to focus instead on selection processes in which some individuals survive, and others die, thus shifting the average characteristics of the population toward those of the survivors.

Indeed, a given organization may have only a very limited capacity to change, because it has invested heavily in one type of equipment or personnel, is limited in the information available to it, is constrained by political factors that resist change, and because it is a prisoner of its own history. Generally speaking, fish cannot learn to fly, and churches cannot mutate into retail stores. However, a process akin to biological evolution by natural selection can change the mix of organizations in a population.

To conceptualize organizations in terms of populations of them, rather than individuals, requires a sociological concept comparable to the biological concept of species. The genetic code of an organism is a kind of chemical blueprint, and all organisms sharing the same general blueprint are members of the same species. Thus the sociological equivalent of a species would have to be a set of organizations that have the same social blueprint, in terms of their formal structures, the patterns of activity within them, and the normative order that defines correct behavior by the human beings who belong to the organization. Thus, the population ecology approach to organizations would look for sets of them that are similar to each other in terms of their structures and how they operate. Such a set of organizations belonging to the same species constitutes a population.

The analogy with biology immediately suggests theories about social organizations. The reason that there are so many different kinds of animals is that the world has a large number of different environments and sets of resources, and each species of animals has evolved to maximize exploitation of one of them. Similarly, organizations exist in such diversity because the human environment is complex. However, this idea is not a fully satisfactory theory, and it is necessary to examine how populations of organizations compete. Hannan and Freeman suggest a fresh way of looking at organizational competition that emphasizes the nature of the environment rather than the strategies of organizational leaders. They launch into an analysis, both mathematical and conceptual, that develops several hypotheses.

According to the biological principle of competitive exclusion, no two populations can continuously occupy the same niche, which means they cannot depend upon the same environmental resources. If the two populations differ in some characteristic relevant for exploitation of the resource, the population that exploits the niche better will drive the other population out. Then only one population will occupy the niche and will be well adapted to it. Thus, the degree of diversity across all the populations reflects the number of distinct resources. If the environment is highly stable, then each niche will tend to be filled by a population of specialized organizations because each such population exploits the resources of a niche very efficiently. But if the environment is constantly changing, then more generalized organizations will have an advantage over specialized ones, because they can exploit the resources effectively even as the resources fluctuate somewhat.

Hannan and Freeman say that their aim is not to take metaphors from biology and apply them to sociology, nor do they think that sociology should be reduced to biology. Rather, they suggest that the abstract theories and mathematical tools developed for biological population ecology should apply equally well to populations of social organizations. They admit that it will be difficult to test such models in sociology, because appropriate data seldom exist. But they are optimistic that progress can be made if researchers begin thinking about populations of organizations, rather than solely in terms of individual organizations.

DiMaggio, Paul J., and Walter W. Powell
  1991 "The Iron Cage Revisited: Institutional Isomorphism and Collective Rationality in Organizational Fields." pp. 63–82 in *The New Institutionalism in Organizational Analysis*, edited by Walter W. Powell and Paul J. DiMaggio. Chicago: University of Chicago Press.

Competition under the conditions of industrial society drove corporations and governments to become highly bureaucratic, running their operations in a highly rational and thus efficient manner. However, bureaucratization developed a momentum of its own, continuing beyond the point at which it was in some sense superior to other forms of organization. DiMaggio and Powell examine the way that processes unrelated to efficiency tend to make organizations in a particular field highly similar to each other. They cite work by a number of other social scientists indicating that diversity tends to decline in well-defined fields. For example, years ago there were many kinds of college textbook publisher, but this diversity declined until there were just two kinds: large bureaucratic "generalist" corporations and small specialist publishers. A field comes into existence through a process of organizational definition that has four parts:

1. Interaction between organizations in the emerging field increases in extent.
2. Clearly defined interorganizational structures appear, involving domination and coalition.
3. The amount of information that must be contended with increases.
4. Organizations develop a mutual awareness that they are engaged in a common enterprise.

DiMaggio and Powell use the term *isomorphism* (having the same shape) for the constraining process that makes each organization in a field tend to resemble the others. They identify three kinds of isomorphism having different causes.

Coercive isomorphism comes about because organizations outside the field (such as the government) and cultural expectations of the society impose common standards across the field of organizations. For example, the government may require the auto industry to adopt a specific set of pollution control technologies, and the legal system imposes the same regulations on all the organizations.

Mimetic processes make the organizations imitate each other, especially when each one faces great uncertainty dealing with its environment. For example, at the end of the nineteenth century Japanese organizations sought to model themselves on their western equivalents, in the assumption that they had learned to deal effectively with problems, and more recently western corporations modeled themselves to some extent on Japanese ones, hoping to duplicate Japanese economic success.

Normative pressures primarily come from professionalization of the central kinds of work carried out by the organizations. Professionalization is the collective struggle of the members of an occupation to define the conditions of their work, to limit the entry of new workers to their occupation, and to establish an ideological basis for their professional autonomy. Professionals bring isomorphism to organizations through the standardized educations they receive, the operation of professional associations, and the relative uniformity of the people recruited to a particular profession.

With this conceptual background, DiMaggio and Powell state a dozen hypotheses concerning isomorphism that could be tested through empirical research.

10
STRATIFICATION

WORKS AT A GLANCE

Functional Analysis

"Some Principles of Stratification" by Kingsley Davis and Wilbert Moore (1945)
"Social Capital in the Creation of Human Capital" by James S. Coleman (1988)

Critical Analysis

The Power Elite by C. Wright Mills (1956)
The Credential Society: An Historical Sociology of Education
    by Randall Collins (1979)
"Bringing the Men Back In: Sex Differentiation and the Devaluation of Women's
    Work" by Barbara F. Reskin (1988)

Occupational Stratification

The American Occupational Structure by Peter M. Blau
    and Otis D. Duncan (1967)

Consequences of Stratification

Social Class and Mental Illness by August B. Hollingshead
    and Frederick B. Redlich (1958)

Stratification is the characteristic of a society that is divided into different social classes or socio-economic strata (layers). The term is also used widely to refer to individual inequality in a society, regardless of whether distinct classes exist. A chief mechanism sustaining stratification in modern societies is the occupational structure, which assigns people to different work positions that possess varying income and influence. However much stratification benefits the rich and powerful, or even benefits the society as a whole, it penalizes the poor and powerless, often in unexpected ways.

In an influential theoretical essay, Kingsley Davis and Wilbert Moore argued that a system of stratification serves important functions for the society as a whole, by motivating talented individuals to play the roles that are crucial to the society's survival. James Coleman argued that a community's norms, values, and social stability provide the basis for individual achievement. Functionalist sociologists—like Davis, Moore, and to some extent Coleman— believe that stratification is necessary for the proper operation of a society. In contrast, critical sociologists generally argue that many aspects of stratification are arbitrary and merely serve the desires for wealth and power of a minority of people.

C. Wright Mills criticized the assumption that American society is based on equal opportunity and democracy. Instead, he argued, a small class of men called the power elite make the important decisions. Randall Collins says that the American educational system is largely a scheme to grab power for highly educated people, even though the knowledge and skills taught in higher education are largely useless. Barbara Reskin says that women face an uphill fight in their struggle for income equality, because men have a variety of tactics to preserve their privileges.

Other sociologists have been neither functionalist nor critical but empirical, developing careful research methodologies for measuring the nature and consequences of stratification. The work of Peter Blau and Otis Duncan on occupational mobility was tremendously influential upon several branches of sociology, in part because it demonstrated statistical methods of analysis that could be employed in a variety of studies, as well as engaging issues of great theoretical significance. Similarly, the study by August Hollingshead and Frederick Redlich on social class and mental illness stimulated many later research projects.

Struggle to change or preserve the stratification system is at the heart of many political debates, and thus it is difficult to prevent the sociology of stratification from becoming politicized. For example, functionalist theorists are generally considered politically conservative, whereas critical theorists are liberal or radical. Perhaps the safest course is to draw intellectual stimulation from theorists who seem to write from both ends of the political spectrum, but be cautious in making policy conclusions about areas in which reliable, systematic research has either not been done, or if it has, has not reached a consensus.

Functional Analysis

Davis, Kingsley, and Wilbert Moore
  1945 "Some Principles of Stratification," *American Sociological Review*
  10:242–249.

Davis and Moore note that all societies are stratified, so they look for the "universal necessity" that creates social inequality in any social system. They approach this question as functionalists, asking what "functional necessity" stratification serves for the society. They suggest that each society has a number of important roles to be filled, each performing a vital task. The society needs to attract able, energetic people to these roles and commit them to the duties of these roles. Stratification accomplishes this, because it offers rewards to induce good people to enter the roles, distributing the rewards across the positions in society so that the most important ones have greater rewards, and the less important ones, lesser rewards. The society must see to it that unimportant roles do not receive high rewards, or good people will be attracted to them, away from the essential roles that must be played well if the society is to survive and prosper.

Four societal sectors have especially important roles: religion, government, economy, and technology. The functional significance of religion is that it supports the ultimate values upon which the society is based, and binds the individual members of society to these values through its rituals and beliefs. Government organizes the society through the laws it enforces, the authority it imposes over institutions, and the defense it maintains against other societies. In economic institutions, wealth flows to the positions that have high status because of their importance to the society. In technology, people with high technical skills gain fairly high rewards, but people with technical knowledge do not become very powerful, because their skills are concerned only with means to attain various goals, and the three other sectors actually integrate the goals themselves. Societies vary in the degree to which the roles are specialized, which of the sectors gets the greatest emphasis, and in other ways. Therefore they also differ in the details of their stratification systems. But in all societies, stratification results from the need to attract the best efforts of good people to the key roles in religion, government, economy, and technology.

Coleman, James S.
  1988 "Social Capital in the Creation of Human Capital." pp. S95–S120 in
  *Organizations and Institutions: Sociological and Economic Approaches
  to the Analysis of Social Structure*, edited by Christopher Winship and
  Sherwin Rosen. *American Journal of Sociology,* volume 94, supplement.

Coleman attempted to bring sociology and economics together in a perspective called Rational Choice Theory. In this influential essay, he applied the economic concept of *capital*, investments or possessions devoted to production and to generating income, to aspects of the society surrounding the individual. Coleman's colleague at the University of Chicago, economist Gary Becker, had already used the term *human capital* to describe attributes a person can acquire that increase his or her capacity to earn income, the chief example being education. In addition to being a sociological theorist, Coleman was a sociologist of education. In this essay, he discussed social factors that assist an individual in acquiring education, thus indirectly giving the person a higher income. Individuals differ in the value of their human capital (e.g., in their educations), and this fact is a chief reason why individuals are distributed as they are in the stratification system. Social capital affects stratification in part by assisting individuals in certain social environments in gaining greater human capital.

The term *social capital* could be applied to many social possessions of the individual. For example, having influential friends can help the individual get a good job. However, Coleman focuses on rather more abstract kinds of social capital that are not directly connected to the individual. One is being immersed in a community where people are trustworthy, fulfilling their obligations and meeting expectations. Another is having a widespread social network that serves to transmit valuable information. And a third is a set of success-oriented community norms and effective sanctions to enforce them. Among the kinds of social structure that facilitate social capital are relatively closed social networks and social organizations that can be put to a variety of fresh uses. A family or neighborhood with strong social capital is better able to keep young people in school and motivate them to get good educations.

Coleman finds these kinds of social capital especially interesting because they are typically *public goods*. This term refers to valuable things from which many people can benefit without having to contribute. For example, a neighborhood watch organization can prevent crime even for the residents who do not participate in it. Therefore, a community faces a serious challenge in motivating individuals to contribute, but if it succeeds in building social capital, its members will be at an advantage in the larger stratification system surrounding the community. Often very elaborate institutions are required to create and sustain public goods. Coleman presents data showing that the school dropout rate is much lower from religious private schools (chiefly but not exclusively Catholic) than from public schools and from non-religious private schools. At the end of his essay, Coleman comments that strong families and neighborhoods are less common now than in the past, and thus the society faces an increasingly more difficult challenge creating human capital.

Critical Analysis

Mills, C. Wright

1956 *The Power Elite*. New York: Oxford University Press.

Mills argues that a national *power elite* has emerged at the pinnacle of American society, a network of men who make whatever major decisions are to be made. Although they have some awareness of their group interests and share many assumptions with each other, they are not exactly what other writers mean by a ruling class. They are not entirely distinct from the larger elites from which they draw their personnel, and their power comes from their position in specific American institutions rather than simply from wealth and prestige. The power elite is psychologically unified because it is composed of men with similar elite origins and educations, socially unified because the men in the national corporations form a close-knit social network, and organizationally unified because men in key positions link corporations with government agencies and coordinate their actions.

Mills disagrees with two viewpoints on the power elite. People who look from a distance at the great events and apparently pivotal decisions of recent history sometimes conclude that the power elite is a conscious conspiracy that wields great power to make these events happen. Others who are close enough to the elite to hear what its members say doubt they have much power but are simply coping as best they can with larger social and economic forces over which they have little control.

In ancient days, the institutions of family and religion held great power, but their influence has declined greatly. Some people imagine that education and science have gained great influence, but Mills doubts this. Instead, he says, three great institutions had come to dominate American society by the middle of the twentieth century: economic corporations, the military domain, and the political directorate. The other institutions are subservient.

Decades earlier, each city had its own local elite, for example the people listed in the *Social Register*, who derived their status from ownership of major local corporations or real estate. But nation-wide hierarchies of power and wealth emerged. Communications technologies permitted the development of a national stratum of celebrities, including sports and television stars who often attached themselves to the power elite. Central to the whole system are the very rich. In the fifty years after the Civil War, men became rich often by cheating investors and using illegal or immoral tactics against competitors, and Mills thinks this has continued. Although technology creates wealth, inventors do not get rich; instead, business operators exploit inventions for their own gain. Often, businessmen become wealthy by getting government contracts or other special favors. War has been a great stimulus to industry, thus enriching those able to take advantage of it. As an industry matures, the number of companies decreases through mergers and bankruptcies until only a few big corporations remain, concentrating their power in the hands of a few owners and executives. The very rich are able to accumulate advantages of many kinds to get and stay on top.

Collins, Randall
1979 *The Credential Society: An Historical Sociology of Education.* New York: Academic Press.

It is widely assumed that education is the ticket to success in modern society, and the single variable that best predicts occupational status is the amount of education people have received. Collins argues this is true not because education actually prepares people for the technical challenges of work, but because universities have succeeded in convincing government and industry to demand educational credentials of employees. The result is a system in which educators and highly educated people throughout the economy unfairly obtain sinecures where they collect high salaries at little effort, while making little real contribution to the society.

The importance of education had increased dramatically over the century before Collins wrote, until it had become central to the stratification system. In 1870, just 2.0 percent of Americans age 17 had graduated from high school, whereas in 1970 the proportion was 76.5 percent. From 1870 to 1970, the proportion of the 18–21 year-old population in college rose from 1.7 percent to 21.1 percent. Collins's book documents in detail how particular professions (chiefly medicine and law) come to be powerful monopolies based on educational credentials, and how the colleges of America reinvented themselves to become bloated organizations with tremendous unearned influence over the stratification system.

The demand for high educational credentials is supported by a technocratic ideology that asserts important jobs in modern society require specialized technical knowledge and that this knowledge must be obtained through formal education in universities and professional schools. Collins calls this ideology "hot air," saying that most higher education does not in fact prepare people to perform better even in most technical occupations. He agrees that the schools contribute greatly to economic productivity by ensuring that most citizens can read, write, and do arithmetic, but he cites much research evidence that schools are a very inefficient place to learn other skills. Managers and professionals learn most of the skills that are critical for their work on the job, through direct experience. The degrees and professional certificates they hold are of benefit to them chiefly by backing up their claims for high salaries and helping them limit competition from people who are equally well prepared to do their jobs but lack these credentials.

Several studies have found that school grades are very poor predictors of occupational performance in later years, except for students with the very high grades often needed to get into elite professional schools. This is true even for professions that the technocratic ideology claims required very stringent high-level training, such as medicine and engineering. Although education may contribute little to productive labor, it can be a valuable asset for people who primarily practice political labor. *Productive labor* is an actual contribution to the total wealth or well-being of a society. *Political labor*, in contrast, is the socially useless effort of maneuvering for advantage within the power system of an organization, forming alliances and shaping people's perceptions of work so that wealth flows into the hands of the person performing the political labor. In that sense, educational credentials are a tool of value chiefly for parasitic individuals and groups, and the growth of education burdens the society with injustice and inefficiency, rather than being a shining example of progress.

Reskin, Barbara F.
  1988 "Bringing the Men Back In: Sex Differentiation and the Devaluation of Women's Work," *Gender and Society*, 2:58-81.

On average, men earn more money than women do. One reason has been that women have commonly been paid less for the same amount and quality of work. When legal reforms required equal pay for equal work, women still earned less because they were concentrated in low-wage occupations. Consequently, considerable effort has been invested to increase women's opportunities to enter high-paying occupations, and some critics have argued there should be equal pay for different jobs of equal value to society. Reskin argues that men will always try to defeat such reforms, often by finding new ways to hold women in subordinate positions. The standard techniques of gender subordination are (1) physical segregation of the sexes, (2) expecting different behavior from them, (3) social separation of males from females, and (4) explicit, gender-based status hierarchies. Men respond to women's challenges by emphasizing how the sexes differ, by refusing to accept traditional female tasks such as home-making, by electing officials who will weaken legal remedies against sex discrimination, and by creating new distinctions within occupations to discriminate against women who enter the occupation. Merely ensuring equal access to all kinds of jobs, and equal pay for work of equal value, may not achieve general equality, because men hold powerful statuses that will allow them to find ways to beat back these challenges from women.

Occupational Stratification

Blau, Peter M., and Otis D. Duncan
  1967 *The American Occupational Structure*. New York: John Wiley.

Blau and Duncan set out to study occupational mobility through a massive survey of 20,700 men administered for them by the U.S. Bureau of the Census, which carried it out in conjunction with the Current Population Survey in

March 1962. Three questions were central to the study: the respondent's current job, the respondent's first full-time job after leaving school, and the kind of work the respondent's father was doing when the respondent was sixteen years old. Occupations were coded into seventeen categories, which Blau and Duncan ranked in terms of income and the men's typical educational background: professionals (self-employed), professionals (salaried), managers, salesmen (other), proprietors, clerical, salesmen (retail), craftsmen (manufacturing), craftsmen (other), craftsmen (construction), operatives (manufacturing), operatives (other), service, laborers (manufacturing), laborers (other), farmers, and farm laborers. Thus, Blau and Duncan could examine *intergenerational mobility* by comparing the respondent's current job with that of his father. They could examine *intragenerational mobility* by comparing the respondent's current job with the first job he got after leaving school.

Much of the analysis uses big tables, with the seventeen occupational categories forming both the horizontal and vertical dimensions, showing how many men answered in particular ways to two of these three questions. For example, one table shows that 9.4 percent of men whose fathers were farm laborers, at the bottom of the status scale, are currently farm laborers themselves. Another 5.7 percent of these sons of farm laborers became independent farmers in their own right, presumably owning their own farms. The largest group, 13.1 percent, became operatives (manufacturing), which means they work on factory assembly lines. In contrast, only 0.6 percent of the sons of farm laborers became self-employed professionals. The fate of sons of self-employed professionals was very different. Only 0.8 percent of them became farm laborers, 16.7 percent became self-employed professionals like their fathers, and 31.9 percent became salaried professionals working for corporations or similar organizations.

The tables show there is some tendency for men to inherit the occupational status of their fathers, although there is also a considerable amount of mobility, both upward and downward. Most of this mobility is a short distance along the status scale, and few men go from rags to riches. More of the mobility is upward rather than downward, in part because men were leaving the farms for the factories, and because technological and economic trends were increasing the need for men in many higher-status occupations. The father's status influenced the son's first job, but it also influenced what job the son currently has, even taking the first job's status into account. That is, background has a continuing influence throughout life. Blau and Duncan found that two barriers between types of occupation are seldom crossed during downward mobility, but are often crossed during upward mobility. Men from white-collar backgrounds are unlikely to take blue-collar jobs, and men from blue-collar backgrounds are unlikely to work on farms. Despite all the historical changes, when Blau and Duncan examined men of different ages (with fathers of different age) and looked at other data sets, they found that the correlation between father's and son's occupation was constant over the span of four decades, suggesting that the American stratification system was stable.

To understand the system better, Blau and Duncan added father's and son's education to the analysis. One theory proposed by other sociologists claimed that the poor become trapped in a vicious circle that keeps them in poverty generation after generation, because they cannot afford the education needed to escape. Blau and Duncan found this was not true for most groups. Education increases the variability in the status men achieve, independently of the men's initial status. Thus men from low status backgrounds are able to obtain somewhat better educations than their fathers had, and many of them rise upward in the status system as a result. Some men from high-status backgrounds fail in their education, and dropping out of education causes them to drop downward in the status system. Even controlling for interactions between the variables, the son's own education predicts his occupational status better than does his father's education or occupation.

The vicious circle may be very real for African American men, however. Blau and Duncan compared African Americans with whites, using a variety of census data as well as their own survey. Being African American made it more difficult to get a good education, but it also made that education less valuable. At a given educational level, whites tended to get better jobs, suggesting that discrimination in the workplace was holding African Americans back even when they were objectively qualified for better jobs. Blau and Duncan speculated that African Americans may have been disappointed by the benefits of education, and thus were not prepared to invest as much in it even when they could. If true, this was a vicious circle, although African Americans were locked into it by discrimination by whites. The data examined by Blau and Duncan were for a period largely before the successes of the Civil Rights Movement, but sociologists today are concerned that the situation may not yet have changed entirely.

This study examines many factors that relate to occupational mobility, such as marriage, immigration, geographic mobility, and the consequences of having many or few brothers and sisters of various ages. By about the year 1900, social scientists had learned that lower-status men tended to have more children than higher status ones. To the extent that men with high-status occupations tend to have few children, their occupations will need to draw men in from other, lower-status backgrounds. And if low-status men have many children, some of them will have to move to higher-status occupations. Thus, one of the forces driving mobility in the American status system was differences in fertility. However, when Blau and Duncan examined recent data, they found that fertility differences across the occupational statuses had almost vanished, except that farm families still tended to be large.

Consequences of Stratification

Hollingshead, August B., and Frederick B. Redlich
  1958 *Social Class and Mental Illness*. New York: Wiley.

Hollingshead and Redlich investigated the ways in which social class was related to the occurrence of mental illness and to the treatment that a mentally ill person received. They did this primarily by collecting detailed information about all the mental patients and psychotherapists or psychiatrists in New Haven, Connecticut, in the latter half of 1950. This was a stupendous effort, which required them to do such things as surveying 876 psychiatrists in New York City who might have patients who commuted from New Haven, and administering a survey to a random sample of 3,559 New Haven households. Whereas Faris and Dunham (Chapter 5) had been concerned with the social disorganization surrounding mental patients, Hollingshead and Redlich were chiefly interested in social class, and their orientation marked a general departure from the Chicago School throughout sociology in favor of an emphasis on social inequality, an emphasis that has persisted for the remainder of the twentieth century.

The measure of social class was Hollingshead's "Index of Social Position," which built on stratification work by several other researchers. It assumed that the community possessed a class status structure, which was determined by a small number of widely accepted "symbolic characteristics" that could be reliably scaled and combined by statistical procedures. This index combined three different measurement scales:

I. **The *residential* scale.** Influenced by the "ecological" approach of the Chicago School (Chapter 7), researchers graded New Haven's neighborhoods from the finest to the poorest, on a six-point scale. Each person living in a given neighborhood received the score representing that neighborhood's quality.

II. **The *occupational* scale.** This was a modification of a system used by the Census Bureau that assigned each person's job to one of seven categories:
   a. executives and proprietors of large concerns, and major professionals
   b. managers and proprietors of medium-sized businesses and lesser professionals
   c. administrative personnel of large concerns, owners of small independent businesses, and semi-professionals
   d. owners of little businesses, clerical and sales workers, and technicians
   e. skilled workers
   f. semiskilled workers
   g. unskilled workers

III. **The *educational* scale.** This was a seven-point scale from "graduate professional training" down to "less than seven years of school."

Based on statistical analysis of survey data on 552 households, Hollingshead developed a mathematical formula for combining the scores on these three scales, then dividing the cases into five social classes, which are described roughly below (with terms Hollingshead himself did not use):

I. The upper class, 2.7 percent of families

II. The upper middle class, 9.8 percent of families

III. The lower middle class, 18.9 percent of families

IV. The working class, 48.4 percent of families

V. The lower class, 20.2 percent of families

In 1950, psychiatrists and their treatments could be divided into two categories. Analytic-psychological (A-P) psychiatrists applied the new "talking cure" of psychoanalysis that assumed mental illness was the result of subconscious psychological conflicts. Directive-organic (D-O) psychiatrists gave authoritative advice and prescribed sedative medications (or heroic treatments such as electric shock and the brain surgery called lobotomy), and they tended not to be up-to-date in terms of current psychological theories. At the time, psychoanalysis was nearing its peak of popularity among highly educated Americans, and psychiatrists at Yale University in New Haven were usually of the A-P type. In contrast, public mental hospital psychiatrists were usually D-O. The two groups read very different journals and were even of very different ethnic origins; 83 percent of A-P psychiatrists were Jewish (as was Sigmund Freud, the pioneer of psychoanalysis), compared with only 8 percent of the D-O group. Since Hollingshead and Redlich wrote, the A-P approach has lost some of its status in psychiatry, and none of the medications used today as specific treatments for mental illness were available to the D-O doctors of 1950. Thus, the two groups were competing psychiatric subcultures, with the A-P group temporarily enjoying much higher professional status at the time of the study. Interestingly, the A-P doctors studied by Hollingshead and Redlich tended to be upwardly mobile, and the highly successful psychoanalytic movement of their day provided them an effective vehicle for social advancement.

As measured by psychiatric treatment, mental illness was more common among Class V (lower class) residents of New Haven than among members of any other class. In the population as a whole, 18.4 percent of individuals belonged to Class V, compared with 38.2 percent of mental patients. The fraction of a group who entered treatment for the first time in a particular span of time is called the *incidence rate*. From June 1, 1950, until December 1, the incidence rate for classes I and II was 97 per 100,000, whereas for Class V it was 139. Thus, people from the lowest social class were somewhat more likely than those from the upper classes to receive treatment. The *prevalence rate* is the fraction of a group under treatment at a particular point in time, and it is compounded from the incidence, the rate at which people complete treatment and may be "cured," and the rate of re-entering treatment for those who had temporarily dropped out. The lowest social class was at a disadvantage in all of these, with a higher incidence, higher re-entry to treatment, and lower cure rate than members of higher social classes. Hollingshead and Redlich attributed this difference chiefly to the extraordinary psychological stresses experienced by poor people and the inferior psychiatric treatment available to them. They also examined the *downward drift hypothesis*, that mental illness strikes people at random throughout society and causes them to drop down in the class system, not finding much evidence for this explanation.

Hollingshead and Redlich examined how social class related to different psychiatric diagnoses, such as the distinction between neurosis and psychosis. *Neurosis* refers to mild problems in which the sufferer remains in touch with reality but experiences impairs functioning and distress. Treatment for it is more common among higher class patients, perhaps because they have especially high standards for the quality of life and performance of roles in society, and thus seek treatment when members of lower social classes would not. *Psychosis* refers to serious mental illness, such as schizophrenia, in which the sufferer loses touch with reality and can hardly function in life. The prevalence of treated schizophrenia was 111 per 100,000 in classes I and II, 168 in Class III, 300 in class IV, and fully 895 per 100,000 in Class V. That is, a member of the lowest class was eight times as likely to suffer from schizophrenia as a member of the upper classes.

Not surprisingly, treatment varied by social class. Fully 46.9 percent of neurotics in classes I and II received psychoanalytic treatments, compared with just 4.9 percent of Class V neurotics. In part, this results from the fact that only richer people can afford this form of treatment, but another factor is the social class relationship between doctors and patients. Ninety-five percent of New Haven psychiatrists belonged to Class I, and the remaining 5 percent to Class II. Upper-class doctors have trouble communicating with lower-class patients, and psychoanalysis seemed designed for well-educated patients who were adept at expressing themselves in words and able to understand the aims of therapy. Especially in psychiatric clinics, lower-class patients were more likely to receive directive and organic treatments. Among psychotics, 67.3 percent of patients from classes I and II enjoyed the relative advantages of private mental hospitals, whereas 89.0 percent of Class V patients suffered the lower standard of care in the state hospitals. Possibly as a result, poor patients stayed sicker longer.

The massive research study by Hollingshead and Redlich was the most significant of many such research projects carried out in the 1950s and 1960s. They provided the intellectual support for major campaigns to increase public knowledge and acceptance of psychiatry, and to invest public resources in psychiatric treatment for those who could not otherwise afford it. Subsequent decades saw continuing controversy over the effectiveness of various kinds of treatment and over the proper role of government in providing them. But a deep sociological appreciation of the dynamic relationship between social class and suffering is an enduring legacy of this research.

11
RACE AND ETHNIC RELATIONS

WORKS AT A GLANCE

The Sociology of Race Relations

Sociology and the Race Problem: The Failure of a Perspective
   by James B. McKee (1993)
"A Theory of Ethnic Antagonism: The Split Labor Market"
   by Edna Bonacich (1972)

Discrimination

"Racial Violence and Black Migration in the American South,
   1910 to 1930" by Stewart E. Tolnay and E. M. Beck (1992)
A Piece of the Pie: Blacks and White Immigrants since 1880
   by Stanley Lieberson (1980)
*The Declining Significance of Race: Blacks and Changing American
   Institutions* by William J. Wilson (1978)

Segregation

The Social Order of the Slum by Gerald D. Suttles (1965)
American Apartheid: Segregation and the Making of the Underclass
   by Douglas S. Massey and Nancy A. Denton (1993)

Throughout the world, conflict between racial and ethnic groups continues to pose severe problems for social stability and human well-being, even though one might have hoped that modern society would have outgrown hostilities of this kind. In the United States, many immigrant groups have assimilated into the larger society, adding elements of their own cultures to the American way of life. In the middle of the second century after the Civil War freed the slaves, however, the status of African Americans remains ambiguous, and the painful legacy of discrimination endures. The selections in this chapter first document the difficulty sociologists had grappling with these problems, and then document the meaning of discrimination and segregation.

James McKee's book is a profound challenge to American sociology, arguing that sociologists contributed little to help African Americans in their struggle for political and economic equality. As Edna Bonacich shows, it may not be enough to overcome racial prejudices, because ethnic groups can develop antagonistic economic situations that fuel racism. Stewart Tolnay and E. M. Beck argue that a main reason why many blacks left the Old South early in the twentieth century was to escape racial violence such as lynchings. In the North, as Stanley Lieberson demonstrates, they faced more severe discrimination than did other immigrants. William Wilson speculates that racism may have declined in significance since the 1960s, and that the poverty of many African Americans reflects the continuing disadvantage of lower-class status.

Based on observational research in one Chicago community, Gerald Suttles documents the enduring separation of ethnic groups. Douglas Massey and Nancy Denton say that racial segregation continues to be a severe problem for African Americans, because many of them are trapped in areas of their cities that lack opportunities. The United States has not yet become a single society, with liberty and justice for all. Thus America needs a vigorous and intellectually courageous sociology of race and ethnic relations. It remains to be seen whether sociologists can meet this challenge effectively.

The Sociology of Race Relations

McKee, James B.
  1993 *Sociology and the Race Problem: The Failure of a Perspective.* Urbana, Illinois: University of Illinois Press.

Despite the number of prominent and talented sociologists and social psychologists who studied white-black race relations over the first two thirds of the twentieth century, McKee says that their work was largely a failure. Most strikingly, they failed to predict the emergence of black activism and race consciousness in the 1960s. However, this was merely an indication of the larger inability of the sociology of race relations to escape the inhibitions imposed by the surrounding white culture and to see the full truth of the black experience in America.

At the beginning of the twentieth century, white racism was bolstered by biologists who confidently asserted the innate inferiority of blacks, and sociologists accepted this false opinion. However, anthropologists like Franz Boas challenged this view. Once biologists realized that individuals inherited a very large number of distinct genes from their parents, many of which affected physical characteristics only in degree, the concept of race lost scientific status within biology.

The first generation of American sociologists, who established the discipline in the 1890s and the first two decades after the turn of the century, were not much interested in race. In the 1920s, however, standard textbooks on social problems began to carry chapters on what was then called either "the race problem" or "the Negro problem." For many sociologists, the discredited idea that blacks were biologically inferior was transformed into the equally unflattering notion that they were culturally inferior, perhaps because slavery had destroyed the vestiges of their African cultures. For a long time, sociologists failed to notice the migration of blacks from southern farms to northern factories, and still considered them a rural people. Few sociologists saw any prospect that blacks and whites could ever mingle on an equal footing, and sociology contributed little to progress in civil rights. By the middle of the 1930s, sociology had become the intellectual home for the study of race relations, but it timidly failed to challenge white bigotry. Sociologists accepted the implacable opposition of whites to black assimilation, even as they thought the only hope for blacks was to become gradually more and more similar to whites. Sociologists were extremely cautious, because they wanted the powerful white establishment to accept their discipline as a valid science, so they avoided the question of racial conflict.

Through his book, McKee suggests that Robert Park was the only white sociologist who had the insight to understand the real situation of blacks in America, and the foresight to know where race relations were headed in the twentieth century. Park had been a writer and press agent for the famous black leader, Booker T. Washington, and he brought a deep personal familiarity with blacks to sociology when he began his scholarly career at the University of Chicago at the age of forty-nine in 1913. Among the most influential teachers in the history of sociology, Park worked enthusiastically with black students, and some of them became influential sociologists in their own rights, notably Charles S. Johnson and E. Franklin Frazier. While recognizing that slavery and rural poverty had left many blacks uneducated and unprepared for industrial society, Park was convinced that they were capable of overcoming these disadvantages in a few generations and of becoming the social, economic, and legal equals of white people. Park disdained social reform movements, however, and he alone of prominent sociologists believed that sooner or later blacks would have to fight for their own rights. Reformers seemed to believe that any gains that blacks experienced would have to come as gifts from the dominant white race, whereas Park believed that conflict must be accepted as an inevitable part of human life, and that oppressed groups had both the right and capability of acting on their own behalf. When Park retired in 1934, sociology lost the only great mind who conceptualized race relations in terms of conflict between race-conscious groups.

In the 1940s and 1950s, many sociologists and social psychologists optimistically decided that white discrimination against blacks was largely a matter of prejudice that could ultimately be overcome. Supposedly, if members of the two races who happened to be of similar status levels were brought together, they would accept each other. In questionnaire studies, the confident and educated white upper-middle class exhibited far less prejudice than the worried and less educated white lower-middle class. Education could prepare blacks for acceptance by whites, and reduce prejudice among the whites. Some of the most influential sociologists began to assert that American culture was a unity, held together by shared values and beliefs, and the fundamental principles of justice and equality provided the basis for integration. If white sociologists had been brave enough to open their eyes, they would have seen signs that their comfortable consensus was false. Black sociologists like Johnson and Frazier knew that their people were developing their own culture distinct from that of the whites, and some studies seemed to indicate that educated whites rejected blacks just as strenuously as the supposedly more prejudiced uneducated whites. Gradually, sociologists had become committed to racial equality, but the means they chose to achieve it were bland intergroup relations educational programs plus modest government desegregation efforts.

Beginning in the late 1950s and extending through the 1960s, most sociologists were astonished to see blacks take the initiative for themselves, in militant action, protest movements, and a growing black consciousness. This rebellion achieved far more rapid change in race relations than had occurred in any similar decade since the Civil War. In his concluding pages, McKee charges that sociology has still, even today, not yet developed a successful approach to the politics of race, including the development of a large but ineffective political "industry" of bureaucrats assigned to manage race relations. The facts that the black power and civil rights movements were only partially successful, and that many of the problems inflicted upon blacks by white society endure, suggest that sociology continues to fail to meet its responsibility to understand "the race problem."

Bonacich, Edna
   1972 "A Theory of Ethnic Antagonism: The Split Labor Market," *American Sociological Review* 37:547–559.

Bonacich seeks to explain hostility between ethnic groups, and believes that economic competition between workers belonging to the different groups provides much of the answer. At the extreme, this hostility takes two forms that are superficially very different. First, extreme ethnic hostility may take the form of *exclusion*, the attempt to keep members of a particular foreign group from entering the society. An example of exclusion is the repeated attempt to prevent Asians from entering California and other far western states. Second, ethnic hostility may create and sustain a *caste* system in which a group suffers restricted rights and opportunities while living within the society. The suppression of African Americans in the Old South illustrates a caste system.

Bonacich argues that ethnic antagonism develops in a labor market that is ethnically split, where the group that will be the victim of antagonism has a lower price of labor than does the group that will develop hostility to them. A *labor market* is the complex social, economic, and cultural system that draws particular individuals to take various jobs, and the term can be applied both to small-scale, specialized occupational systems, and to very large, varied ones. *Labor price* includes not only the wages received by the given group of workers, but also the cost of recruiting them, any side benefits such as lodging or health care, and the cost the employers face in dealing with problems the workers pose, such as strikes or other unrest.

When a new group enters a labor market, a set of dynamics shapes the development of a split. Immigrants from a poor region may migrate in search of work and be willing to accept much lower wages than do more prosperous people who already have the given kind of job. Immigrants may be ignorant of the conditions of the society they enter, and their lack of information may cause them to sign bad contracts or otherwise accept conditions they could actually refuse. Sometimes an immigrant group has the political support of the nation it leaves, as has been the case for people leaving Japan but not for those leaving Mexico. The poorer a group already is, the less relevant the information it possesses, and the weaker its political support, the more likely it is to accept an unfavorable wage bargain with employers in the society it enters. In addition, temporary workers and those merely supplementing other incomes may accept bad employment terms.

Once a split labor market has begun to appear, employers and business leaders may use the cheap labor of the newcomers to break strikes or create new industries. However, in general the capitalists are not in favor of split labor markets. They would prefer a free market of labor in which all workers compete on an equal footing, because the price of labor tends to be lower.

Highly paid labor, the older and established ethnic groups of workers, find their jobs threatened by the newer, cheaper workers. Not only do they stand to lose their jobs, but their wages will decline as well if the new workers are allowed in. If few of the new workers are already in the country, therefore, they agitate for exclusion laws to keep them out. But if the poorer ethnic group is already in the country, then the higher-paid group tries to create a caste system that restricts the poorer ethnic group to bad jobs and withholds rights and resources from them that might let them improve their situations.

Bonacich illustrates exclusion with the case of Australia. Capitalists wanted to import cheap labor from India, China, Japan, and the islands of the Pacific.

White labor was able to organize politically and force the government to institute policies excluding Asian and Polynesian immigrants. South Africa is an extreme example of development of a caste system. When diamonds were discovered in 1869, a class of skilled white miners emerged who were able to develop sufficient political power to prevent the capitalists from quickly employing cheaper blacks. A color line was drawn in the mining industry, preventing blacks from taking the better jobs, and eventually all of South African society was based on apartheid, the economic and social separation of the races within a single country.

Discrimination

Tolnay, Stewart E., and E. M. Beck
  1992 "Racial Violence and Black Migration in the American South, 1910 to 1930," *American Sociological Review* 57:103–116.

In the period 1910–1930, African Americans participated in a "Great Migration" out of the South, many of them moving to northern cities. One factor motivating them to leave some parts of the South may have been to escape racial violence. Tolnay and Beck assembled data on cases in which blacks were lynched by white mobs in ten southern states, a total of 1,893 lynchings from 1882 until 1910, and another 650 lynchings from 1910 to 1930. The researchers then examined data on migration from the United States census, and other variables that might also explain migration, such as the extent of tenant farming and educational levels. Results showed that black migration was indeed high from counties that had high rates of racial mob violence.

Lieberson, Stanley
  1980 *A Piece of the Pie: Blacks and White Immigrants since 1880.*
  Berkeley, California: University of California Press.

Lieberson sets out to understand why African Americans appear to have been less successful in gaining socioeconomic status than the "new" European immigrant groups who came in near the beginning of the twentieth century, such as Italian Americans or Polish Americans. Blacks could be compared with immigrants because many moved from the Old South to the industrial regions that also attracted the Europeans, and because all these groups suffered poverty and discrimination. Lieberson notes that several overlapping theories have been offered. For example, blacks were more visibly different from the "old" European groups (such as the English), and the "new" Europeans could assimilate in a variety of ways, including changing their names. Europeans were drawn in when good economic conditions provided jobs for them, and those who did not adapt well often returned to their homelands. In contrast, job opportunities were often not available when blacks arrived from the rural

South, and the distribution of blacks across the country was very different from that of European immigrants, concentrating them chiefly in poor areas. Some argue that the European immigrants were culturally prepared to succeed in America, which ultimately was based on European cultures, whereas the blacks had only recently come out of slavery, which had impoverished their cultures.

The chief theme of Lieberson's book, however, sets all these theories aside and documents the brute fact that blacks faced much more severe challenges than did the European immigrants, sometimes as the result of historical accidents but very often as the result of racism. Statistics from the first half of the twentieth century demonstrate that mortality rates were much higher among blacks than among the European immigrants, although these, in turn, were slightly higher than for native-born whites. Unlike white immigrants, blacks were systematically prevented from voting and from entering political careers. Segregated education in the South gave blacks fewer days of schooling per year, fewer years, and generally lower quality instruction. Violence against blacks was greater than against white immigrants, as measured for example by the number of lynchings. Although each group was concentrated to some extent in ethnic city neighborhoods, during the first half of the twentieth century blacks went from being relatively unsegregated to highly segregated, over the same period when European immigrants experienced declining segregation. Thus, residentially, white immigrants blended into the surrounding white society, as blacks became relatively isolated from it. Labor unions discriminated against blacks. One advantage for the Europeans was that the number of immigrants was greatly reduced after the 1920s, whereas large numbers of blacks continued to move into the cities, flooding the limited opportunities and possibly causing the prejudice of established white groups to shift from European immigrants to the more visible and more obviously increasing African Americans.

Wilson, William J.
  1978 *The Declining Significance of Race: Blacks and Changing American Institutions.* Chicago: University of Chicago Press.

Wilson argues that the status of blacks in America has been shaped by the changing economic system and that recently their race has become less important in explaining their status than their socio-economic class. The end of legal discrimination against blacks has allowed many to achieve their great potential and enter the middle or even upper classes. However, a substantial number of blacks are hopelessly trapped in the underclass, so poor in opportunities that they are falling ever further behind the rest of the society.

Wilson contrasts two theories of the origins of racism: (1) the theory that the rich and powerful class instigated racism in order to split the working class and dominate it more easily; (2) the split labor market theory of Bonacich (above), in which working class whites generate racism to help them in their conflict with the ruling class. He finds that each theory explains parts of the history of anti-black racism in America, but the changing economic system frequently shifted the importance of these and other factors over the years.

Before the end of the Civil War, most American blacks were slaves under a system that denied full political rights even to many whites, and in which the legal structures that subordinated blacks were so strong that some aspects of racism, such as racist ideologies and neighborhood residential segregation, had not developed extensively. After the Civil War, southern whites of all classes adopted a variety of strategies to keep blacks down. In the North, business owners often found cheap black labor useful, but white workers were sufficiently powerful to develop racist means to preserve their interests against black competition. The story is complicated, but to a great extent the white ruling class was responsible for suppression of blacks in the Old South, whereas the white working class was responsible for racism in the North. Both of the theories involve overt class conflict. Today, the class structure continues to be responsible for the poverty of many blacks, but no longer through obvious conflict in which classes pursue their selfish economic interests by means of racism.

In the middle of the twentieth century, legal barriers to black advancement were swept away, and many talented blacks took their rightful places in the professions, public service, and business. Seeking opportunities in the industrial North, large numbers of blacks have migrated to central areas of the great northern cities. But fundamental economic and technological changes removed many of the opportunities previously enjoyed by the white working class, either shifting jobs geographically outside the central cities or requiring much higher educational credentials for employment. This transformation, combined with rapidly increasing populations of teenage African Americans, greatly magnified youth unemployment with all the social problems that naturally follow, such as poor preparation for adult jobs and crime. Large portions of many cities have fallen into a state of perpetual social and economic crisis. The jobs that are available often do not pay enough for survival, and good performance in them does not lead to better employment. Many of those who do not fall into despair turn to crime, and the result is a demoralized underclass from which few can escape.

Segregation

Suttles, Gerald D.
  1965 *The Social Order of the Slum*. Chicago: University of Chicago Press.

This book was based on nearly three years of participant observation research in a section of Chicago that Suttles calls the "Addams" area. Crowded into half a square mile, the population of twenty thousand is divided into four main ethnic groups: Italian, Mexican, African, and Puerto Rican. (Suttles used the obsolete term "Negro," but here we will use "African" to stress the comparability of all four groups.) Early in the twentieth century, the population was largely Irish, but Italians entered and gradually became dominant. Now the Italians are under great pressure from groups that have only begun to enter and from forces of development in the larger city that are beyond their control. On the west, a vast medical center cut them off from the Italian section called "Western Avenue," and on the east, a new campus of the University of Illinois was constructed despite their opposition. Mexicans and Puerto Ricans filtered in and sought an accommodation with the Italians. The Italians could not prevent construction of the Jane Addams Projects, predominantly African low-income housing that the Italians considered a direct attack by the federal government on their own way of life.

Suttles notes that people who live in a particular area need to develop a moral order, or they will fall into conflict. The Addams area was a poor slum, with the usual high rates of crime, so outsiders were suspicious of its residents. But the residents had every reason to be suspicious of each other. The chief basis of trust was close personal relationships, but far too many people lived in the area for an individual to know personally more than a tiny fraction of them. To some extent small social clubs (which outsiders considered to be gangs) provided a sense of predictability, because a resident could know what to expect from members of a club even if he or she did not know the individual members. Further coherence was provided by fairly rigid division of the population into age and sex groups. This was most clear for the Italians, among whom young men and women were strictly separated from each other to the extent that dating was practically unknown. The largest groupings were those of ethnicity and territory.

About one third of the residents of the Addams area were Italian, a quarter were Mexican, 17 percent were African, and 8 percent were Puerto Rican. Each group had its own language patterns, including special words, intonations, and gestures when speaking English. Social relations within an ethnicity were enhanced by these special understandings. Members of one ethnicity could not comprehend the speech and gesture nuances of others, and this lack of mutual comprehension was a serious handicap to social relations. For example, the Africans felt it was impolite to look directly into a stranger's face, whereas the Italians felt it was impolite not to.

The groups expressed their distinctiveness through varying clothing styles. Only an Italian man would have been seen on the streets wearing just a sleeveless undershirt above his waist, and only the Africans wore ivy league jackets. Because the housing project gave the Africans no opportunity to express their individuality through remodeling their residences, as many Italians had done, the younger Africans turned to short-lasting clothing and hairstyle fads, which only made the conservative Italians more suspicious of them. The ethnic groups differed even in the ways they moved their bodies when they walked.

The four groups competed for eleven parks and playgrounds, seven of which "belonged" to the Italians. "Peanut Park," on the boundary between Italian and African sections, was split between them. Almost all the Italians considered Our Lady of Vesuvio to be their church, and it represented them in the larger community; the other ethnic groups lacked major churches. Of the 267 businesses in the area, 107 "belonged" exclusively to one ethnic group. The proprietors of 92 of these were of the same ethnicity as their clients, and a further 15 specialized in ethnic products. These establishments supported ethnic solidarity and helped provide a sense of social order.

Although each group had prejudices toward the others, the conflict between them was not just a matter of misunderstandings. Rather, they really were in competition for economic resources and for cultural dominance. However, the separations between them, and their fear of each other, minimized direct hostilities. Overt conflict, like other forms of social interaction, took place most commonly within ethnic groups, rather than across them. A person who lacked ethnicity had no one to appeal to, and someone who had good relations with people from another ethnicity was widely suspected of being deviant in other respects as well.

The nation-wide Civil Rights movement encouraged local Africans to demonstrate for the right to use neighborhood swimming facilities. The Italians felt that these facilities "belonged" to them, although they informally permitted some Mexicans to use them so long as the Mexicans did not make an issue of their right to do so. Some Italians said they could have worked out a friendly accommodation with the Africans if the issue had not become a public dispute. Questions of justice aside, the Italians bitterly saw their loss of control over the swimming facilities as a portent of future defeats.

Events could upset the fine balance that prevented violence between the groups. Thinking they were doing a good thing, the social workers of the Chicago Youth Development Project managed to dissolve many of the African "gangs." This opened the Addams area to African gangs from the adjacent Village area, who had not worked out their relations with the three other ethnic groups. The Italians staged a dance, supposedly open to people from all groups, at a Boy's Club that "belonged" to the Africans, who considered the dance an invasion. When a fight broke out among Italians, an African gang from the Village quickly became involved, and the battle reorganized itself along ethnic lines. In retrospect, the chaotic violence that resulted from this breach in the social order of the Addams area was remembered as a "race riot."

Massey, Douglas S., and Nancy A. Denton
   1993 *American Apartheid: Segregation and the Making of the Underclass*.
      Cambridge, Massachusetts: Harvard University Press.

Massey and Denton argue that no group in the United States has been subjected to such intense and sustained residential segregation as African

Americans, and that this segregation has had dire consequences. In 1968, they note, the government commission that had examined the causes of the ghetto riots of the late 1960s had expressed great concern that the United States was dividing into "two societies, one black, one white—separate and unequal." But soon afterward the nation lost interest in the issue of racial segregation, apparently feeling that enactment of laws forbidding discrimination had solved the problem. Yet racial segregation persisted, and many black urban areas have become the home of an underclass that cannot adequately particpate in the wider economy or political system. Some writers (e.g., Oscar Lewis and Edward Banfield) believe that the underclass fails because it is gripped by a "culture of poverty" that copes with hopelessness by being undisciplined and incapable of working for a better future. Massey and Denton reject this theory that a defective culture keeps inner-city blacks poor. In contrast, they say, segregation is the root of the evil of black poverty.

Massey and Denton chart the historical development of black urban ghettos. In 1870, 80 percent of African Americans lived in the rural South, but a century later 80 percent lived in urban areas, half of them in the North. In the early stages of black migration to northern cities, African Americans lived beside whites in many neighborhoods. But as their numbers increased, whites consciously decided to segregate them. Statistics on the concentration of blacks in certain areas of several cities shows not only that such segregation increased from 1860 to 1940, but also that segregation was generally greater in the North than in the South. Between 1900 and 1930, northern blacks were frequently the targets of firebombings, assaults, and even full-fledged race riots, that drove them out of white working-class neighborhoods. During this period, owners of large businesses often tried to hire blacks in the place of striking white workers, and whether out of anger or the cool calculation that terror could drive away the black competition, white workers resorted to such violence.

Beginning in the 1930s, middle class whites resorted to less dramatic means to keep blacks from entering their neighborhoods, including "improvement associations," which employed such tactics as "restrictive covenants" contractually binding property owners from selling to blacks. In 1948 the Supreme Court declared that such covenants were unenforceable. Simultaneously, however, other branches of government were contributing to the creation of black ghettos by financing housing development only in white areas and "red-lining" black districts as undesirable for investment, setting a pattern that private banks and other investment companies soon followed. In the 1960s, educated whites superficially abandoned racially prejudiced attitudes, but discrimination against blacks merely became more subtle. The Fair Housing Act of 1968 was routinely violated by real estate agents who would fail to show housing in white areas to black clients. When courts told cities that racially segregated housing projects were wrong, they did not start locating them in white middle class neighborhoods, but simply stopped building them at all. Massey and

Denton analyze the trends in racial segregation over recent decades, and find that it may have peaked around 1960, but has declined very little since then.

Massey and Denton agree with William J. Wilson that economic changes of recent decades have undermined black urban communities, but they assert that African Americans could have coped with these challenges if they had not been concentrated in segregated neighborhoods. Illustrating their ideas with mathematical simulations, Massey and Denton show that segregation concentrates poverty in black neighborhoods, thus causing a vicious circle or downward spiral. Because the poorest residents often cannot afford to repair their houses, property values begin to fall for everyone. The lack of local wealth means the lack of local jobs, as well, and unemployment causes more unemployment. Crime escalates, conditions in the schools degenerate, and the quality of city services declines. A ghetto counterculture develops, opposed to the surrounding society, in which people are so isolated that they begin to speak a language very different from the "standard" English preferred by the dominant whites. By concentrating poverty in the ghetto, segregation creates an underclass that will be self-perpetuating until segregation itself is somehow eradicated.

SOCIETAL TRANSFORMATION

12
RELIGION

WORKS AT A GLANCE

Differences Between the Protestant and Catholic Traditions

The Diversity of Religious Denominations and Sects

The Growth and Decline of Religious Movements

The sociology of religion has a central theme, which is the emergence and social consequence of religious movements. Durkheim and Weber emphasized the differences between Protestants and Catholics, but later writers gave more attention to the myriad differences among the full range of denominations and sects. Particular religious movements have their origins in the social situations and personal needs of their founders and early generations Successful movements then evolve to serve somewhat different clienteles at the same time that they often cause changes in the social environment.

Perhaps because it states the central theme of the field compellingly, Weber's work on the Protestant ethic stands out among the classics. Gerhard Lenski and Andrew Greeley analyzed survey research data to compare Protestants with Catholics. H. Richard Niebuhr, Liston Pope, and Benton Johnson were more interested in understanding the full diversity of denominations and sects. John Lofland and Rodney Stark observed a small religious cult to develop a general theory of how religious movements recruit converts. Roger Finke collaborated with Stark in historical research on the growth and decline of religious movements.

In some respects, religion is the most sociological of topics, because it is a pure expression of social needs and communication, unrestrained by the materialistic concerns that give economics and technology greater roles in other areas of human life. But religion is clearly shaped by such external factors as social class and national culture. The view that religion is destined to die out as science advances, which was influential in social science for many decades, no longer seems convincing. We now understand that the view of religion contained in the classics was correct. Through religious movements, faith continually reinvigorates itself, having potentially profound effects on human life.

Differences Between the Protestant and Catholic Traditions

Weber, Max
  1904–1905 *The Protestant Ethic and the Spirit of Capitalism*. Translated by Talcott Parsons. New York: Scribner's [1958].

Max Weber examined the remarkable emergence of the capitalist economic system in Europe beginning during the period of the great religious reformers Martin Luther (1483–1546) and John Calvin (1509–1564). Many readers come away from this book with the impression that Weber said Protestantism was the cause of capitalism, but his claims are really more modest than that. Certain forms of Protestantism may have helped capitalism get started, but there were other factors as well, and once capitalism was well established it may not have needed the support of any particular religious doctrines. The book has been tremendously influential throughout sociology, perhaps because it made a good case for the importance of ideas and values in shaping human society, at a time when many other influential social theorists were stressing materialistic factors.

First, Weber outlines the essential features of *capitalism*. It is not simply the greedy amassing of wealth, because greed is found everywhere throughout human history. It does not involve force, as piracy does, but depends upon voluntary exchanges between people. The goal is profit for its own sake, rather than as a means to support a luxurious lifestyle. Money is invested in an enterprise, often by people who do not directly manage its affairs. Wage earners are hired to work for the enterprise, without having a stake in its ownership. The entire operation is managed rationally for pursuit of profit, using the crucially important innovation of systematic bookkeeping. Although economic systems across the continents and the centuries have possessed weak forms of some of these characteristics, fully developed capitalism is a creation of Western Europe that has now spread to its colonies, such as the United States, and thence to every corner of the globe. Weber illustrates the spirit of capitalism with extensive quotations from the American, Benjamin Franklin (1706–1790), who said,"A penny saved is a penny earned."

Then Weber describes *Protestantism*, which can partly be understood in terms of its departures from Catholicism. All religiously intense forms of Christianity stress the spiritual aspects of existence and have the tendency to downgrade the pleasures of this world. Catholicism confined the more intense forms of world-rejection to the monastery. With Protestantism, *worldly asceticism* brought the monastic spirit into the world. Thus Protestants were discouraged from wasting their wealth on pleasures. Protestantism also stressed the fulfillment of duty in worldly affairs, and it considered a person's occupation to be a sacred *calling* ordained by God. Instead of squandering their vitality and wealth on their own pleasures, Protestants invested them in their businesses, and capitalism was born.

In the course of his historical survey, Weber considers the range of different Protestant religious movements prevalent in western Europe after Luther and Calvin. He gives the greatest emphasis to Calvinism, which believed that a person's fate was predestined. Thus, nothing a person could do would save him or her from damnation, unless God determined that he or she should be saved. In its pure form, Calvinism seems ideally designed to stimulate a believer's anxieties, which might strengthen his or her tendency to invest rather than squander wealth, but not well designed to motivate a person to follow God's commandments strictly in hopes that good behavior will earn salvation. Later writers have tended to minimize the importance of Calvinism in creating the spirit of capitalism, and have used the term *Protestant ethic* to describe common values shared by most Protestant denominations.

Max Weber's study of the Protestant ethic was tremendously influential in many branches of sociology, because it seemed to show that values and beliefs could be very powerful in shaping economic behavior. If this is true, then sociology is as important as economics, a more influential and prestigious social science. However, Weber's book was a theoretical argument illustrated with historical information, not a systematic research study undertaken to test his theory. Therefore, Gerhard Lenski attracted considerable attention when he published the first serious test of Weber's theory.

Lenski, Gerhard
  1961 *The Religious Factor.* Garden City, New York: Doubleday.

In 1958, Lenski administered a specially-designed religion survey to a random sample of adults living in the Detroit area. Since 1951 an annual survey called the Detroit Area Study had acquired considerable practical experience in drawing good samples of respondents, training interviewers, and managing large sets of data. A total of 656 people filled out Lenski's long questionnaire, which included many questions about religion, attitudes toward work, and the demographic characteristics of the respondents. For most of his analysis, he divided respondents into four groups: 267 white Protestants, 230 white Catholics, 100 African-American Protestants, and 27 Jews. In a related survey, Lenski obtained comparable data from 57 white Protestant clergy and 49 white Catholic clergy.

Lenski's chief analysis compares white Protestants with white Catholics in the light of Weber's theory of the Protestant ethic. In some ways, Protestants and Catholics in Detroit seem very similar. For example, they equally value earning a good income. But Catholics were less likely than Protestants to have the characteristics needed to get good jobs. Many demanding occupations require a person to break away from family ties, and Protestants were more ready to do this than were Catholics. More firmly embedded in family and community, Catholics tended to have more children, which limited their ability to climb the ladder of success, and they tended to receive less education. Protestants valued independent thinking more than Catholics did.

One of the clearest findings of the entire study concerned the following question: "Do you feel that you have the right to question what your church teaches, or not?" Fully 89 percent of Protestant clergy said they did have this right, compared with only 20 percent of Catholic clergy. Members of the churches were similar to their clergy, with those who attended church frequently being more similar than those who did not. Many of the differences between Protestants and Catholics in Lenski's data are very small, and if he had combined whites and African Americans into a single Protestant group, it would have scarcely differed from Catholics.

Greeley, Andrew
  1989 "Protestant and Catholic: Is the Analogical Imagination Extinct?"
  American Sociological Review 54:485–502.

Greeley uses data from several nations collected by two surveys, the International Study of Values and the International Social Survey Project, to learn whether significant differences remain between Catholics and

Protestants. He hypothesized that Catholics tend to have the *analogical imagination*, whereas Protestants tend to have the *dialectical imagination*. The analogical way of thinking assumes that God is present in the world, expressing Himself through every aspect of creation, and it stresses the *community*. The dialectical imagination believes that God has largely withdrawn from the sinful world, and it stresses the *individual*. Greeley compares the responses of Catholics and Protestants to many questionnaire items. In all the nations studied, Catholics are more likely to stress fairness and equality, values that strengthen the community, whereas Protestants stress freedom and individualism. Catholics often give more emphasis to traditional family values and to being religiously devout. Protestants are more likely to want taxes reduced, to wish the government to stay out of the economy, and to oppose programs to equalize income. Thus, the results generally support Greeley's theory. Interestingly, the particular differences predicted by Durkheim (Chapter 1) and Weber (this chapter) exist only in Germany, because in other nations like the United States Protestants were not any more likely to be lonely (thus prone to suicide) and Catholics were just as likely to work hard (thus following the "Protestant ethic").

The Diversity of Religious Denominations and Sects

Niebuhr, H. Richard
1929 *The Social Sources of Denominationalism.* New York: Holt.

Like many other Christians, H. Richard Niebuhr was disturbed that so many different denominations existed, and he wanted to unify Christianity. He felt that scholarship on the history of religion in America could contribute to this goal by identifying the factors that caused all these denominations to come into existence and remain separate from each other: First, emotional religious sects appeared to serve the special needs of the poor and disinherited, whereas staid, respectable denominations cultivated the middle class. Second, different ethnic groups and immigrants from different nations tended to have their own denominations (such as Norwegian Lutherans separate from German Lutherans). Third, different regions of the country became dominated by different denominations, especially the divides between North and South or old East and frontier West. The fact that different ethnic groups settled in different regions meant that the second and third factors tended to reinforce each other. Fourth, racial divisions were important even within a single denominational tradition, with separate white and black churches. Fifth, as differences of ethnicity and region moderated, denominations often did not merge with each other as we might expect, but increased their superficial differences in beliefs and practices, so that they could justify their existence as independent organizations.

Subsequent scholars have found the greatest inspiration for sociological research in Niebuhr's theory about the transformation of intense religious sects into respectable denominations. Early in their history sects are composed of poor and suffering members who were converted to the new religious movement, and who thus may have strong emotional reasons for preferring powerful religion. When children are born to these converts, they will grow up in the sect, missing the conversion experience that was so important for their elders, and failing to possess the motivations that were behind that experience. Sects tend to regulate the behavior of their members, including avoidance of liquor and other indulgences, so an unintended result may be that the sect members become reliable workers and achieve careers that bring them prosperity and respectable status in conventional society. The second-generation and newly-prosperous members of the sect have less need for the emotionality that had originally marked the sect, and as they become educated citizens of the larger society, they come to expect their clergy to be educated as well. If this process continues for long, the former sect becomes a respectable middle-class denomination.

Pope, Liston
> 1942 *Millhands and Preachers*. New Haven, Connecticut: Yale University Press.

A nationally significant strike by workers at the Loray textile mill in Gastonia, North Carolina gave Liston Pope the opportunity to learn how different religious denominations fit into the social system of a community undergoing economic conflict. The area had always been poor, but around 1900 many residents invested their small savings to build a number of textile mills that could compete with the successful New England mills only because their wage costs were far lower. Workers came from failed farms in the hills. To avoid starvation they were willing to work fifty-five hour weeks, earning just three or four dollars a day. By the end of the 1920s, ownership of the Loray mill had passed into the hands of distant New Englanders who commanded the managers to extract more profit, which they did by making the workers operate more machines at once. Many long-time workers broke down under the stress and were forced to quit, and on April 1, 1929, the rest went out on strike, led by a team of self-professed Communists who had come to town to make Gastonia an example of worker oppression for all the world to see.

The churches had generally been in favor of the building of the mills, because the textile industry offered the entire community its best chance for prosperity. The "respectable" churches of the town were thirty-five Baptist, twenty-nine Methodist, twenty-four Presbyterian, thirteen Lutheran, and three each of the Episcopalian and Roman Catholic denominations. Many of these were subsidized directly by the mills, including the Loray Baptist Church right outside the mill gate, because the mill owners believed that church members made reliable workers. The ministers of these churches were not interested in social or political issues, and they generally believed that the workers would benefit most by humbly accepting the authority of the mill owners.

There were also fourteen houses of worship belonging to tiny sects, many of them in the emotionally intense Holiness Movement. Their emphasis on supernatural glories compensated the very poor for their deprivations, and gave them spiritual honor in place of the social status they could not achieve in the community. The hours spent in these tiny churches, singing and testifying to the power of the Lord, were among the happiest in their drab lives. The sects were not weighted down by educated clergy and trained religious support personnel, and they offered many roles and statuses for people who were nothing more than the servants of brute machines at work. The sect preachers were not oriented toward political action or labor unions, but they were poor themselves and understood the difficult lives of mill workers.

When the strike broke out, the respectable churches quickly lined up behind the mill owners to oppose it. But several of the sect preachers supported the strike, and for a few days they tried to cooperate with the Communist agitators to get a better deal for the poor, exhausted workers. In the night of June 7, the police raided the strike organizers' camp, and in the darkness someone killed police chief O. F. Aderholt. Although no one actually saw who fired the fatal shot, the top Communists were convicted of murder. (Amazingly, they were able to jump bail and escape prison.) Ella May Wiggins, a tobacco-chewing mother of five children who wrote revolutionary songs, was killed on September 14 as she was trying to lead a pro-strike demonstration. Despite several eyewitnesses, no one was ever convicted of her murder, although it seemed certain that strike-breakers for the mill were responsible. Brute force and unequal justice from police and the courts brought the strike to an end. The Loray mill instituted a new policy that no one could get a job unless he or she were a member in good standing of one of the respectable churches that were subsidized by the owners.

Pope's masterful study made the connections between religious organizations and community institutions abundantly clear. He took the abstract ideas of Weber and Niebuhr, and vividly showed how they could describe the range of religious groups in a particular community. Although small in number, the religious sects proved that they had the independence required to criticize the power structures of the society. The numerous, prosperous, respectable churches thought of themselves as defenders of the faith, but they were also defenders of the socioeconomic status quo. Pope's research convinced sociologists that class conflict is reflected in the diversity of churches and sects.

Johnson, Benton
   1963 "On Church and Sect," *American Sociological Review* 28:539–549.

Early writers like Niebuhr and Pope contrasted intense religious sects with more sedate religious organizations called churches or denominations. As the years passed sociologists had ever increasing difficulty applying this distinction to the groups they were studying, until Benton Johnson proposed a radical simplification of the terms. The original church-sect distinction came from the historical work of Max Weber and his student Ernst Troeltsch, which focused on Christian Europe before the nineteenth century. The societies considered by Weber and Troeltsch each possessed a single established religious organization with very close ties to the ruling elite, and enjoying official support from the government. For example, the Church of England was the official religious organization in England, whereas the Roman Catholic Church played that role in a number of other nations. Existing apart from the established church, in many of these societies, were a number of tiny "dissenting" religious sects, which often criticized the government and were persecuted in return, or were so thoroughly separated from the rest of the society that they had no influence. Weber, Troeltsch, and many authors who followed after them defined *church* and *sect* in terms of a large number of differences they had found between particular examples. Liston Pope listed fully twenty-one church-sect differences in his influential book. For example, a sect was interested in heaven, whereas a church was interested in this world; a sect's religious services were filled with emotional fervor, whereas those of a church were passive and restrained.

Johnson pointed out that this was an extremely confusing situation that prevented sociologists from doing clear, accurate analyses. For one thing, newer nations like the United States lacked a single established church to anchor the church side of the church-sect distinction. Another problem was that few of the groups sociologists wanted to call sects had the same characteristics as the older European groups studied by Weber and Troeltsch, and many of them were quite different from each other. To get around this problem, sociologists invented various types of sects, as many as nine in a single study, but the result was even greater confusion.

For Johnson, the only solution was to stop trying to put religious groups into categories. Instead, he proposed reconceptualizing the chief differences between religious groups in terms of how much they accepted or rejected the social environment in which they exist. At one end of this dimension would be the traditional church, which accepts the society around it. At the other end would be nontraditional sects that utterly reject the ways of the surrounding society. Between these extremes, all the other religious groups could be arranged in terms of their degree of acceptance. All the many other characteristics of sects, such as emotionality or biblical fundamentalism, could then be studied separately as variables in their own rights that might or might not correlate with the acceptance-rejection dimension.

Johnson stressed four advantages to this new approach. First, his dimension concerns not only how the religious group acts toward society, but also how society responds to it. At times, Johnson calls the dimension *tension* with the socio-cultural environment, and later writers have agreed that this tension is a two-way street in which society may accept or reject the group, just as the group judges society. Second, the dimension can be measured as finely as needed for the particular research study. When talking very generally, it is still possible to speak simply of *sects*, but when more precision is needed it will be possible to say how far out along the dimension a particular group stands. Third, the dimension allows us to compare a number of different groups in various degrees of tension with their socio-cultural environment, or even to chart the movement of a single group over time. Fourth, it becomes possible to study how a great variety of other characteristics relate to the tension of a group.

The Growth and Decline of Religious Movements

Lofland, John, and Rodney Stark
   1965 "Becoming a World-Saver: A Theory of Conversion to a Deviant Perspective," *American Sociological Review* 30:862–875.

The Lofland-Stark theoretical model of conversion was based on observational field research of the first American branch of the Unification Church, founded in Korea by Reverend Sun Myung Moon. A single woman missionary, Dr. Young Oon Kim, had brought the Unification faith to Eugene, Oregon, where with great difficulty she recruited a handful of followers and brought them down to Oakland, California.

Lofland and Stark encountered the tiny group in Oakland, and they tallied information about the members and about people they met who were interested but did not join. In many cases, they were able to write short life histories of the members, and these stories helped them identify the factors that most converts had in common. Drawing upon the sociological theories that were popular in the early 1960s, they transformed their research findings into a general model. According to Lofland and Stark, for conversion it is necessary that a person:

1. Experience enduring, acutely felt tensions
2. Within a religious problem-solving perspective,
3. Which leads him to define himself as a religious seeker;
4. Encountering the group at a turning point in his life
5. Wherein an affective bond is formed (or pre-exists) with one or more converts;
6. Where extra-cult attachments are absent or neutralized;
7. And where, if he is to become a deployable agent, he is exposed to intensive interaction.

All of the converts to the group examined by Lofland and Stark were extremely frustrated people, often poor with little education, disappointed in romance, and even emotionally disturbed. They felt that their lives should be much better than they actually were, and this long-lasting psychological tension gave them the motivation to seek a radical solution to their problems.

They tended to approach problems from a religious perspective, usually because of a strong religious upbringing. Their problems persisted despite any help they may have received from conventional churches, so they decided they needed a new and better kind of religion. Motivated by their enduring tensions, and guided by their religious problem-solving perspective, they became conscious seekers of new religious involvement. Thus, the first three steps of the Lofland-Stark model prepared them to join a new religious movement, but more was needed before they would actually convert to one.

Each of the prospective converts had reached a turning point in his or her life, a moment when old commitments and lines of action had run their course, and it was time to acquire new ones. At this susceptible point, they met the tiny Unification movement. Had they met some other group, they might have joined it, but accident linked them up with this particular one.

The last three steps of the model concern the relationships and interactions between the convert and other people, both inside and outside the group. Most importantly, the person must develop strong positive feelings (affective bonds) toward people who are already members; these emotional ties pull the person toward the group. If the person had strong bonds to people outside the group, they would pull him or her away from it. So it is also important for the person to lack such extra-cult bonds or that they be neutralized, as in the case of a German recruit who neglected to write his mother in Germany about his involvement. Finally, numerous religious meetings and social occasions with members would transform the individual into a committed member, who could be sent out as an agent to do the movement's work, including recruiting newer members.

Finke, Roger, and Rodney Stark
   1992 *The Churching of America 1776–1990*. New Brunswick, New Jersey.

Many scholars and social scientists assume that religion is slowly declining in strength in a process called *secularization*. According to them, religion is a relic of earlier centuries, destined to vanish as increasing levels of education give people the scientific knowledge to ward off superstitions. Finke and Stark argue instead that religion is a permanent feature of human society. To be sure, the richest and best-educated religious denominations may become secularized, because they are intimately connected to secular (non-religious) institutions of the society, from which they learn to doubt their traditional faith. But these fading denominations merely make room for new religious movements that can take their place. Finke and Stark apply this theoretical perspective to the history of religion in the United States.

From a variety of old records, Finke and Stark calculate that about 17 percent of Americans were members of churches in 1776. A 1980 survey of religious denominations reveals that just over two centuries later the church-member rate was about 62 percent, more than three-and-a-half times as large. Thus, the theory that American society is becoming secularized seems wrong.

At least as measured by the percentage of people who belong to churches, religion has strengthened, rather than weakened, over the years.

Finke and Stark were particularly interested in the "market share" achieved by each denomination, that is, the percent of church members who belonged to the particular group. The population grew rapidly in the nation's early decades, so most denominations gained members. But in terms of market share, three major denominations declined from 1776 to 1850: Congregationalists (from 20.4 to 4.0 percent), Episcopalians (from 15.7 to 3.5), and Presbyterians (from 19.0 to 11.6). Finke and Stark suggest that Congregationalism, especially, may have lost because it became too secular. The Episcopal church was hurt by secularization but also lost ground because it was connected to England, against which Americans fought two wars during this period. Three other denominations grew: Baptists (from 16.9 percent to 20.5), Methodists (from 2.5 to 34.2), and Catholics (from 1.8 to 13.9). Catholics increased largely through immigration, but the Baptists and Methodists grew by recruiting members.

The Baptists and Methodists were very much like religious sects, rejecting many aspects of secular society, including higher education and ostentatious wealth. Methodism arose as a movement within the Church of England. For decades after the revolution, Methodist clergy were passionately dedicated to spreading the word and converting people to a far more intense variety of Christianity than was offered in the Congregational or Episcopal churches. Precisely because they were relatively uneducated, these early Methodist clergy were close to the people, and the movement made extensive use of lay preachers and local religious organizations. Many of these Methodist clergy were *circuit riders*, men who traveled on horseback, carrying little more than a Bible in their knapsacks, taking religion into the frontier lands and establishing tiny circles of believers who quickly grew into churches.

Around the middle of the nineteenth century, Methodism compromised in many ways with the surrounding secular culture. Its clergy began getting higher educations in newly-founded Methodist seminaries, and the lay members often became prosperous leaders of their local communities. Religious fervor waned, and this religious movement moved toward low tension with the socio-cultural environment. The Baptists were similar in many ways to Methodists early in the nineteenth century, but they resisted giving their clergy secularizing educations. Consequently, during the second half of the nineteenth century the Methodists lost market share, while the Baptists gained. Part of the loss occurred in schisms as individual Methodist clergy, members, and entire congregations broke away, many of them forming new high-tension sects of the Holiness Movement that sought to regain the emphasis on supernatural gifts and experiences that the Methodists originally possessed but lost through secularization. Thus, over American history new high-tension religious movements were always ready to take the place of low-tension denominations that had become too secularized.

13
COLLECTIVE BEHAVIOR AND SOCIAL MOVEMENTS

WORKS AT A GLANCE

Panic

The Invasion from Mars by Hadley Cantril (1940)

Social Strain and Relative Deprivation

"Toward a General Theory of Revolution" by James C. Davies (1962)
Theory of Collective Behavior by Neil J. Smelser (1962)

Eclectic Approaches Emphasizing Factors Other Than Strain

Rebellion in the University by Seymour Martin Lipset (1971)
"Resource Mobilization and Social Movements" by John D. McCarthy and Mayer N. Zald (1977)
"Social Networks and Organizational Dynamics" by J. Miller McPherson, Pamela A. Popielarz, and Sonja Drobnic (1992)

Symbolic Politics

Symbolic Crusade: Status Politics and the American Temperance Movement by Joseph Gusfield (1966)

In collective behavior, individuals influence each other informally to engage in roughly the same unconventional behavior. Panic is one category of collective behavior; others are crazes and riots. Social movements are relatively organized attempts to change a significant aspect of society, or to prevent such change. Some authors consider social movements to be a category of collective behavior, and all the authors discussed here consider these forms of social action to be intimately connected. A key issue for theorists in this area is the extent to which collective behavior and social movements are simply mass attempts to solve problems of relative deprivation shared by participants.

In 1938, some radio listeners in the United States got the false impression that their country was being invaded, and Hadley Cantril studied the panic that followed. Theorists such as James Davies and Neil Smelser believe that panic, revolutions, and other forms of collective behavior typically result from relative deprivation and structural strain. Seymour Martin Lipset, John McCarthy, and Mayer Zald believe that other factors are often more important. Miller McPherson, Pamela Popielarz, and Sonja Drobnic consider the ways that social networks shape recruitment and defection to voluntary organizations. Social movements are change-oriented voluntary organizations that compete for members with other groups. Many sociologists agree that generalized beliefs or ideology are important, but Joseph Gusfield has argued that the beliefs underlying a social movement need not be factually correct but might serve a variety of symbolic functions for the believers.

Many sociologists, like Davies and to some extent Gusfield, believe that social movements or instances of collective behavior have relatively simple causes that can be understood through a single factor, usually some form of deprivation or loss. Others, such as Cantril, Lipset, McCarthy, and Zald, believe that a number of factors are at work, each of which must be examined in turn. Still others, notably Smelser, construct elaborate systems that attempt to fit many causes into a single theoretical system.

Panic

Cantril, Hadley
   1940 *The Invasion from Mars*. Princeton, New Jersey: Princeton University
   Press.

On October 30, 1938, the night before Halloween, the Mercury Theatre radio program broadcast a dramatization of *The War of the Worlds*, by British writer H. G. Wells. The program began as if it were a musical evening with Ramon Raquello's orchestra in a New York hotel, when news bulletins interrupted to report that a strange meteorite had struck New Jersey. A few minutes later, the music was replaced by eyewitness observations of the object itself, an immense, yellowish-white cylinder that had blasted a crater in a nearby farm. Soon, war machines emerged from it and began annihilating the United States Army. The public was relatively unfamiliar with science fiction stories at that point in history, and many took the realistic drama for actual news reports. Many thousands of people were frightened by the program, and some panicked.

A group of sociologists, including Hadley Cantril, had been working on a major study of the effect of radio, funded by the Rockefeller Foundation. Quickly securing supplementary grants, they were able to launch a sudden research study. Cantril's team interviewed 135 people who had been frightened, collected newspaper stories, administered surveys, and analyzed polls conducted by other organizations. An estimated 6,000,000 people heard the broadcast; 1,700,000 of them thought it was factual news, and 1,200,000 were frightened or disturbed. It did not take many of these people to flood the telephone switchboards of police and radio stations with worried calls.

Among the factors that encouraged listeners to believe that Martians were actually attacking the earth were the realism of the program itself, the fact that radio had become a standard medium for important announcements, the apparent prestige of the speakers who included expert astronomers, the ease of visualizing specific incidents, the realistically baffled behavior of radio characters themselves, and the unified quality of the total experience. Many listeners tuned in late, and others tuned in only because friends who were worried by the broadcast telephoned them. These people missed the beginning of the program when it was clearly labeled a fiction drama.

Questionnaires and interviews allowed Cantril to investigate how listeners had tried to verify the impressions they got from the program. Some checked internal evidence from the broadcast against things they already knew. For example, a few had read the first science fiction magazine, *Amazing Stories*, and recognized the style. Or they noticed that events in the story were moving unrealistically fast. Some others checked external evidence, for example turning to other stations on the radio or checking the program listing in the newspaper. A number of listeners tried to check external evidence but failed for some reason. One person looked out the window and saw a strange greenish glow on the horizon. Failure to reach parents on the telephone was taken as evidence they had been destroyed. A street full of cars was seen as proof that people were fleeing, and an empty street was seen as evidence the way had been blocked so they could not flee. Other listeners were so confused they didn't even try to check the truth of the invasion report.

People who failed to verify the report tended to be more frightened than those who did so. Listeners with less education and relatively poor people were more likely to panic and less likely to use effective means for testing the veracity of the report. Cantril argued that some people have more critical ability than others, whereas some are especially suggestible or anxious. If two or more people listened to the program together, or if friends called each other on the phone, one person's reaction would be influenced by those of the others. Some listeners perceived themselves to be relatively safe for the time being, for example, those distant from the supposed invasion point in New Jersey.

The Martian invasion panic was greatly stimulated by the fact that the world really was in great danger at that point in history. Hitler had taken Austria and was in the process of seizing part of Czechoslovakia. Less than a year later, the Second World War would break out in Europe, and most people already sensed it coming. A decade into the Great Depression, many people had good reason to be terrified about their economic futures, and it seemed that social norms were disintegrating around them. Listeners had become used to hearing alarming news reports on the radio, and it seemed plausible that a new horror could erupt at any moment.

Social Strain and Relative Deprivation

Davies, James C.
  1962 "Toward a General Theory of Revolution," *American Sociological Review* 27:5–19.

Davies argues that revolutions are caused by the extreme dissatisfaction of many people, but certain circumstances are far more favorable to their occurrence than others. When people are extremely poor and miserable they typically do not start revolutions, because they must devote all their energies simply to surviving. When people are poor and have little political power they are not likely to rebel if conditions are gradually improving, because they have hope. Revolution is most likely to occur when "a prolonged period of objective economic and social development is followed by a short period of sharp reversal."

Davies distinguishes a person's *actual need satisfaction* (what the person actually gets in life) from his or her *expected need satisfaction* (what the person wants and feels he or she deserves). During times of progress, people come to expect more in the future than they have at present. If the progress continues for a long time, people will adjust to ever greater opportunities. Then, if progress ends and conditions deteriorate, people will become extremely dissatisfied. Expected need satisfaction will continue to rise, as actual need satisfaction falls, so the gap between the two will grow to an intolerable degree and produce a revolution. Davies offers several examples from history, beginning with Dorr's Rebellion and the Russian Revolution.

In the early decades of the nineteenth century, Rhode Island developed along a somewhat different path from the neighboring New England states. The growth of textile factories drew whole families to give up farming in Rhode Island, whereas in Massachusetts many families kept their farms and only the wives and daughters took factory jobs. This meant Rhode Island workers were more vulnerable to economic depressions. Originally, only a very small fraction of the men were allowed to vote in elections, and suffrage (the right to vote) grew more slowly in Rhode Island than elsewhere. (Women were excluded from the vote in most parts of the United States for many decades.) In 1840, 17 percent of the national population voted (not counting slaves), compared with only 8 percent in Rhode Island. But conditions improved until a severe economic slump started in 1835. Independent suffrage associations met in 1841, without the approval of the state government, enacted a new constitution, and held an unofficial election in which all men could vote. On May 17, 1842, the People's Legislature tried to take over a state arsenal, and the months of violence called Dorr's Rebellion broke out. By January 1843, the rebellion had been suppressed, but the official legislature compromised and gave all men the right to vote.

Russia was slower than many other European nations to industrialize and to develop democratic institutions. After increasing unrest, the serfs (oppressed peasant farmers) were emancipated in 1861, and higher wages in factories drew many to the cities. Reforms in the judicial system reduced the grinding injustice of earlier years, and economic conditions improved for many people. War with Japan, beginning in 1904, caused an economic recession that led to abortive rebellion in 1905 and to increased political repression. A moderate economic recovery ended when war broke out with Germany in 1914 and was followed by extreme suffering. Having been defeated earlier by Japan, Russia was in the process of being defeated by Germany when full-scale revolution broke out in 1917. The catastrophic result was the establishment of the Soviet Union, which lasted for more than seventy years.

Davies argues that in both Rhode Island and Russia, the rebellion occurred only after a period of progress had ended in an economic and political retreat in which people's rising expectations were severely frustrated by a fall in the actual satisfaction of their needs.

Smelser, Neil J.
1962 *Theory of Collective Behavior.* New York: Free Press.

Smelser was a disciple and collaborator of Talcott Parsons (Chapter 1), and this book is the most complex influential example of structural-functionalism. Like Robert K. Merton's work on anomie (Chapter 5), it stresses the importance of strain between different elements of the culture in motivating unconventional behavior, and it conceptualizes culture in terms of a more-or-less unified structure composed of such elements as norms and values. This book offers very complicated charts of concepts arranged in hierarchies, and then uses them to map the processes by which various kinds of collective behavior and social movements arise. Central to Smelser's view of society are four components of social action:

1. **Values** are the goals that guide social action. They are the most general

component of social action, and they unify the society.

2. **Norms** are rules that define how the values are to be realized. More specific than values, they range from formal regulations to unconscious understandings about proper behavior held by members of the group.
3. **Mobilization of motivation into organized action** means elements of the culture that define the roles and the clusters of roles that are societal institutions. Here Smelser places families, churches, corporations, and other institutions, plus the reward structures that cause individuals to play the roles that these institutions require.
4. **Situational facilities** are the most specific component of social action, consisting of the resources and barriers that assist people in attaining their goals or prevent goal attainment. Many of these are mental, such as the practical knowledge that people may possess, whereas others are physical, such as the tools required to do a particular job.

These four components of social action form a hierarchy, from most general (values) to least general (facilities). Smelser illustrates this conceptualization by stating that American education is based on the value of free public schooling, supported by norms that all children of certain ages may attend school, where people playing roles of teachers and pupils are organized in particular settings, and such facilities as books and techniques of instruction are available. In addition, he identifies seven levels of specificity within each of these four, creating a complex intellectual structure of twenty-eight categories. He says the hierarchy functions as a system, and redefining any component requires redefining all the components below it, but not those above it.

Smelser defines collective behavior as "mobilization on the basis of a belief which redefines social action" (p. 8). *Mobilization* is the process by which the actions of a large number of people come to be coordinated so that many are doing essentially the same thing or seeking the same goals. The model of how mobilization takes place has six steps:

1. **Structural conduciveness.** A particular kind of collective behavior cannot take place without certain preconditions that permit it. For example, financial panics cannot occur in societies that lack financial markets.
2. **Structural strain.** This is not merely frustration felt by many people, but impairment in the relations between the components of action as they are organized in the society, so that parts of the culture fail to function properly. The existence of a class of poor and oppressed people, who are denied the full benefits of citizenship even when they obey society's norms, is an example of strain.
3. **Generalized belief.** This is an ideology that identifies the source of the strain and says what to do about it. For instance, religious revival has been presented as the solution for many different problems.
4. **Precipitating factors.** These are dramatic events, unimportant in themselves, that trigger action based on the generalized belief. A random fist fight between two individuals might touch off a riot.

5. **Mobilization of participants.** Communication brings many people to-gether to find a solution to their common problem. The growth of local civil rights organizations, recruitment of members, and coordination of activities across a wide geographic area is an example of successful mobilization.
6. **Social control.** The institutions of society may work against mobiliza-tion at any point in this chain, most obviously at the end when forces opposed to an emerging social movement respond to it. The govern-ment might attempt to improve the political or economic conditions of deprived groups, or it might send military forces to suppress their rebellion.

For a full-blown case of collective behavior to arise, each of these six de-terminants of collective behavior must be favorable. Smelser argues that they become important in roughly the order he numbers them, from structural con-duciveness to social control. Thus his theory is a *value-added* model. This is a term from economics that describes a process in which each step adds to the effect of the ones that came before, in a set sequence. To make an auto-mobile fender, iron is dug from a mine, refined and made into steel sheets that are stamped into shape, attached to the other parts of the car body, then painted. It does no good to paint the iron ore right when it comes out of the ground; each step must come only after the earlier steps have made their con-tribution.

Often collective behavior involves what Smelser calls *short-circuiting*. This is a kind of error, in which people respond to a problem with a lower-level component of social action by jumping to a higher component and assuming that redefining it in terms of a new generalized belief will solve the problem at the lower level. The illustration Smelser gives is the "Sputnik" panic in the late 1950s, when the United States was jolted by the Soviet Union's launch of the world's first artificial satellite. When Smelser wrote, the full facts of this episode had not yet come out, and it was still believed that the United States was incapable of launching satellites in 1957, and that the Soviet Union was technologically more advanced. In fact, the American technology was already superior, but different political decisions had been made in the two countries about the priorities for military rocketry. In any case, the launch of Sputnik I precipitated a kind of panic, in which Americans responded in a short-circuited manner, blaming alleged inferiority of the educational system or of the institutions of science, and responding to this generalized belief by pour-ing resources into education and setting up a well-funded space agency.

Much of Smelser's analysis focuses on the development of generalized be-liefs, and he argues that five different kinds of belief produce the five princi-pal forms of collective behavior. *Hysteria* defines an ambiguous situation as extremely dangerous, thus triggering panic in which people rush away from the threat. *Wish-fulfillment* makes people think they can gain their heart's desire through rushing toward something in a craze or fad. *Hostility* focuses people's intense dissatisfaction on a particular target, causing a hostile out-burst or riot against that target. *Norm-oriented beliefs* convince people that some set of societal rules needs to be changed, thus creating a norm-oriented social movement. *Value-oriented beliefs* produce the form of collective be-havior with the most general aims, social movements that seek to reconstitute the fundamental value structure of the society. Published at a time when struc-tural-functionalism was about to lose its preeminence in sociology, Smelser's *Theory of Collective Behavior* summed up decades of work by other people in a complex intellectual structure that was the epitome of functionalist thought.

Eclectic Approaches Emphasizing Factors Other Than Strain

Lipset, Seymour Martin
 1971 *Rebellion in the University*. Boston: Little, Brown.

Beginning at the University of California at Berkeley in the academic year 1964–1965, a wave of student rebellion swept American college campuses, abating in the early 1970s. Students rallied, published radical literature, staged sit-ins, and seized administration buildings. At the peak of this revolt, some of the nation's leading universities were paralyzed: Columbia in 1968, Harvard in 1969, and the University of California at Santa Barbara in 1970. Among its fea-tures were opposition to the Vietnam War, which was then in progress, and experimentation with free sex and drug use. Many alternative explanations have been offered for this striking period of youth revolt, and Lipset employs both questionnaire survey data and historical studies to understand its sources.

Some commentators blamed the uprising on opposition to the Vietnam War. This opposition intensified soon after the military draft was tightened on seniors and graduate students in 1967–1968. Others cited disappointment over the meager results of the Civil Rights Movement. Still others blamed the per-missiveness of child rearing philosophies followed by parents in the late 1950s and early 1960s, who presumably failed to give their offspring discipline or re-spect for authorities.

The rebels criticized the universities, saying that college administrators de-nied students their rights and that the teachers devoted their time to research for the military and big corporations rather than to teaching. However, opin-ion poll data showed that most students were satisfied with their educational institutions and that dissatisfaction had not increased prior to the student re-bellion. The polls also showed that the students dissatisfied with their schools were also dissatisfied with the nation, so apparently the criticism came largely from a group of youths who were generally disaffected with American insti-tutions rather than being the result of unusual strains objectively experienced by students at the time.

Problems with all explanations that stress particular historical conditions are that rebellion has been common at American universities since the birth of the nation, that many previous wars had also been unpopular, and that comparable youth rebellions occurred in many nations not involved in Vietnam. Serious but non-political student rebellions took place at Harvard in 1790, 1807, and 1830. The University of Wisconsin has been a hotbed of left-wing politics since before World War I, and Berkeley is set in a community that has been among the most liberal since the beginning of the twentieth century. Lipset believes that traditional American culture began to unravel in the 1920s, and the collapse of the 1920s' counterculture during the Great Depression drew many young people toward leftist politics. World War II and the early years of the Cold War with the Soviet Union suppressed radical political activity, but it was only a matter of time before it would reappear, which it did in the sixties.

The popular press often portrayed the 1960s rebellion as a "generation gap," suggesting that young people were at odds with their parents. However, the majority of college youth were conservative or moderate, and only small numbers were deeply involved in the counterculture. The student rebels tended to be the children of liberal or even radical parents, many of whom had been involved in the political radicalism of the 1930s. Lipset argues that leftist politics thrives among affluent, well-educated people engaged in intellectual or welfare occupations, and their children carry on the family political traditions when they go to college. To some extent the student rebels blamed their parents for being hypocrites, espousing the same political values but failing to act upon them. Compared with other decades, the connection between youth movements and adult political organizations was weak during the sixties, and the young radicals sensed they had to make the revolution on their own.

The student rebels appeared to be more intelligent and academically able than non-rebels, but this is chiefly because the revolt tended to be concentrated at elite universities where most of the students had these qualities. Within these universities, conservative or professionally-oriented student leaders tend to have grades just as high as those of the leftist leaders. Lipset argues that most radical movements find their first recruits among the privileged classes, whose prosperity allows them the luxury of exploring new cultural trends, and only later attract people from the deprived classes that more logically ought to support them.

To some extent the youth rebellion of the 1960s was so impressive simply because at that time so many more young people were in college than ever before. Gradual cultural changes had been taking the nation away from the proverbial Protestant ethic for decades, and the prosperity and mass media of the sixties intensified the trend. The Vietnam War added a focus for discontent, which allowed the hard-core radicals to recruit more widely throughout the student body, but as the United States withdrew from the conflict this focus for radicalism faded. Ironically, one of the results of the episode was that faculty at many institutions were given lighter teaching loads, thus giving students less to be satisfied about.

McCarthy, John D., and Mayer N. Zald
  1977 "Resource Mobilization and Social Movements: A Partial Theory,"
  American Journal of Sociology 82:1212–1241.

McCarthy and Zald say that the dominant theories of social movements have been wrong to stress the frustrating deprivations experienced by people who feel they have legitimate grievances. Rather, they say, there are always many discontented people in society, far more than required to explain the existing social movements. When movements do arise they often seem unrelated to any increase in discontent, and many participants do not, in fact, suffer from relative deprivation. McCarthy and Zald say that sociologists would do better to examine the factors and processes that allow social movements to become organized, especially the ways that successful movements exploit resources in their social environment.

A newer perspective on social movements, called the *resource mobilization perspective,* stresses five areas of research:

1. How does a social movement bring together the money and labor needed for success?
2. What are the characteristics of the formal organizations that constitute the core of a successful movement?
3. What roles are played by individuals and organizations outside the movement itself?
4. How can we model the flow of resources toward or away from the movement?
5. How do rewards and costs explain the actions of individuals and organizations with respect to the movement?

McCarthy and Zald recognize that various degrees or levels of organization can exist. They use the basic term *social movement* for a set of change-oriented beliefs that some members of the population possess. Often, an opposing set of beliefs arises against a social movement, and they call this a *countermovement.* A *social movement organization* is a formally structured part of a movement or countermovement, often legally incorporated with a standard name and a headquarters office. All such organizations working for the goals of a particular social movement constitute a *social movement industry.* For example, the Civil Rights Movement has consisted of a number of formal organizations, plus a considerable number of individuals who share its general aims. From this general perspective, sociologists can develop many specific hypotheses and conduct studies that examine factors beyond mere relative deprivation in understanding how social movements arise and develop toward failure or success.

McPherson, J. Miller, Pamela A. Popielarz, and Sonja Drobnic
1992 "Social Networks and Organizational Dynamics," *American Sociological Review* 57:153–170.

McPherson, Popielarz, and Drobnic administered a survey to 1,050 adults living in ten Nebraska communities, asking them to say when they joined or left any voluntary organizations during their lives and inquiring about their social relations. A group cannot recruit new members unless current members develop social relationships with outsiders, yet those relationships can also pull members out. McPherson, Popielarz, and Drobnic suggest that strong ties between members stabilize a group, but weak ties to outsiders destabilize it (see Granovetter in Chapter 3). A tie between two people is strong if they see each other often, if they share a number of friends, and if they are similar in age, education, and other personal characteristics. Results confirmed the importance of social relationships for voluntary organizations. The more friends a person has within a group, the longer he or she is likely to remain a member. In contrast, ties to people outside a group reduce the time a person will remain a member. Weak ties to outsiders are more disruptive than strong ties, because a weak tie is more likely to put the person into contact with competing voluntary organizations that might recruit him or her. Weak ties form bridges to very different parts of the larger community, thus opening up the individual's social world.

Symbolic Politics

Gusfield, Joseph
1966 *Symbolic Crusade: Status Politics and the American Temperance Movement*. Urbana: University of Illinois Press.

Compared with Europe, the United States has been relatively free of sharp class divisions and conflict. Gusfield says that moral issues have therefore often taken the role that economic issues might have played. A cultural group can promote the prestige and power of its way of life through moral reform crusades that push its values ahead of those of competing groups. Drinking of alcohol, versus abstinence, was a distinguishing mark of competing ethnic groups. Alcohol policy has therefore become a weapon in the cultural and economic struggles that rage beneath the relatively quiet surface of American society.

Gusfield draws a distinction between class politics and status politics. *Class politics* is based on rational calculation of the group's economic interests, and it promotes policies that are designed to improve the group's material position in society. *Status politics* is concerned with the prestige of the group in society, using political processes symbolically to enhance the honor of the group. Sometimes the same policy may serve both of these purposes, but often a particular effort in status politics may serve the prestige of two or more groups whose economic interests are quite different. At the same time, a single group's needs for material benefit and symbolic prestige may generate conflicting political agendas.

Rural, native-born Protestants in nineteenth-century America respected temperance, and their culture stressed the values of self-control and hard work. The changing economic system and an influx of immigrants transformed society and threatened the dominant groups. Catholic immigrants especially came from societies where alcohol was an accepted part of social life, so alcohol came to represent conflict between Protestants and Catholics. New England aristocrats saw their power slipping in the 1840s, and they emphasized temperance among a number of issues that symbolically defended their status. Lower-status Protestant groups adopted the declining aristocracy's values as a way of increasing their own prestige. By the mid-1870s, women were gaining status by taking leadership roles in the temperance crusade. Gusfield employs a variety of kinds of historical data, such as prohibition voting statistics, to support his thesis that the temperance movement was not a reaction to objective problems caused by alcohol, but instead was a symbolic attempt to preserve or gain social status.

14
POLITICAL SOCIOLOGY

WORKS AT A GLANCE

Democratic Political Institutions

Political Man by Seymour Martin Lipset (1960)

Partisans and Parties

Power and Discontent by William A. Gamson (1968)
The Party Network: The Robust Organization of Illinois Republicans
by Mildred A. Schwartz (1990)

Revolutions

Revolution and Rebellion in the Early Modern World
by Jack A. Goldstone (1991)
"Ideology as Episodic Discourse: The Case of the Iranian Revolution"
by Mansoor Moaddel (1992)

Political sociology is an interdisciplinary field that overlaps some of the territory of political science but is rooted in such central areas of sociology as stratification, organizations, and social movements. It differs from the sociology of collective behavior by focusing on relatively stable political institutions and upon such regularized political processes as elections. But political sociology draws heavily upon insights from the study of collective behavior in understanding those great transformations of the political realm known as revolutions and the ways that political institutions are challenged by mass rebellions.

Perhaps the central question of political sociology is how social conflict can be expressed through democratic institutions, and this is the issue that Seymour Martin Lipset addressed in many of his essays. William Gamson has explored the ways that political power and popular discontent interact to produce public decisions. Mildred Schwartz applied organizational theory and network analysis to the Illinois Republican Party, concluding that it was a robust organization capable of surviving defeat and innovating in pursuit of victory. The most extreme and often decisive political processes are revolutions. Jack Goldstone argues that a revolution does not succeed unless the government is already weakened by crisis, and Mansoor Moaddel shows that revolutionary ideology grows from political discourse during episodes of conflict.

Thus, political sociology concerns itself with the mechanisms that cause both stability or instability in the system that allocates positions of authority in the government and that determines what decisions government leaders will make. Political leaders depend upon the support of constituencies. Partisans within constituencies form interest groups that seek to select leaders and to influence them once they are in office. Under extreme circumstances, the government can become weak enough, with a factionalized elite and dissatisfied populace, that political revolution can succeed in toppling it. All political processes are shaped by ideology.

Democratic Political Institutions

Lipset, Seymour Martin
  1960 *Political Man*. Garden City, New York: Doubleday.

This is a series of essays, drawing upon data from many studies, about the social conditions that favor democracy. Lipset conceptualizes his topic as follows: "Democracy in a complex society may be defined as a political system which supplies regular constitutional opportunities for changing the government officials, and a social mechanism which permits the largest possible part of the population to influence major decisions by choosing among contenders for political office" (p. 45). He also phrases the central question of his book in terms of social stability: "How can a society face continuous conflict among its members and groups and still maintain social cohesion and the legitimacy of state authority?" (p. 22). Thus, democracy is a political system that manages conflict by involving most of the population in the decision process in a manner that convinces them to accept decisions that do not always favor their individual or group interests.

"Economic Development and Democracy" documents the fact that prosperity is more favorable to democratic institutions than is poverty. Lipset examines the recent political histories of European, Latin American, and English-speaking nations, showing that the more democratic nations have higher per capita incomes, are more urban, and proportional to population have more doctors, cars, telephones, radios, and copies of newspapers. Importantly, nations in which the people are more educated are likely to be democratic. Education may be more important than wealth, because it instills the knowledge and flexibility of mind that are necessary for democracy. Economic hardship logically increases the strength of radical, anti-democratic dissatisfaction, whereas national prosperity increases the security and thus the patience even of those who have less than the average share of wealth. In addition, the gap between rich and poor may be narrower in the most prosperous and democratic nations.

"Social Conflict, Legitimacy, and Democracy" examines how groups can be made to feel that existing political institutions are the best ones for the society, even if particular leaders and decisions may be wrong. Legitimacy is absolutely crucial during the period when a society is only just developing democratic institutions. A crisis of legitimacy can occur if the status of major traditional institutions is threatened, or if major societal groups are excluded from the political process. Thus legitimacy requires a fine balance between conservative and liberal forces. Lipset argues that some nations facilitated this transformation by preserving their monarchies, thus maintaining the loyalty of traditionalist groups even as the political process was gradually opened up to groups that previously had been excluded. Nations differed in how effectively they managed the entry of industrial workers into the political process. Britain did a better job than Germany, with resultingly greater political radicalism in Germany. Three major issues have posed a challenge to political legitimacy in Western nations: (1) deciding the proper role of the church in public affairs, (2) admission of lower strata such as industrial workers to full economic citizenship, and (3) determining how the national income will be distributed across social classes.

"Working-class Authoritarianism" asserts that members of the working class tend to have a rigid and intolerant orientation toward political issues. Because of their lower level of education, working class people tend to see complex political debates in simplistic terms of good and evil. Therefore, they have often supported extremist movements that were not healthy for democracy. Lipset offers data from opinion polls in many nations illustrating this claim. Psychological explanations suggest that the limitations and stresses of working-class childhood produce adults who lack confidence and habitually submit to authority, at the same time that they are isolated from the ideas and organizations of democratic society. This essay has been the focus of tremendous debate over the years, and subsequent studies have both supported and undercut its argument.

"Elections: The Expression of the Democratic Class Struggle" notes that political parties tend to represent the interests of economic classes, and that stable democracies thus manage competition between the classes peacefully in continual election campaigns that tilt the balance back and forth between the major classes. In industrial societies, the chief party division is between those that represent the lower classes and those that represent the middle and upper classes. Lipset notes that there can be exceptions to this rule, and economic class is not the only social cleavage in modern society. But poll data from many nations support the theory that major parties are chiefly class based. In Britain, the Labour Party obtains its chief support from the lower classes, and the Conservative Party, from the middle and upper classes. In the United States, despite the relatively blurred class lines, the Democratic Party is more strongly connected to the lower classes, and the Republican Party, to the upper classes.

"American Intellectuals: Their Politics and Status" examines the paradox that leftist politics is especially strong among groups that seem to do well in the American economic system: scholars, artists, philosophers, authors, and journalists. Lipset considers several possible explanations. Creative artists reject the idea that their art can be judged entirely in terms of its dollar value in the market, and thus they tend to reject the values of business. Never having had an entrenched aristocracy, America lacks a really conservative cultural tradition that might be the ideological home for many intellectuals. The very fact that intellectuals create new concepts and images sets them in opposition to tradition. And despite the fact that university professors and many other intellectuals are well paid, they tend to feel unappreciated by society, so they scorn it. Lipset suggests that one source of this unjustified sense of being an underprivileged group is that many intellectuals suffered rejection by their high school classmates, and they have never quite gotten over this painful adolescent experience.

Partisans and Parties

Gamson, William A.
  1968 *Power and Discontent.* Homewood, Illinois: Dorsey.

This work of theory integrates two perspectives on how political power and popular discontent interact to produce public decisions. The *influence perspective* sees politics as a conflict in which interest groups and political parties seek to shape the outcomes not only of elections but also of government decision-making processes. The *social control perspective* focuses instead on how government leadership operates to achieve the goals of society most efficiently at the least cost to the leaders themselves.

Gamson uses the term *authorities* for government officials who make binding decisions on behalf of the society, and *partisans* for members of the public who are affected by these decisions and may seek to influence them. Partisans may be considered a *constituency* for a particular policy and they often form *interest groups* with varying degrees of *solidarity*. Several factors can promote solidarity for an interest group, including symbolic expressions such as a special name or slogan, being treated as a group by non-members, having a high rate of social interaction among members, and possessing a common style of life, norms, and values.

In Gamson's analysis, a crucial dimension is the degree of *trust* a particular group of partisans has in government leaders. Related to trust is the degree of *efficacy* the partisans feel, which is their perception that they can influence the decisions of government leaders. People who have little trust and little feeling of efficacy are *alienated*. Trust is a major source of power for government leaders, and the loss of trust can be disastrous. Gamson offers the example of President Lyndon Johnson, who was widely trusted in the summer of 1964 when he used a naval incident that occurred in the Gulf of Tonkin to increase American involvement in the Vietnam War. However, the bloody toll of this war, and Johnson's apparent inability to bring it to an end, eroded public trust severely, so that in 1967 he was unable to get the Congress to support his policies in Latin America. When trust is lost, it is hard for a leader to take decisive actions that might restore it, and Johnson was forced to decide against seeking re-election.

It is not easy to define political influence. Suppose a unified partisan group loudly demands the government take a particular action, and it does. We cannot easily be sure whether the group's influence made the government take that action, or whether it might have adopted the same policy even without the noisy partisan group. Gamson uses two probabilities, P_a and P_b, to define influence. The first, P_a, is the probability the government will take an action that is preferred by a particular partisan group, after the group has attempted to exert influence. The second, P_b, is the probability that the government will take that action, even if the group does nothing. A partisan group can be said to have influence if and only if P_a is different from P_b.

However, influence situations can often be extremely complicated. For example, a civil rights group might want a city to adopt an open housing ordinance, but a neighborhood group might not want this. The civil rights group begins to agitate for open housing, but this action causes a reaction from the neighborhood group, who then begin agitating against the ordinance. Before both groups started up, the chance that the ordinance might be passed could be 60 percent, and after both groups were in action the probability might still be 60 percent. Even though the civil rights group might get its preferred outcome, its actual influence on the decision could have been completely counterbalanced by the influence of the neighborhood group. Thus, influence is a difficult concept to use. It is important, however, so Gamson devotes several sections of his book to consideration of what influence means and how it can be measured.

Gamson suggests three kinds of influence a partisan group can exert: constraints, inducements, and persuasion. *Constraints* are disadvantages the group can cause the authorities, or the threat of such punishment if the authorities do not do what the partisans want. *Inducements* are advantages the partisans can give the authorities, ways the partisans can reward the authorities if they do what the partisans want. *Persuasion* consists of arguments that convince authorities that the partisan's preferred decisions are best, or of other factors such as trust in the partisans' judgment that convince the authorities to take action preferred by the partisans. A partisan group's capacity to use constraints and inducements depends on the variety of resources it may possess, from money to the numbers of votes it can cast in elections to its ability to cause trouble through political demonstrations.

Authorities have several potential responses to discontent. If partisans are discontented but lack resources, or have resources but are relatively content, the authorities can probably ignore them. Otherwise, the authorities may have to accept influence and do what the partisans want. But there are other options if the cost of the action to the authorities would be high. Social control may resist the partisans's influence by keeping partisans out of the society or the organization, by blocking partisans's access to the government and insulating authorities from their attempts at influence, by imposing sanctions on the partisans (which under extreme circumstances may even mean killing them), by persuading them to give up their desires, or by coopting partisans's leaders and granting just enough of the partisans's wishes to take the steam out of their crusade without in fact giving them all they want.

Gamson believes it is often possible to predict which kind of influence a partisan group will attempt to use. A group that trusts the authorities will attempt to influence them chiefly by persuasion, because it thinks authorities are committed to the same goals as the group and merely needs to be shown the right way of achieving them. A group that is neutral in its degree of trust will emphasize inducements, appealing to the self interests of the authorities by offering them rewards for making the decisions the group prefers. And a group that is thoroughly alienated from the authorities will resort to constraints, believing that only threats can prevent the authorities from going against the group's preferences. In return, authorities will use persuasion to control groups that trust the authorities and use inducements and sanctions to control neutral groups. Authorities will try to insulate themselves from highly alienated groups in the belief there is no way to change their attitudes. Because there are many potential interest groups in society, and many issues that government must deal with, Gamson's theory describes a constantly-shifting set of influences and attempts at social control, a dynamic interplay between partisans and authorities.

Schwartz, Mildred A.
  1990 *The Party Network: The Robust Organization of Illinois Republicans.*
  Madison: University of Wisconsin Press.

Schwartz studied the Illinois Republican Party from the standpoint of organizational sociology, chiefly by means of extensive interviews with two hundred individuals holding a variety of positions in the party, supplemented with published information, documents from the state party headquarters, plus observation of campaign rallies and a state convention.

Political parties have been defined in a number of ways. For example, a party has been described as a group that seeks to elect people to public office under a particular label (such as "Republican"), regardless of how well or poorly organized the group is. Schwartz conceptualizes organization chiefly in terms of the network of links between individuals and positions that forms the social structure of the party. In the abstract she refers to *party actors,* whether they are individuals or organizational subunits such as a committee, and examines the ways that party actors of different kinds are linked by relatively stable patterns of interaction. Thus, she defines a political party as a network of "individual or collective units sharing a party name whose activities have some recognizable partisan purpose" (p. 11). The nucleus of party existence is the collective effort to capture a single public office. The chief theoretical problem for the sociology of parties is how attempts to capture different offices will link up into a widespread effort to place members of the party into many offices. Schwartz argues that the Illinois Republican Party is an exceedingly robust organization, capable of surviving electoral defeat and possessing considerable stamina for constant political struggle despite the precariousness of political leadership.

Party actors include Republican incumbents of elective office, members of party committees (both local and national to the extent that they work for the success of the state organization), and other groups that contribute to the party regularly and significantly influence it. Schwartz studied twenty-three kinds of party actor: U.S. senator, U.S. congressman, governor, constitutional officer (such as state attorney general or treasurer), state senate leader, state senator, state house leader, state representative, local officeholder, Republican National Committee member, national committeeman, State Central Committee (including staff as well as members), state central committeeman, county chairman, local committeeman, Republican Senate Campaign Committee, Republican Congressional Campaign Committee, State Senate Campaign Committee, State House Campaign Committee, United Republican Fund, interest group, advisor, and financial contributor.

Schwartz collected data on which of these actors interacted regularly with each other, and analyzed these data using a technique called *block modeling,* which identified blocks of actors that were united by dense interaction patterns. The three kinds of actor who were most central to the party's network of relations were actually those that stood formally outside the party: financial contributors, interest groups, and advisors. Contributors, of course, are an essential component of the informal wing of the party, often providing the financial resources needed to win an election. Fully 400 interest groups were registered to lobby in Illinois, and several of these worked exclusively with the Republican Party, rather than with both parties. Although some political advisors worked with contributors and interest groups, others provided technical assistance directly to candidates and party committees. Most closely connected to these three members of the informal wing of the party were the governor, U.S. senator, state senators, and state representatives.

Party actors operate within an environment that provides resources and shapes their activities. The crucial elements of this environment are the varied constituencies that potentially provide support. Of the twenty-three party actors, nine are linked directly to the electorate, whereas the fourteen others serve other interests. The electorate is not a unity. Voters in primary contests are a very selective group, compared with those who vote in general elections. Some office holders are elected state-wide, whereas members of the U.S. House of Representatives serve individual congressional districts, and local elected officials have geographically very narrow constituencies. The leaders of the state senate and house have the members of these legislative bodies for their constituencies. The various party committees and the informal wing of the party have parts of the party apparatus or special interests for their constituencies.

Individual people in these party positions both cooperate and compete with each other. Office-seekers with different constituencies have little incentive to help each other, whereas people seeking different offices from the same constituency may often cooperate. Naturally, individuals seeking the same office compete even if they are members of the same party. Schwartz found that there tend to be more primary challengers within the party seeking office in those counties where the party is more likely to win the general election.

During the time of Schwartz's study, the Republican party had developed a relatively coherent conservative ideology. A potential conflict exists between two aspects of this ideology. Cultural conservatism seeks to preserve traditional family and religious values. Capitalist dynamism favors the free market and individual entrepreneurship. Many social scientists have concluded that capitalist dynamism tends to erode traditional norms and values, yet members of the Republican party had no difficulty blending cultural conservatism with capitalist dynamism, and many voters responded favorably to this combination.

Some political analysts say that a *strong party* is most effective, whereas others advocate a *weak party*. A strong party is highly disciplined, with a shared ideology and a centralized organization possessing a well-defined hierarchy of authority. Schwartz found that the Illinois Republican Party was a *loosely coupled organization,* in which the various party actors have considerable independence and the authority hierarchy is unable to impose strict discipline. Thus, the party appears weak. But this means that it is highly adaptive. When some leaders lose hotly contested elections, others are ready to come forward to take their place. Although the party is weak in discipline, it is strong in ideology. Shared beliefs and values integrate the loosely coupled parts of the organization and sustain individual enthusiasm even through times of electoral defeat. An adaptive party, like the Illinois Republicans, has the following four key features:

1. It must be a loosely coupled system.
2. It is a rational, goal-directed system.
3. It is a cultural system, ideologically distinct from other parties and providing powerful symbols.
4. It is a system of power, directed to achieving control over uncertainty.

Revolutions

Goldstone, Jack A.
1991 *Revolution and Rebellion in the Early Modern World.* Berkeley:
University of California Press.

Goldstone argues that political rebellions and revolutions are not isolated events but often occur simultaneously in several nations, because the same underlying causes are at work over a wide geographic area. His premier example is the wave of political unrest that swept Europe and Asia around 1640, causing revolution in England and China, and major revolts in France, Turkey and many nations between. He theorizes that revolution is likely to occur when a society experiences three severe problems simultaneously that are often accompanied by a fourth:

1. **State financial crisis.** The government has great difficulty raising enough money to meet its ordinary obligations and thus is in no position to react effectively to an emergency such as war.
2. **Severe elite divisions.** The influential groups in society are divided among themselves, with different elite factions competing with each other to such a degree that it is difficult to get them to cooperate in responding to serious issues.
3. **High potential for mobilizing popular groups.** Social conditions make it relatively easy to mobilize ordinary citizens to support rebellion. Some of these conditions are grievances, like those caused by high prices and low wages. Others are structural conditions such as an unusually large number of young people in the age distribution of the population or an unusually large number of workers in weakly-ruled cities.
4. **Increased salience of radical ideologies.** The first three problems tend to fuel ideological movements, promulgating heterodox cultural and religious ideas. On the basis of these ideas, radical groups are able to organize opposition to the state.

This is a theory of state (governmental) breakdown, as much as it is a theory of revolution. Revolutions will not succeed if the state is strong, but financial crisis and divisions among the elite can weaken it sufficiently for popular rebellions to make headway if numbers of people can be mobilized around radical ideologies. The states studied by Goldstone, from England to China, were similar in many respects. Their economies were based heavily on agriculture. Their territories were ruled by hereditary monarchs who existed in some tension with other authorities both at the local level and in religious and cultural institutions. A literate elite was sufficiently independent to be critical of the way the government was doing its job, and the general population was divided into groups with complex relations to the state and the elite groups. Finally, extensive trade within the societies had produced widespread markets in which price changes could have great effects on many kinds of people. These conditions set the stage for political rebellion. Goldstone says that any combination of eight factors can be present in political crisis:

1. loss of confidence in the state
2. elite revolt against the state
3. popular revolts, whether rural or urban, against the state or elites
4. widespread violence or civil war
5. change in political institutions
6. change in the status of elites
7. change in economic organization and property ownership
8. change in the symbols and ideology that justify stratification

All of these characteristics were present in the twentieth-century Russian and Chinese communist revolutions. Goldstone says that all but two (change in the status of elites and change in economic organization) were present in the English Revolution of 1640. Other writers had attributed the English Revolution and other rebellions to the rise of capitalism or the stresses caused by war. Although Goldstone's theory gives changing prices in a widespread market a role in generating rebellion, he says that the emergence of modern capitalism was not a factor. He acknowledges that war can contribute to the problems faced by a state, but he says it is not the most important cause.

For the fundamental mechanism of his theory, Goldstone turns to demography. He explains that the simultaneous rebellions across Europe and Asia came at the end of a time of unusual population growth. Earlier, repeated plagues had kept the death rate high, but for a century before 1640 these diseases had been rare, so the population expanded rapidly. This meant increased competition for a limited number of elite positions, and it meant rising prices coupled with decreasing wages. Thus, members of the elite were thrown into greater competition with each other, and members of the general public faced severe economic stresses that made them receptive to political mobilization. Rising prices greatly increased state expenditures, for example by greatly increasing the cost of feeding the armies, but revenues did not increase accordingly. Goldstone offers several mathematical analyses that show

how a medium-sized increase in population can create a disproportionally large change in some other variable, such as prices or competition for elite positions.

The English Revolution of 1640 illustrates this theory. The Black Death struck England in 1348–1349, and plague returned periodically thereafter. Consequently, the population size in 1500 was not much different from what it had been in 1300. Prices were stable from 1380 to 1500. From about 1500 to 1640, epidemics were more rare and the English population increased from about two million to five million. Consequently, grain prices increased by 600 percent, and ordinary people suffered because their wages did not keep pace. The general population growth meant the number of sons of aristocratic or gentry (land-owning) families increased more rapidly than the elite positions open to them, and one sign of the hot competition for status was a great increase in college enrollments. Unfortunately for the state, many of its ordinary revenues failed to increase, and net income may have actually declined. For example, the system for renting out lands belonging to the king had been set up during a period of stable prices, and leases were often for ninety-nine years at a fixed rate. Custom duties for wine and cloth were determined by the quantity of the imported product rather than its value. The state turned to ever more desperate money-raising schemes, until it was deeply in debt. When a Scottish army entered England, King Charles I was unable to respond effectively, and the monarchy was swept aside by a revolution that placed dictator Oliver Cromwell in power. Revolutions, Goldstone says, produce not democracy but authoritarianism. After a brief period the English aristocracy reasserted itself and the monarchy was reestablished with Charles II. From 1650 to about 1750, epidemic diseases allowed the population to rise only slightly, from 5.2 million to 5.7 million, wheat prices stopped rising, college enrollments declined, and political conflict was more moderate.

Goldstone applies the same analysis to the French Revolution, the Ottoman Crisis in Turkey, and the Ming-Qing dynastic transition in China. At the end of his book, he warns that the American state has entered a period of financial crisis that needs to be addressed so that unanticipated threats do not trigger political revolt in the United States.

Moaddel, Mansoor
1992 "Ideology as Episodic Discourse: The Case of the Iranian Revolution," *American Sociological Review* 57:353–379.

In 1979, the Shah of Iran was deposed from power by a movement led by the religious figure Ayatollah Khomeini. Over the following months an explicitly Islamic government consolidated its power. Moaddel argues that the three main existing theoretical perspectives on revolutionary ideology fail to explain the role of ideas in this major revolution. First, *subjectivist models* state that social crisis causes many individuals to feel intense tensions that make them vulnerable to ideologies offering revolutionary solutions to their problems. Although Iran experienced some social and economic setbacks, they were not severe, and the generally rising prosperity reduced socioeconomic motives for revolution. Second, *organizational models* argue that competing political organizations mold ideologies to justify their existence. To some extent, this applied to the Shah's government, but the traditional religious elite (the "ulama") failed to develop ideologies to counter secularization and did not unite against the Shah. Third, *Marxian models* tend to consider ideology merely the expression of class interests, and revolutionary ideologies are a reflection of a revolutionary class, such as workers who want to overthrow capitalists. Although at times ideology was connected to class interests in Iran, the people supporting competing ideologies had varied class backgrounds, and the revolutionaries were seldom workers or peasants as Marxists would have expected them to be.

Moaddel offers a fourth theory, which considers ideology to be a force in itself, not merely a tool of other forces. Ideology operates in often unexpected ways during episodes of conflict. Over a period of years, the Shah progressively consolidated his power until his government was extremely repressive. The fact that the United States supported his regime tended to discredit the liberal ideologies associated with America. The Shah suppressed traditional religious customs, unintentionally strengthening the prestige of religion among his opponents. When a religious regime replaced the Shah, it was constrained to a very great extent by the Shi'i tradition of Islam that prevailed in Iran. For example, merchants and landowners were protected from exploitation by the new government because Islamic religious traditions favored them. Thus, ideology can be shaped during some political episodes, in an episodic process of political discourse, but it also shapes politics in powerful ways.

15
SOCIAL CHANGE

WORKS AT A GLANCE

Technological Determinism

Social Change by William Fielding Ogburn (1922)
Becoming Modern: Individual Changes in Six Developing Countries
    by Alex Inkeles and David H. Smith (1974)

Cultural Trends

Social and Cultural Dynamics by Pitirim A. Sorokin (1937)
The Lonely Crowd by David Riesman (1950)

Integration of Technology
and Culture

The Coming of Post-Industrial Society by Daniel Bell (1973)
"The Rational Reconstruction of Society" by James S. Coleman (1993)

Social change is not merely the result of collective behavior or of religious and social movements. Many social scientists stress the importance of technical invention, and some give it the key role. *Technological determinism* is the view that technological innovation is the engine of history, and that technology itself is largely self-generated. Other social scientists believe that very large-scale cultural trends are also important, and that these vary in their connection to technology.

William F. Ogburn was a technological determinist who believed that social change resulted from four processes: invention, accumulation, diffusion, and adjustment. Often inventions occurred faster than society could adjust to them, and the result was an uncomfortable cultural lag in which the institutions of society were poorly integrated. Alex Inkeles and David Smith collected questionnaire data from six developing nations to test the theory that industrial technology was creating a uniform, world-wide set of values. Pitirim A. Sorokin believed that culture evolved in long cycles, quite apart from technology, whereas David Riesman believed culture was steadily transforming human personality in a possibly unhealthy direction. Both Daniel Bell and James Coleman were convinced that social change has rendered many traditional institutions of society obsolete, and the science of sociology must be used to create viable new institutions for the future.

Technological Determinism

Ogburn, William Fielding
  1922 *Social Change*. New York: Huebsch.

Ogburn asserts that human history is largely the story of four interrelated steps in a process of technical development:

1. invention
2. accumulation
3. diffusion
4. adjustment

Invention is the process by which new forms of technology are created. Although inventors tend to be far more intelligent than the average, invention is not primarily an individual accomplishment. Rather, inventions are collective additions to an existing cultural base that cannot occur unless the society has already gained a certain level of knowledge and expertise in the particular area. For example, the telegraph was created by combining a number of existing elements, such as electricity, coils, batteries, signaling, and alphabet codes. Until these had already been developed, it could not be invented. Ogburn devotes an entire chapter of his book to a long list of inventions and discoveries that were made independently by two or more people, illustrating the fundamental role of culture in preparing the way for such innovations.

Some societies show great cultural inertia, and institutions such as religion can retard innovation. In the absence of such disturbing influences, technology will grow as new inventions are added to the existing cultural base.

Accumulation is the growth of technology because new things are invented more rapidly than old ones are forgotten. When humans learned to work iron, they did not abandon copper; instead they used both metals for different purposes. A cultural object tends to persist because it is useful. Sometimes an old invention is forgotten because it has been rendered obsolete by more recent inventions. A shift in the way a society makes a living can allow an entire sector of technology to languish. For example, if a particular society gives up hunting for cattle herding, it will lose some of its knowledge about hunting even as it gains new knowledge about herding. Other things being equal, the rate of invention tends to increase over time, because an accumulating cultural base provides the material for an ever greater number of new inventions. Accumulation of inventions is encouraged if many separate social groups contribute their inventions.

Diffusion is the spread of an idea from one cultural group to another. Invention is more difficult than borrowing, so isolated cultures tend to progress only slowly. One reason for the increased rate of invention is the increasing contact between societies, itself the result of inventions in transportation and communication. But diffusion stimulates invention as well, because ideas from different societies can combine to form novel ideas that required cultural contributions from all of them. The impact of sudden diffusion on a society can be tremendous, as when horses were introduced to the Native Americans of the Great Plains, or when Japan opened its previously closed doors to western technology. Thus, invention, accumulation, and diffusion can pose a profound challenge to a society.

Adjustment is the process by which the non-technical aspects of a culture respond to invention. Social change does not generally occur smoothly, but in a series of jumps, some of them small, and others quite large. One reason is that important inventions come along only rarely, but when they do they are decisive in their impact. One aspect of a culture may resist change because it is tied to a number of important institutions that have achieved a fine balance or equilibrium. To change that key element will have such great consequences that people resist altering it, especially those groups that have vested interests in the status quo. Traditions, habits, the often conservative force of education, and social pressures toward conformity all resist change. Thus a decisive new invention can create a tremendous strain in the culture that may not quickly dissipate.

Problems of adjustment to invention often involve what Ogburn calls *cultural lag*. This is a maladjustment that comes about because the various parts of modern culture are not changing at the same rate. Rapid progress in one area may demand progress in another area related to it, but the adjustment is delayed, perhaps for many years. Early in the history of the United States, the land was covered by vast forests, and the individual woodsmen with their hand axes could do little damage chopping as much as they wanted. But then improved lumbering technology, and the technology-caused growth of population and markets, posed a dire threat to the forests. Decades passed before society adjusted to the new technologies and began to realize that it had to shift from uncontrolled exploitation of the forests to conservation, which meant reforestation and a whole host of measures to preserve the environment. Between the development of the technology and society's adjustment was a period of cultural lag.

Ogburn's theory of the transformation of the family is especially provocative. The traditional farm family may have possessed a well-integrated culture, in which men and women performed different but equal roles with economic, educational, protective, recreational, and religious functions. The woman's economic function was especially important, and she made many of the things the family needed, including clothing and food preserves. But over the course of the nineteenth century, factories stole her significance as a manufacturer of clothing and preparer of food. Technology-caused economic development made it possible to afford public schools, and the increasing sophistication of industry required increased formal education, so the growth of schools robbed mothers of their traditional function as child educators. According to Ogburn, women's traditional role declined in importance, and women in consequence became relatively powerless and oppressed by men. The obvious solution was for women to gain equal rights in employment and other public activities, but this came about only slowly over a period of decades marked by cultural lag.

Inkeles, Alex, and David H. Smith
　1974 *Becoming Modern: Individual Changes in Six Developing Countries.*
　　Cambridge, Massachusetts: Harvard University Press.

Inkeles and Smith are concerned with the development of "third world" societies, and they theorize that modernization requires their citizens to gain attitudes and capabilities that are radically different from those traditionally socialized into members of their cultures. They note with sadness that many nations that were freed from the bonds of colonialism have since slid backward, economically and socially, rather than advancing. And they suggest that the conditions of people living in these nations will not improve until they abandon the ways of the past and adopt the attitudes and behavior appropriate for citizens of industrial societies. They develop and test these hypotheses through a massive questionnaire survey translated into the appropriate languages and administered to nearly 1,000 young men in each of six developing nations: East Pakistan (Bangladesh), Nigeria, Chile, India, Argentina, and Israel (among Oriental Jews).

Much of their work is an empirical struggle to develop a comprehensive definition of *modernity* and to determine statistically if its elements really fit together into a single cultural and psychological whole. The institutions of modern society, chiefly factories, need workers who respect technical competence rather than religious tradition, who follow abstract instructions, who rely upon objective evidence to make judgments, and who can follow strict time schedules. Thus, the first step in developing the concept is to say that successful urban factory workers are likely to be more modern in their thinking and behavior than are isolated rural farmers.

In constructing their elaborate questionnaire, Inkeles and Smith postulated that modernity could be conceptually divided into many different dimensions. A dozen of these were individual characteristics: openness to new experiences, readiness for social change, development of complex opinions, possession of much information, orientation toward the future rather than the past, a sense of being able to control the environment, favoring long-term planning, believing that the world is predictable, valuing technical skills, having aspirations for achievement in education and occupation, respecting the dignity of other people, and understanding industrial production. Areas of life in which modernism is very different from traditionalism include the following: family, women's rights, birth control, religion, aging, politics, communications, consumerism, social stratification, work commitment, national identity, and citizenship.

Using many questionnaire items related to all of these concepts, Inkeles and Smith developed measures of Overall Modernity (OM). They began with 166 items The six members of the international research team then judged how well each item reflected the core meaning of modernity, and 79 items were selected by five of the six raters to form the OM-1 scale. By similar procedures, 23 secondary modernity items were selected, 17 items measuring modern political involvement, and 47 items concerning modern behavior. Then the researchers carried out elaborate statistical analysis to see how the items clustered in the actual responses of the six thousand men. Spread out over many pages of the book, this statistical analysis leaves much room for criticism from sociologists who doubt that modernity is a single complex of attitudes and behavior. But Inkeles and Smith discovered a large number of items that did correlate significantly with each other. Defining this cluster of items as modernity, they set out to explain it, looking at factors such as education and factory work that shape the character of a person.

In the developing nations under study, many of the men had received little or no schooling, but those who had received a few years were far more modern than their uneducated peers, and each additional year of school had the expected effect. Exposure to modern mass media, such as radio and newspapers, also made a man more modern. Factories were similar to schools, in that years spent in them added to a man's modernity. All this may seem obvious, but some other obvious hypotheses turned out to be false. Some factories were more modern establishments, both in terms of technology and the way they were organized, than were others. Yet the men in more modern factories were not themselves more modern than men working in much cruder establishments. Sociologists might think that living in a city rather than in rural areas would increase a person's modernity, but this turned out not to be true when education and factory experience were controlled. Rural people who have good educations or who participate in modern agricultural experiments such as cooperative farms can score quite high on tests of modernity. Importantly, several analyses showed that people from very traditional families can become modern if they gain formal education, and a person who completes childhood under traditional conditions still can become modern in adulthood.

It is not easy to harmonize the approach of Inkeles and Smith with the idea that substantial cultural diversity can and should be maintained as nations develop economically. Their research was predicated on the notion that modernity is a single cultural complex that must replace traditional cultures, stressing rationality and cosmopolitanism. Although there is much room for debate, the data presented by Inkeles and Smith support this position. On the other hand, they found that modernity did not cause psychological stress or necessarily disrupt social relationships.

Cultural Trends

Sorokin, Pitirim A.
  1937 *Social and Cultural Dynamics*. 4 vols. New York: American Book
    Company.

Sorokin was an official in the moderate Russian government that was overthrown by Lenin during the First World War. He barely escaped execution and came to the United States, where he founded the sociology department of Harvard University. Thus Sorokin had good personal reason to wonder about large-scale social phenomena like revolutions, wars, and the rise and fall of civilizations. He was not convinced that gradual technological development assured that history would be a story of inexorable progress, and he theorized that the dynamics of cultural and social change could be destructive as often as constructive.

Sorokin's 1937 four-volume publication is one of the largest works of sociology, about three thousand pages long and covering the entire sweep of Western history. But the core idea is a relatively simple theory of how civilization rises and falls in a series of long cycles. A key question is how culture can become unified and whether the great cultures we call civilizations are integrated wholes. After considering various earlier authors and the different ways that the institutions of a culture might be integrated, Sorokin concludes there is great variation in the degree to which the parts of most cultures fit together. Some are merely accidental collections of beliefs and practices that were thrown together by history, whereas others exist only in opposition to some external threat. But Sorokin theorizes that the really successful cultures, the ones that have an enduring impact on history, probably are integrated wholes. Their beliefs, practices, and institutions are functionally integrated, each supporting the others and each dependent upon the others. Furthermore, at the heart of each integrated culture there exists an idea or a perspective on existence that renders the whole logically consistent.

The basis of a logically integrated cultural system are elements of thought and meaning that relate to one of two realms. First are *internal* elements that concern the inner experience of people, their images, ideas, volitions, feelings, and emotions. Second are *external* elements, the objects, events, and processes that exist outside the person but are meaningful only in so far as they relate to inner experience. Thus, for Sorokin, elements of culture that concern the external are subordinate to those that concern the internal. Cultural systems vary in the emphasis they give to internal versus external; that is, they vary in whether they are ideational (internal), sensate (external), or a mixture of the two. The essence of a culture can be found in its major premises concerning four general questions:

1. the nature of reality
2. the nature of the needs and ends to be satisfied
3. the extent to which these needs and ends are to be satisfied
4. the methods of satisfaction

An *ideational* culture considers reality to be essentially spiritual rather than material. The goals it sets are mainly spiritual ones, and it seeks to satisfy spiritual needs as completely as possible. To accomplish this, it minimizes or eliminates physical needs, but there are two ways it can do this. First, an *ascetic* ideational culture suppresses carnal desires and seeks to detach from the world of the senses, viewing both as illusions. The individual dissolves in a supernatural reality. Second, an *active* ideational culture accepts the same premises as the ascetic, but it tries to reform society in accordance with its spiritual vision.

A *sensate* culture believes that reality is whatever the sense organs perceive. It does not believe in any supernatural world. Its aims are physical or sensual, and it seeks to achieve them through exploiting or changing the external world. Sorokin identifies three varieties. First, an *active* sensate culture uses technology and empire-building to take charge of the material world. Second, a *passive* sensate culture indulges itself in pleasures of the flesh. Third, a *cynical* sensate culture adapts to the surrounding conditions in a calculated attempt to profit; superficially it might appear ideational because it does not dominate the material world, but fundamentally it is merely the most devious of the brands of sensate culture.

Some cultures are mixtures or transitional types. Sorokin emphasizes the most logically integrated of these mixed types, which he calls the *idealistic* culture, because it is a concerted attempt to blend the ideational and sensate types.

After describing the types, Sorokin devotes the greater part of his four volumes to charting the trends in various aspects of culture over the course of Western history: art, literature, music, warfare, economy, family, government, philosophy, law, technology, and science. For example, he tabulates what proportion of the great paintings were spiritual (ideational) versus sensual (sensate) over the centuries. His general conclusion is that the classical civilization of Greece and Rome collapsed when it became highly sensate. The new, Christian civilization that arose on its wreckage began with a highly ideational culture, then evolved through an idealistic phase into its present condition, which is extremely sensate.

Perhaps at its birth, a civilization bases itself on a coherent set of spiritual beliefs that give it strength. To the extent that its ideational culture is successful, it grows and develops. As time passes, it slowly loses a grip on its spirituality, doubt sets in, and the culture becomes progressively more sensate. At the extreme it is so thoroughly sensate that it lacks a spiritual core and dissolves or is conquered by a stronger civilization that is still in an ideational or idealistic phase.

Sorokin does not say that Western civilization is about to fall, although a collapse as devastating as that suffered by ancient Rome is always a possibility for an advanced sensate society such as ours. Rather, Sorokin asserts merely that we are entering a major transition period that is bound to be grim, cruel, bloody, and painful. If Western civilization can orient itself again toward the spirit rather than the senses, it can be reborn.

Riesman, David
1950 *The Lonely Crowd*. New Haven: Yale University Press.

When Riesman wrote, many anthropologists, psychologists, and sociologists were interested in the way that culture, social structure, and individual personality influence each other. Many writers believed that each distinctive type of society tended to be peopled by individuals with a corresponding type of character. For Riesman, changes in technology and population are closely linked to changes in character. Over the last several hundred years, he believes, changing conditions of Western societies have shifted the emphasis from tradition-directed to inner-directed to other-directed forms of character.

Tradition-directed individuals dominated pre-industrial societies. The individual must conform to a rigid, age-old culture sustained through innumerable rituals, religion, and a complex structure of clans, castes, or other social divisions. Because many children die of disease or starvation before they reach adulthood, the society needs a high birth rate to survive, and a high proportion of its citizens are children. Heavy emphasis is placed on the extended family, which reinforces tradition. In part because the culture is simple and uniform, children learn to act like adults at a very early age, as they must do in these economically precarious societies. The society regulates population by encouraging a high birth rate, but when the population rises beyond the carrying capacity of the technology, harsh traditional measures (from killing girl babies to warfare) reduce the numbers. The psychological mechanism that guides behavior is the fear of *shame* for failing to follow the unquestioned traditions of the society.

Inner-directed individuals are most at home in societies undergoing transition from ancient to modern forms, which are marked by a feeling of vitality. These people possess a strong set of internal values, socialized into them by demanding parents, without the extended families of earlier times or the mass media of later times to diffuse their influence. Under conditions of rapid change, the ancient traditions no longer hold, and the individual is controlled by a powerful system of goals and psychological habits ingrained during childhood. Advances in technology have raised the level of wealth and reduced death rates, so the population grows rapidly. This expanding population, in turn, increases markets and thus the opportunity for individual achievement in the relatively undeveloped commercial and industrial sectors of the economy. The individual is encouraged to live up to the inner ideal and constantly experiments with greater and greater self-mastery His or her character remains firm throughout life, and successful examples of this type create new enterprises and take advantage of expanding frontiers. The individual who deviates from internalized values feels *guilt*.

Other-directed individuals fit into the complex social institutions of modern society. They find their values in the group that surrounds them, and they adapt to the new groups they enter, as growing up and pursuing a career take them through many social environments. The birth rate has declined and the society has lost dynamism. Early school attendance places children in the hands of teachers who devalue skill and emphasize cooperation. The increasing intrusion into the home by mass media erodes the former socialization role of parents. To be other-directed means to be especially sensitive to the desires and expectations of others, and this characteristic helps such people succeed in the group-oriented work environment of modern bureaucracies. Advancement comes from improving one's social skills, and approval from one's peers becomes the prime goal. The emotion that supports conformity is *anxiety*.

Riesman believed that middle class, mid-century Americans were torn between the competing styles of character. Some tradition-directed individuals were still found among the working class and among rural people, but the middle class had become a battleground between the older inner-directed type and the newer other-directed type. Riesman admits a good deal of admiration for the inner-directed character, but vast bureaucracies cannot tolerate these lone wolves. They were well adapted to the old frontiers of expansion and production, but now the need is to open up internal frontiers of ever greater consumption. The mass media drive out inner-directed people and their values from all areas except politics. In political affairs, inner-directed activists are moralizers who fail to understand the need for compromise. Their life experiences are progressively more disappointing, and their mood becomes one of indignation when it is not despair. And yet other-directed individuals suffer in modern society, as well, so attentive to the social environment that they lose touch with their own feelings. They are seized by a terrible loneliness in the midst of the crowd from which they desperately want approval. In the end, the issue in modern society is how to preserve a healthy degree of autonomy without becoming anomic.

Integration of Technology and Culture

Bell, Daniel
  1973 *The Coming of Post-Industrial Society*. New York: Basic Books.

This book is an influential example of social forecasting. Bell knows that forecasts cannot predict the future with any precision, but they can sketch the limits of what is possible and identify key issues that policy makers will have to address. Theory without facts is sterile, but the sociologist cannot simply observe the facts. Rather, observation must be guided by theory, and only ideas can render facts meaningful. Thus, we can speak of different kinds of societies with full awareness that many different conceptual schemes are available, even though we choose to employ a particular one. Arranged conceptually in terms of how production is accomplished and how knowledge is used, societies can be described as *pre-industrial, industrial,* or *post-industrial.*

A society has three parts: the social structure, the polity, and the culture. For a given type of society, each of these three is oriented toward a particular *axial principle*:

1. The *social structure* consists of economy, technology, and the system of different kinds of work. In modern society, the axial principle for the social structure is *economizing*, which means allocating resources in terms of economic efficiency.

2. The *polity* is roughly synonymous with the political system. It regulates the distribution of power between groups and manages their disputes. The modern axial principle for polity is *participation*, as groups jostle to share power more or less democratically.

3. The *culture* comprises shared meanings and the expressive symbols that communicate them. Today, its axial principle is the desire for personal *self-fulfillment*.

In prior decades, these three were linked by a common value system, but they have become increasingly disconnected. The transformation of industrial society into post-industrial society chiefly concerns changes in the social structure. However, Bell rejects simple theories of technological determinism. The polity and culture can respond in a number of different ways to the challenges posed by post-industrial social structure. Their options can be understood best by recognizing five components of the "post-industrial" concept (p. 14):

1. **Economic sector:** the change from a goods-producing to a service economy
2. **Occupational distribution:** the pre-eminence of the professional and technical class
3. **Axial principle:** the centrality of theoretical knowledge as the source of innovation and of policy formulation for the society
4. **Future orientation:** the control of technology and technological assessment
5. **Decision-making:** the creation of a new "intellectual technology"

Bell examines each of these at length. Service jobs have always been common, but now highly-educated service workers are becoming dominant through their activity in universities, research institutes, professions, and government. An increasing proportion of all employed people will be in technical occupations, broadly defined. At the highest levels, the crucial knowledge is theoretical in nature, stressing abstract symbols and scientific understanding. Because advanced technologies have many unintended consequences, including harmful ones such as environmental pollution, it will be essential to manage technology on a large scale. Thus the exponential growth of science and technology requires us to develop new information technologies, rooted in advanced social science.

Bell foresaw that the transition from industrial to post-industrial society would greatly weaken the labor unions, which had held the corporations somewhat in check. New institutions would be required to subordinate corporations to the needs of the society. Economic markets cannot deal with *free goods* that should be available to everyone (such as clean air and pure water) or with *externalities* that affect people not involved in a particular economic transaction (such as pollution from a factory harming people who neither work there nor buy its goods). An economic value system overemphasizes private goods to the expense of public goods, with often pathological results. For example, economists count the output of a steel mill as part of the Gross National Product (GNP). But they also add the cost of cleaning up its pollution to the GNP, apparently unable to recognize the difference between benefit and harm. We need to offset economics with sociology, to address questions of social justice and the proper balance between the public and private sectors.

This will require a system of social accounts that provides information on the social costs and benefits of alternative policies, putting economics in the broader context of human needs. The system would begin with a series of social indicators, fundamental information collected by social scientists to chart social change and the consequences of particular government actions. These would measure mobilization of human resources in four areas: (1) the social costs and net benefits of innovations, (2) the nature and magnitude of social ills such as crime and family disruption, (3) performance in meeting social needs like housing and education, and (4) opportunities for socio-economic mobility. Such a system would place great responsibilities upon social scientists and upon intellectuals in general, creating a meritocracy in which the most intellectually capable and educated individuals essentially ruled the world. Other groups in society might protest such a radical change in the organization of human society, so political opposition will be among the most difficult challenges blocking the creation of a just and efficient post-industrial society.

Coleman, James S.
  1993 "The Rational Reconstruction of Society," *American Sociological Review* 58:1–15.

  Generations of sociologists have tried to understand the great historical process of change that has transformed traditional societies into the modern world. Coleman argues that engineering has turned a primordial natural environment into a constructed technological environment, and that human beings have yet to realize the central challenge of this evolution. Primordial social institutions based upon the family are inexorably losing strength. Coleman notes the tremendous decline in the proportion of the population in agriculture, from 84 percent in the United States in 1810 to less than 5 percent in the 1980s, which is connected to the loss of traditional community based on family ties. Similarly, the family has declined as women in ever greater numbers entered the labor force and children went to school. Coleman says we have failed to realize that the social capital on which primordial social organization depends has vanished (see Coleman's essay on social capital in Chapter 10). It is impossible to repair traditional institutions, because the world that sustained them is rapidly dying. We must find a new basis for social life by consciously constructing fresh institutions.

  The best historical example of a purposively constructed organization is the corporation. A corporation is a fictitious person lacking flesh and blood but capable of acting in court and the marketplace. This idea emerged over a period of centuries, supported by the principle that the individual humans associated with a corporation were not liable for its debts. Wherever primordial social organization has become ineffective we must create other novel institutions and modify existing ones in imaginative ways. For example, parents have lost much of their former incentive to raise children to be productive members of society. Therefore, governments will have to find new ways of motivating parents and will take over much of the decision-making power concerning how children are socialized. Coleman shows that the decline of primordial, family-based societies has coincided with the emergence of the science of sociology, thus implying that sociologists of the future will have heavy responsibilities in constructing the needed social organization.

16
DEMOGRAPHY

WORKS AT A GLANCE

Demographic Transition

"The Theory of Change and Response in Modern Demographic History" by Kingsley Davis (1963)

"Lessons from the Past: Policy Implications of Historical Fertility Studies" by John Knodel and Etienne van de Walle (1979)

Immigration

"Immigration," by Edward Jarvis (1872)

Sex Ratio

Too Many Women? The Sex Ratio Question by Marcia Guttentag and Paul F. Secord (1983)

Population Explosion or Collapse

How Many People Can the Earth Support? by Joel E. Cohen (1995)

"The Family that Does Not Reproduce Itself" by Nathan Keyfitz (1987)

Demography is the study of the dynamics of human populations, emphasizing birth (fertility), death (mortality), and migration (emigration and immigration). In some respects demography is among the most scientific of sociological subdisciplines, because it is possible to measure the number of people in the population precisely.

For a number of years, demographic transition theory was extremely influential. As stated here by Kingsley Davis, this theory held that modernizing societies first experience a drop in mortality, maintaining high fertility rates and thus enduring a population explosion, before dropping birth rates bring the population back into balance. However, demographers such as Knodel and van de Walle are critical of this theory, because it does not accurately describe what happened historically to the industrial nations, and there is little reason to believe it will apply to developing nations.

Since his work in the early 1840s (Chapter 1), Edward Jarvis had realized that sociological data could be of tremendous political significance, and he devoted considerable effort throughout his life to make sure that the data were as accurate as possible. In the immigration debate of the 1870s as now, wild speculations based on false impressions could unnecessarily aggravate hostilities between groups, and a rational immigration policy required an accurate understanding of the facts. Therefore, Jarvis analyzed carefully the birth and immigration trends to determine objectively whether immigration was swamping the country.

In addition to immigration, gender relations and population growth are major social controversies today. Marcia Guttentag and Paul Secord argue that the sex ratio—the balance between males and females in the population—shapes the relative power of the two genders and the roles they will play in the family and the larger society. Joel Cohen says it is very difficult to explain why a society has the birth and death rates it does and to predict population trends into the future. However, he judges that the numbers of human beings will continue to grow rapidly and that the earth cannot forever sustain this population explosion. In contrast, Nathan Keyfitz is concerned that the populations of educated groups are collapsing, and he cannot imagine what government policies might reverse this discouraging trend.

Demographic Transition

Davis, Kingsley
  1963 "The Theory of Change and Response in Modern Demographic History," *Population Index* 29:345–366.

A central concern of demographers has been understanding the historical transition from traditional societies to modern ones. Traditional societies have high birth rates and high death rates, which balance to keep the total population of the society roughly constant. Technological and economic development improve public health and medicine, which in turn extend the life span and reduce death rates. For a few generations birth rates stay high, causing rapid population growth, sometimes called population explosion. Eventually, birth rates also lower until they are again in balance with death rates. Both fertility and mortality are low, and the population is again roughly constant, but at a much larger size than before this demographic transition. In theory, the advanced industrial societies of the world (from Canada and the United States to western Europe to Japan) have completed this transition, but the developing nations of the world are still in the midst of it, thus causing the present massive population growth of the planet. In his influential article, Davis attempts to explain the decline in fertility experienced by Japan and western Europe.

Davis says that the decline in fertility was not caused by starvation or poverty brought on by growth of the population beyond what the land could sustain, a popular idea in demography since Thomas Malthus discussed it in 1798. Rather, developing nations became more prosperous during the period of transition. Nor is the explanation a shift in societal values, Davis says, because there is little evidence that values exist other than as a shorthand way of describing people's actual behavior. Instead, people experience the consequences of lowered mortality in their own families, as adults live longer and fewer children die before adulthood, and they choose to limit fertility as a way to take advantage personally of the opportunities for economic improvement that would be threatened by too many children. Although modern birth control techniques help prevent pregnancy, fertility in fact declined well before they were available. In all the societies considered by Davis, who devotes special attention to Japan and Ireland, a variety of practices reduced fertility: postponing marriage to later in life, not marrying at all, contraceptive techniques including both modern and traditional methods, migration away from the geographic region of high fertility, and abortion or even infanticide.

Knodel, John and Etienne van de Walle
   1979 "Lessons from the Past: Policy Implications of Historical Fertility
      Studies," *Population and Development Review* 5:217–245.

Demographic transition theory has become highly controversial, and there are grave doubts whether the lowered fertility characteristic of contemporary Europe will become standard throughout the world as other nations modernize. Recently, historical demographers have examined what happened in various parts of Europe. Knodel and van de Walle doubt that economic development inevitably brings down the fertility rate, and they cite European historical data to support this skepticism. The European societies of three hundred years ago were quite different from today's developing nations, because Europeans tended to marry relatively late in life and often not marry at all, so it is not at all clear that much of the world is simply going to repeat the demographic history of Europe. Surveying much European historical demography, Knodel and van de Walle find more evidence against the theory that fertility decline requires economic development:

1. Fertility declines took place under a wide variety of social, economic, and demographic conditions. For example, high educational levels and low child mortality rates were not associated with reductions in the birth rate.
2. Methods of limiting births were not widely known or practiced, even though many births were unwanted. Before the drop in fertility rates, couples seem to have produced about as many children as they biologically could, and the loss of children through death did not increase the number that would be born into the family as one would expect it would if parents were controlling their childbearing.
3. Increases in the practice of family limitation and the decline of marital fertility were essentially irreversible processes once under way. Although birth control is a highly private matter, demographers can measure its introduction in historical statistics when the age at which mothers give birth to their last child drops significantly.
4. Cultural setting influenced the onset and spread of fertility decline independently of socioeconomic conditions. Remarkably, despite their huge socioeconomic differences most of the European provinces greatly reduced their fertility at the same time, 1880–1910. However, cultural barriers slowed communication of birth control ideas, and fertility limitation is encouraged by the relatively high status of women in the culture.

Immigration

Jarvis, Edward
  1872 "Immigration," *Atlantic Monthly* 29:454-468.

In the middle of the nineteenth century, Americans discussed the consequences of immigration, just as they do today, and social scientists contributed demographic analyses to the debate. In 1870, Frederic Kapp published an article in the journal of the American Social Science Association (a predecessor of the American Sociological Association), building on earlier calculations by Louis Schade and apparently showing that fertility rates among recent immigrants were so high their children would swamp the country. Conversely, it seemed that fertility rates were so low among descendants of the people who had been in the country since the first census in 1790 that they would soon be a minority. Jarvis suspected that Kapp and Schade had make several mistakes in their calculations, and he set out to correct them.

Demographers are usually at the mercy of government agencies that collect the data they need for their work, and they employ a variety of quantitative techniques to compensate for the gaps in the official statistics. Jarvis's article illustrates the level of scientific sophistication achieved by the demography of his time. The data available to him were fragmentary, but perhaps he could fit the pieces together. Beginning in 1819, the United States Government required all people who entered the country at the ocean and Great Lake ports to register. Estimates by other demographers filled in the period back to 1790. But no records existed of the people who entered the country by land. At the time, the inflow from Canada was significant, while that from Mexico was small, so Jarvis turned to Canadian data. Statistics on immigration to Canada, along with information about mortality rates and Canadian census data, allowed Jarvis to estimate that 395,000 immigrants vanished from Canada and must have gone on to the United States by land. Combining all these calculations, Jarvis estimated that 8,000,000 immigrants entered the United States from 1790 through 1870.

A different approach to immigration depends upon the data collected in the 1850, 1860, and 1870 censuses of the United States, which asked people where they had been born. On the basis of his earlier calculations, Jarvis carefully estimated the number of immigrants who entered in each decade, projected how many of each decade group should have survived until each census given a likely mortality rate, and found that his projections matched the census reports very closely.

On the basis of a single table in the 1850 census reports, Schade had calculated that births in the United States exceeded deaths by only 1.38 percent. Jarvis points out that Schade had apparently failed to notice that the figure he took to be births during the year actually referred to the number of children under one year of age living at the end of the year, which is a very different thing. Under the conditions of the time, many infants would have been born and died during that year, and not showed up in the tally of living children at the end and thus not in Schade's birth rate. Jarvis calculated that for every 100,000 children living at the end of the year, 115,000 had been born, and 15,000 of them died. Jarvis found that Schade had missed at least 390,000 children.

Jarvis then turned to life tables developed by insurance companies that needed to know what rates they should charge for life insurance. These gave very good information about the life expectancies of people in each age group, which then could be used to project the number of people surviving to any given year. He also examined the different age distributions in the native-born and immigrant populations, which placed a larger portion of immigrant women in the child-bearing years. Birth rates apparently were higher for immigrants, but so were death rates. After a long series of calculations and verifications, Jarvis arrived at his best estimates. In 1860, a total of 26,957,000 people of European descent lived in the United States. Kapp had estimated crudely that only 29 percent of them were descended from people who were already in the country in 1790. Jarvis's far better calculations showed that the correct number was 71 percent.

Sex Ratio

Guttentag, Marcia, and Paul F. Secord
  1983 *Too Many Women? The Sex Ratio Question*. Beverly Hills,
    California: Sage.

Demographers are concerned not merely with the total numbers of people who are born, died, or enter and leave a society by migration. They also study the population characteristics of segments of the society, and among the classic variables is the balance between women and men. This is traditionally measured by the sex ratio, the number of males per 100 females. If the sexes are numerically balanced, the sex ratio is 100. A number like 110 indicates that there are more men than women, whereas a number like 91 means there are fewer men than women. Guttentag and Secord are concerned with the social consequences of sex ratios that are far above 100 ("too many men") or far below 100 ("too many women"). They note that the sex ratio in the United States was always above 100 until the 1940s, but afterward dipped well below 100. That is, the nation went from a historical surplus of males to a surplus of females.

The sex ratio has especially great social consequences for unmarried individuals in the age range when people are generally getting married and having children. Conventional marriage, of course, pairs one woman with one man, so if there are fewer men than women many of the women will be unable to find mates. Much of the American excess of females occurs at the older age groups because women tend to live longer than men. Women tend to marry men who are two or three years older than themselves. The "baby boomers" born when the birthrate was rising rapidly after the Second World War were in a marriage squeeze. Since women tend to marry men older than themselves, when the population is increasing they take their husbands from birth cohorts that were smaller than their own. Guttentag and Secord look at the data for women aged 20–24 years old in 1970. If their potential husbands were in the 22–26 age group, they were seeking men in a situation with a sex ratio of only 84. And if their potential husbands were 23–27, then the sex ratio was 67! Thus, only two out of three women could possibly marry husbands three years older than themselves. Guttentag and Secord suggest that these highly unfavorable sex ratios greatly affected relations between men and women in the early 1970s, establishing new cultural patterns that have persisted despite more favorable sex ratios in recent years.

The numerical balance between the sexes affects their relative power, but not in the most obvious way that a majority may dominate a minority. Guttentag and Secord distinguish two kinds of power that relate to the sex ratio in very different ways:

1. *Dyadic power* is the capacity of one individual to make a good bargain with a member of the other sex, because he or she belongs to the rarer gender. When the sex ratio is high, women have dyadic power, because

each of them could potentially find another suitor if the man she is interacting with does not treat her well. Men compete with each other for the attentions of the relatively few available women, so they are forced to give women much in the relationships. However, if conditions were reversed, and the sex ratio were low, the scarce men would be in the stronger bargaining position, and women would have to give more.

2. *Structural power* is the capacity of one gender to exert power over the other because it has gained control over important institutions of the society, is wealthier, and is able to determine the moral values. Potentially, either gender could hold structural power, but over the course of human history men have generally done so. This fact has shaped the effect of dyadic power.

Other things being equal, when the sex ratio is high, women hold dyadic power, because men compete for their affections. This was the case in the early European Medieval period, when the legends were told of bold knights doing deeds of valor to win fair ladies, and in the Old South before the Civil War, where a similar chivalry supposedly marked men's behavior toward women. However, when the sex ratio is high but men hold extreme structural power, dyadic power may not do women much good. Especially among the richer classes, women may be confined to their homes and placed under extreme social restrictions, locked up like rare jewels, pampered but imprisoned. Guttentag and Secord examine a number of societies across history, including Athens and Sparta in classical Greece. In Athens, where the sex ratio was high, women of respectable families led extremely restricted lives, but in Sparta, where the sex ratio was low, women were more liberated, although not achieving full equality with men.

Examining the contemporary situation in the United States, which is similar in many respects with other industrial nations, Guttentag and Secord outline the potential social consequences of a low sex ratio or "too many women." Most directly, women will tend to marry at a slightly older age; more of them will never marry; there will be more divorced women; and more of the divorced women will not marry again. One might think that the reverse would be true for men, for example that they would marry young because it is easier for them to find attractive mates. But Guttentag and Secord find that this is not the case. Because men have dyadic power, they do not need to give women as much, so they are not under as much pressure to make commitments. Therefore they are reluctant to marry and quick to divorce, compared with men in high sex ratio societies. Both because many women must get along without a man, and because many women feel exploited by men, a low sex ratio inspires women to seek greater independence from men and socioeconomic equality with them. Given that men have only moderate structural power in modern societies, one result is a major realignment in relations between the sexes, in which women largely achieve equal rights. At the same time, supports for the traditional family are weakened.

Guttentag and Secord report that the most severe shortage of men they were able to find in their survey of documented human history was among contemporary African Americans. Among the likely consequences of a persistent low sex ratio are some of the social problems often said to be especially severe in the black community: births outside of marriage, families without a father present, and unstable relations between young black women and men that require black women to be unusually resourceful in their careers and in raising their families. Guttentag and Secord point out that most black marriages endure until the death of one spouse, and one should not falsely conclude that relations between the sexes among African Americans are inherently problematic. But an unbalanced sex ratio is undoubtedly one of the problems especially burdening the American black community, aggravated by and aggravating the other problems that this group of citizens faces.

Population Explosion or Collapse

Cohen, Joel E.
  1995 *How Many People Can the Earth Support?* New York: W. W. Norton.

Cohen shares the widespread concern that the earth's population is increasing so rapidly that humans will soon reach the point at which natural resources and ecology can no longer sustain them. However, he is exceedingly critical of the attempts demographers have made to project rates of population growth into the future, and of other scientists to estimate the total *carrying capacity* of the planet. Simply defined, carrying capacity is the number of people the earth can support indefinitely. Demographers have ignored the concept of carrying capacity, even though it is widely used outside demography, and Cohen approaches it critically with the intellectual tools of a demographer.

To provide perspective for understanding the future, Cohen surveys the past history of human population, acknowledging that estimates of the human population in past years are rather uncertain. Comparing various serious estimates of the total human population in 10,000 B.C., Cohen concludes that the number was probably between 2 million and 20 million, and that the invention of agriculture increased this number to between 170 million and 330 million by 1 A.D. This is a big jump in numbers, but the growth rate was imperceptible, perhaps as little as 1/50 of a percent per year, and probably not more than 1/20 of a percent. The development of world trade, the so-called industrial revolution, and improvements in public health and the economy stimulated increased rates of population growth later on. By 1750, the total population was in the range of 650 to 850 million, and it reached 1 billion before 1850, 2 billion around 1930, 3 billion around 1960, 4 billion in about 1974, and it passed 5 billion in about 1986. In 1995, the approximate population of the planet was 5.7 billion, and it was increasing about 90 million each year, an annual growth rate of 1.6 percent. Thus, at the end of the twentieth century, the human population was growing at a greater rate than ever before, as well as by larger absolute numbers each year.

Demographers use a variety of statistical methods to calculate estimates of the future population. The simplest is *mathematical extrapolation*, taking the current growth rate and running it forward some number of years. If there were 5.7 billion people in 1995, then this method estimates there would be $5.7 \times 1.016 = 5.7912$ billion in 1996, $5.7912 \times 1.016 = 5.8838592$ billion in 1997, and roughly 6.7 billion in 2005 (a 1.6 percent growth rate means each year has 1.016 times the population of the previous year). One source of inaccuracy in this method is that it does not take account of the age distribution of the population, and age groups differ greatly in terms of how much they contribute to population change. The *cohort-component method* takes account of the differing rates of fertility and mortality of the different age cohorts. This method unreasonably assumes that the factors influencing the rates are constant over time, whereas *system models* attempt to incorporate whatever knowledge social scientists have about these factors. For example, increased education for women tends to delay the age at which they have their first child, thus reducing the total number of children they will produce, so projections of educational change can feed into mathematical models of population change.

Unfortunately, none of these methods produce really reliable projections of population more than a very few years into the future, because social scientists simply do not understand the factors influencing birth rates with any precision. Cohen gives several examples of confident population projections published by official agencies that turned out to be seriously flawed. For example, every year from 1960 through 1977, the British government census bureau predicted what the country's population would be in the year 2001. In 1965, it predicted 60.5 million would be counted by the 2001 census. Each year the estimate increased, until it peaked at 75.5 million in 1965. From then on, the estimate declined, until in 1977 it fell to 57.5 million.

Estimates of the total world population are especially uncertain. The birth rates in rich industrialized nations are very low, whereas rates in developing countries are high, and no one can be sure how rapidly they will decline, if at all. In 1990, about 77 percent of the world's population lived in nations with high fertility rates. One of the more reasonable projections published by the United Nations suggested that world population would reach about 11.5 billion around the year 2150 and level off afterward, but this estimate was based on a set of assumptions rather than on good understanding of the complex factors that influenced fertility and mortality.

Cohen examined all serious estimates of the earth's human carrying capacity that had been published, and found that they ranged widely from fewer than one billion (a sixth of current population) to 1,000 billion. As an example of how credible estimates are calculated, he performed his own analysis of how many people could be sustained by the world's current supply of fresh water, using various assumptions about how much of it was required to grow food at varying mixtures of grains and meat. Efficient use of water with a good diet, under the assumption that 9,000 cubic kilometers of fresh water was available each year, yielded an estimate that the earth could sustain 7.8 billion people, a number that may be reached early in the next century. But Cohen's estimates of carrying capacity ranged from a low of 1.1 billion to a high of 137.5 billion. He concluded that carrying capacity was a very dubious concept, because it depended upon very shaky estimates of the efficiency of future human technology and highly subjective notions of the necessary quality of life. Despite the uncertainties in estimating carrying capacity, Cohen believes that unrestrained population growth cannot continue. If it is to avoid war over resources, he says, the world must rely upon six main approaches to lowering fertility:

1. promoting contraception through education and low-cost delivery of contraceptives
2. developing the poor economies of the world so their birth rates will become low like those of the developed nations
3. improving the survival of children so parents will not feel the need to produce many of them
4. improving the education and social status of women, thus empowering them to choose low fertility
5. educating men to value lower fertility
6. a combination of the above five approaches

Keyfitz, Nathan
   1987 "The Family that Does Not Reproduce Itself." In *Below Replacement Fertility in Industrial Societies*, edited by Kingsley Davis, Mikhail Bernstam, and Rita Ricardo-Campbell. Cambridge, England: Cambridge University Press.

Keyfitz notes that a modern society will remain constant in population if each couple produces about 2.1 children and the age distribution has stabilized so that neither an unusually large nor unusually small proportion of the population is in the child-bearing years. The figure is slightly larger than 2.0 because a fraction of all children born will not live to be adults and have the opportunity to contribute to fertility. However, Keyfitz says, couples in Western Europe produce on average only 1.6 children, so the population will shrink rapidly as soon as the age distribution stabilizes. He remarks that Austria has withstood assaults by Turks, Russians, French, and Germans, but its low birth rate threatens to destroy it by shrinking the population twenty-five percent in each generation. Recognizing that his topic is controversial, Keyfitz undertakes an uninhibited examination of the causes of the impending population collapse in industrial societies.

Keyfitz argues that causes operating on several different levels set the conditions in which couples will decide whether or not to have a child at a particular point in time. Modern contraceptive techniques and treatments for infertility give most couples a choice, and the current low level of fertility is far less than human biology permits.

A key economic factor is that women now are employed in great numbers, and studies show that as women's wages grow the number of children they produce declines. Small families allow women to invest more of their time in earning money. Keyfitz thinks this cannot be the whole explanation, because it does not say why women are increasingly interested in jobs. It cannot just be that they want money, because decades ago husbands earned far less than they do today, yet women did not rush into employment back then. Keyfitz argues that socio-political causes underlie the economic changes and thus are the real explanation for the fertility decline.

Perhaps both employment and leisure activities have become more attractive in recent years. Decades ago, work meant hard labor in a factory, but today it increasingly means pleasant activity in offices. Although some of the drudgery of child-raising has been reduced, the fact that so many children move away from their parents upon reaching adulthood means that investing in children may seem pointless. Education steals the child from the home, and parents play a diminished role in shaping the child in comparison with school and the mass media. Thus, parents may derive less pleasure now from their children than they did in earlier decades, at the same time that many dazzling forms of adult recreation have become available. Few parents now rely upon their children to support them in old age, so the economic returns from investing in children are slight. Modern society emphasizes gratification in the present, rather than investing in a long-term future, so the value of a future generation has declined.

The development of gender equality, among the most significant political changes of the twentieth century, also has a role in reducing fertility. Traditional societies with high fertility invariably assigned females and males to very different roles, beginning at an early age. What Keyfitz calls a vast conspiracy surrounded the individual female, forcing her to play the roles of submissive daughter, wife, and mother. He explains that nobody had to plan such a system or even be aware of its nature. Rather, male-dominated societies might come into being spontaneously in earlier centuries. Such societies would out-compete more gender-equal societies, which would have lower rates of population growth. Even today, Keyfitz observes, male-dominated Islamic society retains its high fertility, and thus it may wind up demographically swamping low-fertility European society many centuries after it failed to conquer Europe by the sword.

Keyfitz is skeptical that governments can adopt intentional policies to keep their populations from shrinking. He imagines that the United States might need an additional four million births per year. If women could be induced to bear a child for $10,000 per year for the five pre-school years, then the cost would be $200,000,000,000 annually. Keyfitz ends his essay on a concerned and skeptical note. He cannot believe that America is prepared to pay enough money to keep the birth rate at the replacement level, nor that Americans would be willing to abandon the value of equality.

GLOSSARY

Accumulation: The growth of technology because new things are invented more rapidly than old ones are forgotten.

Adjustment: The process by which the non-technical aspects of a culture respond to invention.

Alienation: Lack of trust in government leaders coupled with the feeling that it is not possible to influence their decisions.

Analogical imagination: A way of thinking supposedly common among Catholics that assumes God is present in the world, expressing Himself through every aspect of creation, and that stresses the community rather than the individual.

Anomie: A state of normlessness in which the society fails to provide a coherent set of values and norms; for the individual, anomie is the state of being without effective rules for living.

Apartheid: The racist system that was in effect in South Africa for about two generations that sought to separate the races, relegating blacks to an inferior status.

Baby boom: The period for about two decades after the Second World War when the fertility rate was high compared with the years before or after.

Bureaucracy: A system for organizing work and other group activities according to a set of formal rules and procedures that define how participants should behave, usually in the form of a hierarchy of authority.

Capitalism: An economic system where money is invested in enterprises that employ free wage labor and systematic bookkeeping in the rational pursuit of profit.

Carrying capacity: The number of people the earth (or some part of it) can support indefinitely.

Caste: A group within a society whose rights are defined differently from those of other groups and who are not permitted to blend with other castes.

Church: The established religious organization in a society, having an alliance with the state and the ruling class. In Benton Johnson's definition, a church is a religious group that accepts the social environment in which it exists.

Class politics: Political action that is based on rational calculation of the group's economic interests, promoting policies that are designed to improve the group's material position in society.

Clique: An area within a larger social network where the individuals are linked by many social relationships and thus function like a cohesive group.

Cohort: A set of people who were born at approximately the same time, for example, those born in a given year or a given five-year period.

Collective behavior: Episodes in which people influence each other informally to engage in a particular kind of behavior. Major categories are panics, crazes, and riots.

Commitment mechanism: An institutional arrangement that functions to bind an individual to an organization.

Concentric zone model of urban development: The theory that cities tend to form a series of rings, like an archery target, with the central business district in the middle and zones of various kinds of industry or residential type surrounding it.

Conjugal role-relationship: The manner in which the roles played by a husband and wife tend to be similar and shared (joint), or different and unshared (segregated).

Connected social network: A network of social relationships in which the people tied to a given person tend to be tied to each other as well.

Constituency: The set of people in the society who are potential supporters for a particular policy or political leader.

Construction of reality: The process by which a set of phenomena is made meaningful through social definitions.

Control theory: A sociological explanation that says people are more likely to commit deviant acts if their ties to society are weak.

Conversion: The process of joining a religious movement, usually conceptualized in terms of a radical transformation of the person involved.

Craze: A form of collective behavior in which people rush toward something they want

Cult: A deviant religious group, sometimes defined as one with a single, authoritarian leader, or as one with novel or exotic beliefs and practices. Because many journalists and opponents of new religions have used this term disparagingly, most sociologists of religion now prefer the term New Religious Movement (or NRM).

Cultural lag: A maladjustment in the culture that comes about when rapid change in one area is not immediately matched by concomitant change in other areas that are closely related to it.

Definition of the situation: One of several alternative ways of interpreting the meaning of an event or setting, usually socially constructed.

Delinquency: A consistent pattern of deviant behavior performed by a child or adolescent, including acts such as alcohol use or driving an automobile that might not be deviant if performed by an adult.

Delinquent subculture: A subculture in which performance of the roles requires the individual to engage in delinquent behavior.

Democracy: A political system that permits the largest possible part of the population to influence major decisions and in which regular opportunities exist for changing government officials.

Demographic transition: The historical evolution of a society from a situation of high birth and death rates to one of low birth and death rates, often with a population explosion occurring during the transition because mortality decreases before fertility does.

Demography: The study of the dynamics of human populations, emphasizing birth (fertility), death (mortality), and migration (emigration and immigration).

Deskilling: A process in which the nature of a job changes in such a way that it requires less skill of the workers, thus typically causing their status and bargaining power with management to decline.

Deviant behavior: Actions that violate the norms of a society and tend to receive condemnation and punishment when they are discovered.

Dialectical imagination: A way of thinking supposedly common among Protestants that assumes God has largely withdrawn from the sinful world, and that stresses the individual rather than the community.

Diffusion: The spread of a technical idea or other element of culture from one group to another.

Dispersed social network: A network of social relationships in which the people tied to a given person tend not to be tied to each other.

Dramaturgical approach: A form of symbolic interactionism that analyzes how people play roles, using concepts and analogies from the theater.

Dyad: A social unit consisting of two people and the relationship between them.

Egoism: A condition in which social relationships are unstable and society lacks solidarity. In Durkheim's theory, egoism can lead to egoistic suicide.

Endogamy: Marrying a person from one's own social group.

Exchange theory: One of the major theoretical perspectives in sociology, stressing that people enter into exchanges with each other to obtain rewards.

Exclusion: The policy of trying to prevent a particular group from entering the society.

Extended family: A large family group, linking members of three or more generations and often including many relatives of the same generation.

Functionalism: *See structural-functionalism.*

Generalized belief: An ideology that identifies the source of problems faced by a group of people and says what they should do about it.

Group: A more-or-less exclusive set of individuals who have relatively stable and extensive relations among themselves and possess a sense of shared identity or purpose.

Growth machine: A socio-political arrangement that unites business and government groups in favor of policies encouraging economic growth.

Human capital: Attributes a person can acquire that increase his or her capacity to earn income, such as education.

Ideational: A form of culture that considers reality to be essentially spiritual rather than material, thus demanding strong religious commitments.

Incidence rate: The fraction of a group who enter some category in a particular span of time, such as the number per 100,000 who enter psychiatric treatment during a given year.

Influence perspective: An approach in political sociology that sees politics as a conflict in which interest groups and political parties seek to shape the outcomes not only of elections but also of government decision-making processes.

Inner-directed: A personality style in which the individual possesses a strong set of internal values, socialized into him or her by demanding parents.

Intergenerational mobility: Movement up or down in the society's stratification system that takes place from one generation to another.

Intragenerational mobility: Movement up or down in the society's stratification system that takes place within a single generation, that is, the mobility experienced by an individual or cohort of individuals.

Invention: The process by which new forms of technology are created.

Isomorphism: The tendency of each organization in a particular field to resemble the others.

Labeling theory: An explanation of deviant behavior that emphasizes how social reaction can cause a person to play the role of deviant.

Labor market: The complex social, economic, and cultural system that channels individuals into various jobs.

Looking-glass self: *See social self.*

Medicalization: The process through which a form of deviance comes to be defined as an illness rather than as a sin or crime.

Merchant capitalism: A form of free market economy that emphasizes profit through buying and selling, rather than profit from industrial production.

Meritocracy: A system in which the best and most capable individuals rule the world.

Millennial movement: A religious movement that believes Christ or some other supernatural force will soon transform the world into an ideal society that may last a thousand years (the millennium).

Mobilization: The process by which the actions of a large number of people come to be coordinated, so that many are doing essentially the same thing or seeking the same goals.

Modernity: A set of personality characteristics that suit a person to play valuable roles in modern society, including such traits as openness to change, complex opinions, and orientation to the future rather than to the past.

Natural attitude: The unquestioning orientation with which people confront the world of every-day life.

Network: A structure of social relationships linking a number of individuals directly or indirectly.

Neutralization: Symbolic redefinition of a deviant act that reduces the perpetrator's blame.

Norms: Rules that regulate behavior, setting standards for proper or improper acts in given situations; more specific than values, they define how the society's values should be realized.

Nuclear family: A small family group consisting just of a married couple and their children.

Objectivation: The process by which people come to believe that socially-constructed meanings are really objective and could not be otherwise.

Opinion leader: An influential person who tends to adopt innovations and then convinces others in the network to adopt them as well.

Organization: A collectivity oriented to the pursuit of relatively specific goals and exhibiting a relatively highly formalized social structure.

Organizational ecology: A perspective on social organizations that considers the competitive and cooperative relations linking large numbers of them operating within a particular environment.

Other-directed: A personality style in which the individual finds his or her values in the surrounding group, adapting to the shifting values of new groups while pursuing a career that takes him or her through many social environments.

Panic: A form of collective behavior in which people rush terrified from something they fear.

Paranoia: A form of mental disorder in which a person suffers from delusions of grandeur and persecution.

Participant observation: A research technique in which the sociologist shares in the activities of a group while studying it.

Party: A network of individuals and suborganizations bearing a clear political label and seeking to elect people to public office.

Post-industrial society: The most modern form of society, in which service professions are more important than manufacturing, the professional and technical class dominates other elites, and theoretical knowledge is central for the formulation of policy.

Power elite: A network of highly influential persons who make the major decisions in the society.

Primary group: The set of social relations surrounding an individual that are characterized by intimate, face-to-face interaction and enduring cooperation.

Profession: An occupation, such as medicine or law, whose practitioners claim to possess such specialized knowledge that they should be allowed to set their own standards for practice of the occupation.

Proposition: A statement about the relationship between properties of nature, part of an explanation in formal theory.

Protestant ethic: A set of values supposedly held by many Protestants that stresses duty, self denial, and hard work.

Relative deprivation: A frustrating condition in which people experience a low level of satisfaction compared with that enjoyed by other people or with that which the sufferers believe they should enjoy.

Residual deviance: The violation of norms that are so taken-for-granted by members of society that their language does not give it a formal name.

Resource mobilization theory: A perspective on collective behavior and social movements that stresses the ways their participants gain resources from their social environment and employ them strategically to achieve their aims.

Riot: A form of collective behavior in which people rush against something they hate; sometimes called a hostile outburst.

Schism: A social process in which a religious organization splits into two parts, one of which is often a religiously intense sect that is antagonistic to the parent organization.

Sect: A religious group in opposition with the established church of a society. In Benton Johnson's definition, a sect is a religious group that rejects the social environment in which it exists.

Secularization: A historical process through which religion becomes progressively weaker because of the spread of scientific concepts and other aspects of modernization.

Sex ratio: The numerical balance between the sexes, traditionally measured as the number of males per 100 females.

Sexual dimorphism: A significant difference in the biological natures of the two genders manifested in behavior as well as in physical appearance.

Sensate: A form of culture that believes reality is whatever the sense organs perceive, thus tending to be sensuous and, in the modern era, scientific.

Social capital: Attributes of an individual's social environment that increase his or her capacity to earn income.

Social control perspective: An approach in political sociology that focuses on how government leadership operates to achieve the goals of society most efficiently at the least cost to the leaders themselves.

Social disorganization: The condition of a society when its social life is chaotic, its population is unstable, and its institutions fail to mesh with each other.

Social fact: For Durkheim and his followers, a phenomenon that belongs to society and cannot be understood simply in terms of the desires and actions of individuals.

Social movement: A relatively organized attempt to change some significant aspect of society, or to prevent such change.

Social self: The set of ideas the individual has about himself or herself, which were derived from communication with other people.

Sociogram: A diagram representing the structure of social relationships among a set of individuals.

Sociometry: The branch of sociology devoted to the measurement and analysis of the network of social relationships connecting a number of people.

Status politics: Political action that is concerned with the prestige of the group in society, using political processes symbolically to enhance the honor of the group.

Strain theory: The view that a lack of integration between the values and norms of a society will cause deviance; the individual is forced to commit deviant acts because he or she lacks the opportunity to achieve the culture's goals by conforming.

Stratification: Division of a society into socioeconomic strata (layers), social classes, or other forms of individual inequality.

Structural-functionalism: A school of thought describing society as a set of institutions that exist in a clear structure of relationships to each other, held together by a shared set of values.

Subculture: A set of norms, roles, and values that differ from those of the surrounding culture, usually followed by a particular group or network of people.

Subcultural deviance theory: An explanation of deviant behavior that says an individual will be influenced toward one or another behavior pattern by the people with whom he or she has contact; if they are criminal, so will the person be.

Symbolic interactionism: One of the major theoretical approaches in sociology, emphasizing the communications that provide the individual with a personal identity and with socially-scripted roles to play.

Technological determinism: The view that technological innovation is the engine of history, and that technology is largely self-generated.

Tradition-directed: A personality style in which the individual conforms to a rigid, age-old culture sustained through innumerable rituals, religion, and a complex structure of clans, castes, or other social divisions.

Vacancy chain: A series of positions in an organization linked by the movement of individuals from one to another in sequence; the chain begins when a person leaves the organization, creating a vacancy, into which the next person moves, leaving another vacancy, and so on.

Values: The most general principles that guide social action; shared definitions of abstract goals that should be achieved.

Zone of transition: A ring of factories and decaying residential buildings around the central business district, in the concentric zone model of urban development.

SUGGESTED READINGS

1. The Scope of Sociology

Clark, Terry N.
1973 *Prophets and Patrons: The French University and the Emergence of the Social Sciences*. Cambridge, Massachusetts: Harvard University Press.

Durkheim, Emile
1915 *The Elementary Forms of the Religious Life*. London: Allen and Unwin.

Jarvis, Edward
1855 *Report on Insanity and Idiocy in Massachusetts*. Boston: White. Reprinted in 1971, Cambridge: Harvard University Press.

Pickering, W. S. F.
1984 *Durkheim's Sociology of Religion*. London: Routledge and Kegan Paul.

Pope, Whitney
1976 *Durkheim's Suicide: A Classic Analyzed*. Chicago: University of Chicago Press.

Stark, Rodney, and William Sims Bainbridge
1997 *Religion, Deviance and Social Control*. New York: Routledge.

2. Exchange and Symbolic Interaction

Blumer, Herbert
1969 *Symbolic Interactionism: Perspective and Method*. Englewood Cliffs, New Jersey: Prentice-Hall.

Boudon, Raymond
1981 *The Logic of Social Action*. London: Routledge and Kegan Paul.

Cooley, Charles Horton
1911 *Social Organization*. New York: Scribner's.

Denzin, Norman K.
1994 "Symbolic Interactionism." Pp. 4444–4452 in *The Encyclopedia of Language and Linguistics*, edited by R. E. Asher. Oxford: Pergamon Press.

Mead, George Herbert
1934 *Mind, Self, and Society*. Chicago: University of Chicago Press.

Stark, Rodney, and William Sims Bainbridge
1996 *A Theory of Religion*. New Brunswick, New Jersey: Rutgers University Press.

3. Groups and Social Networks

Cook, Karen S., and Joseph M. Whitmeyer
1992 "Two Approaches to Social Structure: Exchange Theory and Network Analysis," *Annual Review of Sociology* 18:109–127.

Marsden, Peter V.
1990 "Network Data and Measurement," *Annual Review of Sociology* 16:435–463.

Shaw, Marvin E.
1981 *Group Dynamics*. New York: McGraw-Hill.

Wilson, Stephen
1978 *Informal Groups*. Englewood Cliffs, New Jersey: Prentice-Hall.

4. Family

Cherlin, Andrew J., and Frank F. Furstenberg, Jr.
1994 "Stepfamilies in the United States," *Annual Review of Sociology* 20:359–381.

Furstenberg, Frank F., Jr.
1990 "Divorce and the American Family," *Annual Review of Sociology* 16:379–403.

Goode, William J.
1963 *World Revolution and Family Patterns*. New York: Free Press.

Juster, Susan M. and Maris A. Vinovskis
1987 "Changing Perspectives on the American Family in the Past," *Annual Review of Sociology* 13:193–216.

Moen, Phyllis, and Elaine Wethington
1992 "The Concept of Family Adaptive Strategies," *Annual Review of Sociology* 18: 233–251.

Young, Michael, and Peter Wilmott
1973 *The Symmetrical Family*. New York: Penguin.

5. Deviance and Control

Cohen, Albert K.
1955 *Delinquent Boys*. New York: Free Press.

Gottfredson, Michael R., and Travis Hirschi
1990 *A General Theory of Crime*. Stanford: Stanford University Press.

Miller, Walter B.
1958 "Lower Class Culture As a Generating Milieu of Gang Delinquency," *Journal of Social Issues* 14:5–19.

Sampson, Robert J., and John H. Laub
1992 "Crime and Deviance in the Life Course," *Annual Review of Sociology* 18:63–84.

Shaw, Clifford and Henry D. McKay
1929 *Delinquency Areas*. Chicago: University of Chicago Press.

Wolfgang, Marvin
1958 *Patterns in Criminal Homicide*. Philadelphia: University of Pennsylvania Press.

6. Labeling and Relativity

Becker, Howard S.
1963 *Outsiders*. New York: Free Press.

Conrad, Peter
1992 "Medicalization and Social Control," *Annual Review of Sociology* 18:209–232.

Goffman, Erving
1961 *Asylums*. Garden City, New York: Doubleday.

Gove, Walter R.
1970 "Societal Reaction as an Explanation of Mental Illness: An Evaluation," *American Sociological Review* 35:873–884.

Pfohl, Stephen J.
1985 *Images of Deviance and Social Control*. New York: McGraw-Hill.

Schur, Edwin M.
1965 *Crimes Without Victims: Deviant Behavior and Public Policy*. Englewood Cliffs, New Jersey: Prentice-Hall.

7. Community and Urban

Baldassare, Mark
1992 "Suburban Communities," *Annual Review of Sociology* 18:475–494.

Caplow, Theodore
1982 *Middletown Families: Fifty Years of Change and Continuity*. Minneapolis, Minnesota: University of Minnesota Press.

Gans, Herbert J.
1962 *The Urban Villagers*. New York: Free Press.

Hoover, Dwight W.
1990 *Middletown Revisited*. Muncie, Indiana: Ball State University.

Lynd, Robert S., and Helen Merrell Lynd
1937 *Middletown in Transition*. New York: Harcourt, Brace.

Warner, W. Lloyd, and Paul S. Lunt
1941 *The Social Life of a Modern Community*. New Haven, Connecticut: Yale University Press.

8. Work, Occupations, and Professions

Abbott, Andrew
1988 *The System of Professions: An Essay on the Division of Expert Labor*. Chicago: University of Chicago Press.

Althauser, Robert P.
1989 "Internal Labor Markets," *Annual Review of Sociology* 15:143–161.

Freidson, Eliot
1984 "The Changing Nature of Professional Control," *Annual Review of Sociology* 10:1–20.

Rosenbaum, James E., Takehiko Kariya, Rick Settersten, and Tony Maier
1990 "Market and Network Theories of the Transition from High School to Work," *Annual Review of Sociology* 16:263–299.

Spenner, Kenneth I.
1988 "Social Stratification, Work and Personality," *Annual Review of Sociology* 14:69–97.

Starr, Paul
1982 *The Social Transformation of American Medicine*. New York: Basic Books.

9. Organizations

Barnett, William P., and Glenn R. Carroll
1995 "Modeling Internal Organizational Change," *Annual Review of*

Sociology 21:217–236.

Chase, Ivan D.
 1991 "Vacancy Chains" *Annual Review of Sociology* 17:133–154.

DiMaggio, Paul J., and Helmut K. Anheier
 1990 "The Sociology of Nonprofit Organizations and Sectors," *Annual Review of Sociology* 16:137–159.

Fligstein, Neil, and Robert Freeland
 1995 "Theoretical and Comparative Perspectives on Corporate Organization," *Annual Review of Sociology* 21:21–43.

Singh, Jitendra V., and Charles J. Lumsden
 1990 "Theory and Research in Organizational Ecology," *Annual Review of Sociology* 16:161–195.

Zucker, Lynne G.
 1987 "Institutional Theories of Organization," *Annual Review of Sociology* 13:443–464.

10. Stratification

Dahrendorf, Ralf
 1959 *Class and Class Conflict in Industrial Society.* Stanford, California: Stanford University Press.

Hauser, Robert M., and David L. Featherman.
 1976 *Occupation and Social Mobility in the United States.* Madison, Wisconsin: University of Wisconsin Institute for Research on Poverty.

Jacobs, Jerry
 1989 *Revolving Doors: Sex Segregation and Women's Careers.* Stanford: Stanford University Press.

Jencks, Christopher
 1972 *Inequality.* New York: Basic Books.

Treiman, Donald J.
 1977 *Occupational Prestige in Comparative Perspective.* New York: Academic Press.

Tumin, Melvin M.
 1953 "Some Principles of Stratification: A Critical Analysis," *American Sociological Review* 18:387–394.

11. Race and Ethnic Relations

Frazier, Edward Franklin
 1957 *Black Bourgeoisie.* Glencoe, Illinois: Free Press.

Glazer, Nathan, and Daniel Patrick Moynihan
 1970 *Beyond the Melting Pot.* Second edition. Cambridge, Massachusetts: MIT Press.

Patterson, Orlando
 1982 *Slavery and Social Death: A Comparative Study.* Cambridge: Harvard University Press.

Portes, Alejandro, and Cynthia Truelove
 1987 "Making Sense of Diversity: Recent Research on Hispanic Minorities in the United States," *Annual Review of Sociology* 13:359–385.

Snipp, C. Matthew
 1992 "Sociological Perspectives on American Indians," *Annual Review of Sociology* 18:351–371

Van den Berghe, Pierre
 1978 *Race and Racism: A Comparative Perspective.* New York: Wiley.

Williams, Robin M., Jr.
 1994 "The Sociology of Ethnic Conflicts," *Annual Review of Sociology* 20:49–79.

12. Religion

Bainbridge, William Sims
 1997 *The Sociology of Religious Movements.* New York: Routledge.

Cohn, Norman
 1961 *The Pursuit of the Millennium.* New York: Harper.

Glock, Charles Y., and Rodney Stark
 1965 *Religion and Society in Tension.* Chicago: Rand McNally.

Lofland, John
 1977 *Doomsday Cult, Enlarged Edition.* New York: John Wiley.

Richardson, James T., Mary White Stewart, and Robert B. Simmonds
 1979 *Organized Miracles.* New Brunswick, New Jersey: Transaction.

Stark, Rodney, and William Sims Bainbridge
 1985 *The Future of Religion.* Berkeley: University of California Press.

13. Collective Behavior and Social Movements

Jenkins, J. Craig
1983 "Resource Mobilization Theory and the Study of Social Movements," *Annual Review of Sociology* 9:527–553.

Lo, Clarence Y. H.
1982 "Countermovements and Conservative Movements in the Contemporary U.S.," *Annual Review of Sociology* 8:107–134.

McPhail, Clark, and Ronald T. Wohlstein
1983 "Individual and Collective Behaviors with Gatherings, Demonstrations and Riots," *Annual Review of Sociology* 9:579–600.

Obershall, Anthony
1973 *Social Conflict and Social Movements*. Englewood Cliffs, New Jersey: Prentice-Hall.

Rosengren, Karl Erik, Peter Arvidson, and Dahn Sturesson
1975 "The Barsebäck 'Panic': A Radio Programme as a Negative Summary Event," *Acta Sociologica* 18:147–162.

Turner, Ralph H., and Lewis M. Killian
1987 *Collective Behavior*. Englewood Cliffs, New Jersey: Prentice-Hall.

14. Political Sociology

Brint, Steven
1985 "The Political Attitudes of Professionals," *Annual Review of Sociology* 11:389–414.

Burstein, Paul
1981 "The Sociology of Democratic Politics and Government," *Annual Review of Sociology* 7:291–319.

Eisenstadt, Shmuel N.
1963 *The Political Systems of Empires*. New York: Free Press.

Jenkins, J. Craig, and Kurt Schock
1992 "Global Structures and Political Processes in the Study of Domestic Political Conflict," *Annual Review of Sociology* 18:161–185.

Skocpol, Theda
1979 *States and Social Revolutions: A Comparative Analysis of France, Russia, and China*. New York: Cambridge University Press.

15. Social Change

Durkheim, Emile
1933 *The Division of Labor in Society*. New York: Macmillan.

Gilfillan, S. C.
1963 *The Sociology of Invention*. Cambridge, Massachusetts: MIT Press.

Lubeck, Paul M.
1992 "The Crisis of African Development," *Annual Review of Sociology* 18:519–540.

Portes, Alejandro
1973 "The Factorial Structure of Modernity," *American Journal of Sociology* 79:15–44.

Rogers, Everett M.
1960 *Social Change in Rural Society*. New York: Appleton-Century-Crofts.

White, Lynn
1962 *Medieval Technology and Social Change*. Oxford: Oxford University Press.

16. Demography

Espenshade, Thomas J.
1995 "Unauthorized Immigration to the United States," *Annual Review of Sociology* 21:195–216.

Hirschman, Charles
1994 "Why Fertility Changes," *Annual Review of Sociology* 20:203–233.

Kasarda, John D.
1985 "Social Mobility and Fertility," *Annual Review of Sociology* 11:305–328.

Malthus, Thomas
1798 *An Essay on Population*. New York: Dutton.

Nathanson, Constance A.
1984 "Sex Differences in Mortality," *Annual Review of Sociology* 10:191–213.

McNicoll, Geoffrey
1992 "Changing Fertility Patterns and Policies in the Third World," *Annual Review of Sociology* 18:85–108.

Wrong, Dennis H.
1964 *Population and Society*. New York: Random House.

INDEX